... but give me Amsterdam

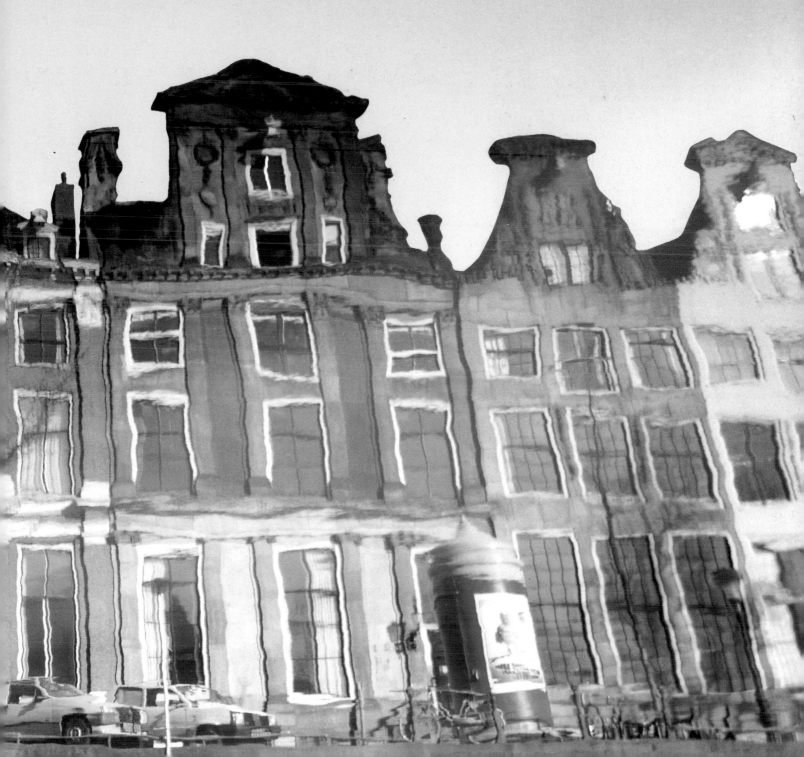

... but give me

Jules B. Farber

Amsterdam

Kosmos–Z&K Uitgevers, Amsterdam/Utrecht

For Barbara

© Text 1995 Jules B. Farber
© Photography: *see* Illustration Credits
All rights reserved
Cover design: Studio Jan de Boer
Book design: Ton Ellemers, BNO
D/1995/0108/235
NUGI 471/644

Contents

7 *Foreword*

S. PATIJN, BURGOMASTER OF AMSTERDAM

9 *Name Dropping*

FAMOUS, INFAMOUS VISITORS

14 *Heart and Soul*

ESSENCE OF THE CITY

31 *The Dam*

VORTEX OF THE COUNTRY

39 *Royal Link*

AMSTERDAM/HOUSE OF ORANGE, UP & DOWN
RELATIONSHIP

45 *Monument Life*

AMIDST UNIQUE HISTORICAL INHERITANCE

51 *Jordaan*

CUSTOMS, HUMOR, MUSIC, IDIOMATIC LANGUAGE

59 *Mokum*

JEWISH REFUGEES' IMPRINT ON LOCAL LIFE

69 *Once-Holy Place*

AMSTERDAM MIRACLE, RELIGIOUS UPHEAVALS

77 *French Accent*

NAPOLEONIC OCCUPATION TO CURRENT
GALLIC PRESENCE

84 *Americana*

HISTORICAL, ARCHITECTURAL, CULTURAL
INHERITANCES

92 *Nippon on the Amstel*

JAPANESE BUSINESS COMMUNITY LIFE

99 *Chinatown*

ORIENTAL OASIS IN OLDEST QUARTER

101 *Russian Relations*

EARLY TRADERS, CZAR PETER, ROYAL LINKS

107 *The Arts*

CORNUCOPIA OF CULTURAL OFFERINGS

128 *Design for Living*

AMSTERDAM SCHOOL TO
AVANT GARDE

135 *Leisure*

COSMOPOLITAN FORMS OF RELAXATION

143 *Protests*

CENTURIES OF LOCALS IN REVOLT

149 *... and the World*

GLOBE-SPANNING EXPEDITIONS, EXPLORATION,
TRADING

157 *Three Mainports*

HARBOR, SCHIPHOL, TELEPORT

170 *Business Scene*

INTERNATIONAL FINANCIAL SERVICE CENTER

189 *Illustration Credits*

Three white St. Andrew's crosses, in the form of Xs on a black column centered on a red background, constitute the Amsterdam coat of arms. While the column depicts the city's water site, the crosses representing the apostle were probably inspired by the shields of a prominent 13th century family with many Crusaders in its fold. In 1489, Maximilian of Austria granted the rights for his imperial crown to surmount the coat of arms. Not only was this prestigious, but the mercantile Amsterdammers had practical benefits. Ships bearing this implied protection of the emperor could sail and trade everywhere. Early in the 16th century, two lions were added as bearers of the coat of arms. With great pride, the gilded emperor's crown was placed on the 5-meter-high Western Church tower in 1638. In recognition of the Amsterdammers' courageous resistance to the Nazi occupiers during World War II, Queen Wilhelmina bestowed the right to incorporate 'Heroic, Resolute, Merciful' on the coat of arms in 1947.

Foreword

As I write these words (September 1995), I have not yet read the contents of this book, … *but give me Amsterdam*, that you, reader, have in your hands!

Some titles speak so profoundly for themselves that one can not put down the book in question. In the pages that follow, some twenty essential aspects of fascinating Amsterdam are examined. Amsterdammers of very varied backgrounds speak out! However, as they express their evaluations of Amsterdam, one thing is certain: a moment came in their lives, as it did in mine, when they decided to do their best for Amsterdam. Why? Because the city deserves this now as it always has through the centuries.

Is this unfounded local chauvinism?
You, reader, know better!

S. Patijn, burgomaster of Amsterdam

Guy d'Avesnes, an early noble arrival, granted city rights in 1306. While the mercantile burghers were proud of their new status as citizens, the year 1275 when the toll privilege was granted is considered the actual start of their civic history.

Name Dropping

Famous, infamous visitors

Countless famous and infamous people have been attracted to Amsterdam for all kinds of reasons: love, literature, peace, exile, music, movies, history, religion, reverence, promotion, politics, illicit power or, like the crowned heads of yesteryear, for a massage. As a curtain-raiser, a small, random selection:

Musical notes

Wolfgang Amadeus Mozart, advertised as a virtuoso — an eight-year-old composer and performer (he was actually nine!) — and his sister, fourteen-year old Nannerl (really fifteen!), lived in the Gouden Leeuw (Golden Lion), with their promoter father, Leopold, for four months in 1766. Their first concert took place in the hall above the Hollandsche Manege (Dutch Riding Academy), then on the Marnixstraat, at the end of the Leidsegracht. At first, Leopold had refused to let his two prodigy children come from

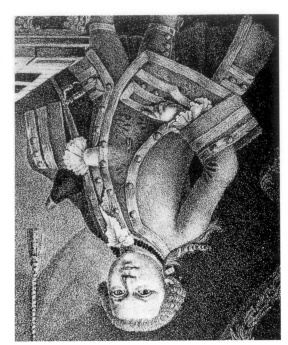

England to Holland, even to perform for Prince Willem V of Orange in The Hague, since he found the Hollanders *ein bisschen grob* (somewhat boorish). Royal pressure on Leopold, extended through the Dutch ambassador in the United Kingdom, finally resulted in his acquiescence to crossing the Channel to Holland.

But it took quite some advertising by papa Mozart to buoy up lagging sales for the concert. Promises of a duet on one harpsichord, a rarity in those days, and that Wolfgang would play all audience requests brought in the crowds. 18th century hype!

An unobtrusive marble plaque on an undistinguished 19th century brick façade superimposed on the building at Prinsengracht 506 reveals (in Italian): 'In this house the great composer and violinist Pietro Antonio Locatelli lived, worked and died.' One of the major figures in Italian baroque music, Locatelli was virtually forgotten until a 1950s revival.

Wolfgang Amadeus Mozart in 1763 when he was seven and his sister Nannerl was twelve. Three years later, papa Mozart and his children moved into an Amsterdam hotel near the Dam for four months while he promoted their concerts.

Pietro Antonio Locatelli, one of the great Italian baroque composers and violinists, lived and worked in Amsterdam.

Rolling Stones 1995 concert. Live CD recording of *Stripped* in Amsterdam's pop temple, Paradiso, for a small group, while thousands watched the performance on huge video screens on the Museum Square.

John Lennon and Yoko Ono during their bed-in at the Amsterdam Hilton in 1966.

was before the Concertgebouw (Concert Hall) was completed in 1888 and the Amsterdam Concertgebouw Orchestra, initiated that same year, developed into one of the world's leading symphony orchestras. Brahms' criticism, justified or not at the time, has been resoundingly drowned out in the ensuing century by enthusiastic bravados of renowned conductors, composers and solo performers who prize their performances with the great orchestras and smaller ensembles in the Dutch capital of music. The Concertgebouw's love affair with Gustav Mahler was evident in extensive celebrations in 1995 (see 'The Arts').

Quite a different kind of musician, over a century after Brahms, chose Amsterdam as his world stage to protest for peace. John Lennon, and Yoko Ono, was ensconced in Suite 902 of the Amsterdam Hilton in 1969 for a bed-in. The pop star, knowing his pulling power with such a mega media event, literally had the press at his feet as he and his bride talked non-stop about peace from ten a.m. to ten p.m. for seven days straight. It was quite a performance — far from the usually packed concert halls. Shades of the sixties revisited: Mick Jagger and the Rolling Stones were back in the Dutch capital in 1995 for a live CD recording of *Stripped* in the Paradiso pop temple. Tight security controlled the 530 fortunate persons, including Crown Prince Willem Alexander, who were allowed to enter. An estimated 100,000 fans jammed the Museum Square to watch the broadcast of the world's greatest rock and roll band performance on gigantic video screens. The Stones chose the Paradiso, according to Jagger, because it's the best place in Europe to do this'.

Franz Liszt came to Amsterdam to perform his *Graner Messe* on the Moses and Aaron Church organ in April 1866.

Johannes Brahms, after conducting his *Third Symphony* in Amsterdam in 1879, commented: 'You are good people but bad musicians.' This

Making Movies

'Amsterdam As Film Decor', researched by a small Dutch magazine, *Furore*, revealed more than 500 locations used for 171 domestic and foreign productions during more than 50 years.

The all-time top film location in the Dutch capital is the Staalstraat, a picturesque, narrow street which epitomizes every director's dream of an old Dutch setting.

Some years back, an unexpected location was found in the middle of the Bijenkorf department store's roof tower on Dam Square. Charlie Chaplin, in *The Great Dictator* (1940), stood before a window overlooking rooftops in the capital of a fictive European country, Tomania. The towers in view — the Stock Exchange, St. Nicholas Church and the Old Church — are all in Amsterdam and were filmed from that store roof. In the movie, a man jumps out of that window to test the 'world's smallest parachute' for the dictator. This scene was actually montaged in Hollywood, where Chaplin played a double role as a barber in the ghetto and as the dictator Adenhoid Hynkel.

A random sampling of some directors and their stars reflect the seductive variety of the Amsterdam scene.

Roman Polanski chose Amsterdam as the setting for his contribution to *Les plus belles escroqueries du monde* (1964). Robert Mitchum in *The Amsterdam Kill* (1977) raced through the city as an American drug agent. Isabelle Adjani and Gérard Depardieu starred in *Barocco* (1976). Catherine Deneuve in *Courage ... Fuyons!* (1979). Sean Connery alias James Bond, pursued a diamond smuggler in *Diamonds Are Forever* (1971). George Stevens directed Millie Perkins, Joseph Schildkraut and Shelly Winters in *The Diary of Anne Frank* (1959). Agnès Varda directed *L'Une chante, l'autre pas* (1976) about French women coming to Amsterdam for abortions. Joseph Losey directed Monica Vitti and Dirk Bogarde in *Modesty Blaise* (1966). Orson Welles directed and starred in *Mr Arkadin* (1955). Don Siegel brought Burt Reynolds and David Niven to town for the filming of his *Rough Cuts* (1980). Rex Harrison was in Amsterdam for *A Time to Die* (1983). Jacques Tati directed and starred in *Traffic* (1971).

Claude Lelouch directed *Vivre pour vivre* (1967) with Yves Montand, Candice Bergen and Annie Girardot. Dutch director George Sluizer filmed

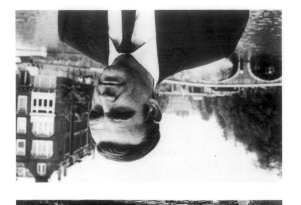

Sean Connery as James Bond in *Diamonds are Forever*

Speedboat crashing into the canal in *Amsterdamned*.

Gerard Depardieu and Isabelle Adjani in *Barocco*, filmed on the Egelantiersgracht in the Jordaan quarter.

Diary of Anne Frank deportation scene was shot on the Staalstraat.

Charlie Chaplin in *The Great Dictator*. Locations were shot from the Bijenkorf department store rooftop, but the actor only appeared before the cameras in Hollywood.

Amsterdam has been the setting for hundreds of foreign and Dutch films.

Many more international and Dutch films were set in Amsterdam, but, undoubtedly, the most controversial production centered on *La Ragazza in Vetrina* (Girls Behind Windows) in 1960. Though filming and photographing in the red-light district is traditionally taboo, an unwritten law enforced by the prostitutes' souteneurs, Italian director Lucio Emmer presumed he had properly arranged everything. Permission had been granted by City Hall. Payments for lost income and inconvenience were made to prostitutes, café proprietors and residents. Even the Salvation Army's Good Will Center located nearby pitched in by contributing extras.

But problems mounted. A Protestant City Council member protested, while the Dutch Royal Marine objected to two 'clients' wearing their official uniforms. Emmer and his electrician came to fisticuffs with Utrechtse Appie, the neighborhood's most renowned pimp. Emmer and some of his equipment ended up in the canal.

The movie, probably the only one ever filmed on location in the centuries-old red-light district, had a sad ending — it was banned in Italy!

Royalty

Though there were no luxury hotel accommodations back in 1578 and the ensuing centuries, royal visitors flocked to Amsterdam. William of Orange, also known as William the Silent, was the first overnight guest in the converted St. Cecilia cloister soon called the Prinsenhof. Other Dutch princes and foreign royalty followed, including Maria de' Medici, the widowed Queen of France, and Louisa Maria Gonzaga, Queen of Poland. In time this complex became the Admiralty, later served as the Town Hall, and in recent years, became the Grand Hotel Amsterdam.

Another run of royals to Amsterdam, starting in 1870, was instigated by something far beyond a regal back-rub. This was due to Dr. Johann Georg Mezger, who had taken up residence in the struggling, new Amstel Hotel. Reputed to be the pioneer in raising remedial gymnastics and massage to a more precise medical science, a forerunner of physiotherapy, he achieved worldwide fame for his revolutionary treatment and was soon sought after by royalty. They came in droves, accompanied by their large staffs, to stay in the hotel for treatment by Dr. Mezger. His patients included the Queen of Romania (nicknamed Carmen Sylvia), the Queen and

Anthony Perkins and Bibi Anderson in *Twice a Woman* (1978).

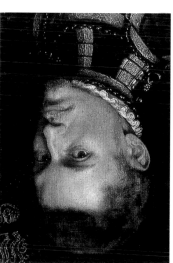

Willem of Orange, first royal guest in the former St. Cecilia cloister, which was rebuilt to become the Prinsenhof.

Right: Maria de' Medici was honored with a splendid water spectacle on the Rokin when she visited. Her lodgings were in the Prinsenhof.

Crown Prince of Sweden, former Empress Eugénie of France, the Prince and Princess of Wales and their children, Czarina Marie Fedorovna and her daughter Olga, the Shah of Persia, with a 40-man retinue, Austrian Empress Elisabeth (Sisi), wife of Frans Jozef I; and many members of the French and German aristocracy. Queen Juliana and Prince Bernhard's silver wedding anniversary in 1962 drew all the world's remaining royalty, including the Shah of Iran and Empress Fara Dibah, Queen Elizabeth and Prince Philip and many other royals. The wedding of Princess Beatrix and Claus Von Amsbergen in 1966 drew many of the future (now present) kings and queens. They came again in 1980 for the coronation of Queen Beatrix.

Anyone who is anyone has come to Amsterdam at some time during the last seven centuries. They continue to come: the great literary lights, the *glitterati*, the heroes of celluloid and sound

who are today's royalty, the movers and shakers, the captains of industry and heads of state. Amsterdam welcomes them all, without blinking, blasé about these celebrities who come to enjoy this wonderful city. But the infamous are not welcome. The despised Chilean ex-dictator Agusto Pinochet, who slipped in for arms purchases, was quickly discovered, declared *persona non grata* and whisked out of town!

Prinsenhof, 1620 view. It evolved through the centuries from royal lodgings to become the Admiralty, later the Town Hall, and, most recently, the Grand Amsterdam, a luxury hotel.

Crowned heads from all over the world came to celebrate the 25th wedding anniversary of Queen Juliana and Prince Bernhard in 1962. The Amstel Hotel was the party venue.

Heart and Soul

Essence of the city

A msterdam is a charming, dynamic, hustling, tolerant, greedy, seedy, beautiful, enlightened, socially-oriented, politically eruptive, warm, welcoming, *gezellig*, schizophrenic kind of place. It is more a worldly village than a cosmopolitan capital. It is eternally young at heart, despite its more than 700 years, and

'coolly' self-assured, sane and civilized. It acts like a capital, but lets the lawmakers get on with their endless debates in The Hague. It plans for the future while zealously guarding its past. It uses its heritage to serve today and adapt to tomorrow. During more than seven centuries of history — often with glorious highpoints, but sometimes with depressing lows — Amsterdam managed to change with the times, roll with the punches and still remain the same wonderful place that cannot really be compared with any other city in Europe, or even in the world. It's not Venice, despite the obvious similarities. Built on the water and interlaced by canals, both are reputed for being tolerant and cosmopolitan, for art and democracy, for maritime trade, banking and printing. However, Amsterdam's canals were dug based on a planned pattern, have fresh water and a controlled level, while the Venetian canals were randomly built, are filled with seawater and are subject to the tides. While

Southern Church steeple which Rembrandt viewed from his home.

In the inner courtyard of the Amsterdam Historical Museum, formerly a medieval cloister and orphanage, sun seekers enjoy lunch or drinks.

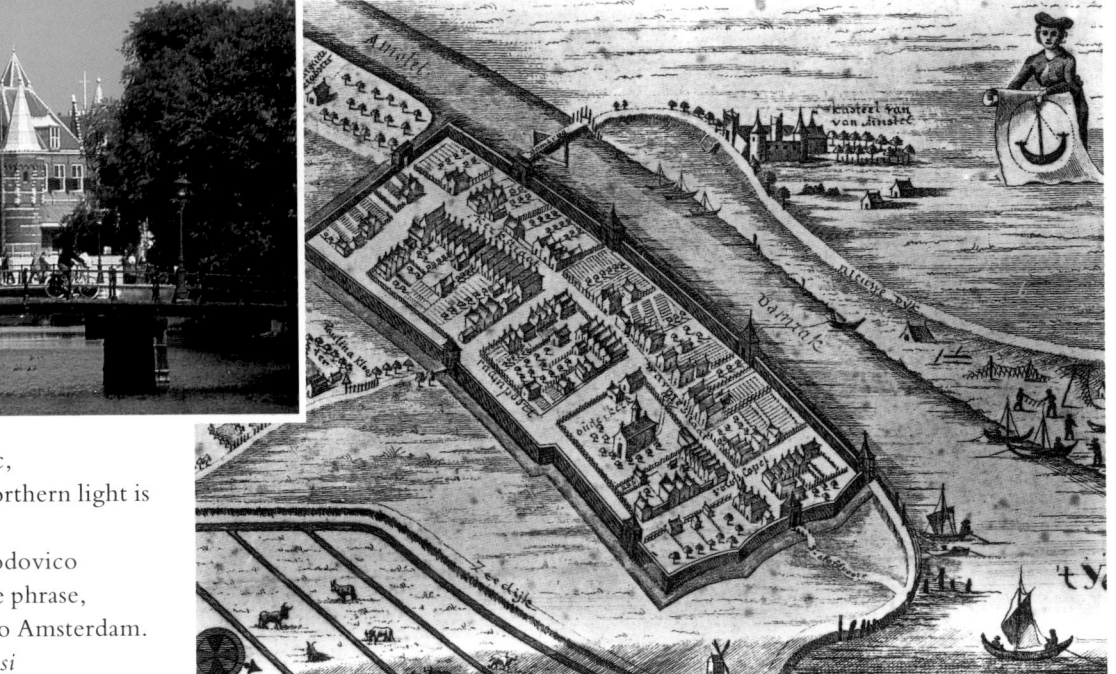

Venice has a special southern magic, Amsterdam's ambiance in a cold northern light is truly unique.

In 1567, the Florentine traveller Lodovico Guicciardini was the first to use the phrase, 'Venice of the North', in relation to Amsterdam. In his *Descriptione di tutti i Paesi Bassi* (Description of all the Netherlands), he wrote: 'And by reason of the air, the water and the seat of the place, and for convenience and the great number of canals, which are to be found down almost every street, and for other reasons, this city is similar almost to that of Venice ... This city will rightly become the Venice of the North.'

By the mid-17th century, when Amsterdam had overshadowed the Italian lagoon city, the Dutch writer Constantijn Huygens, in his *Stede-stemmen*

(City Voices), profiled Amsterdam with prideful chauvinism as 'Twice-Venice', referring to the canals, twice as many quays as the Adriatic port with Amsterdam's trade extending both east and west, while Venice's was limited to the Mediterranean.

Water has been part of Amsterdam life since the very start. Earliest inhabitants lived by fishing

Left: The Weigh House is being converted into a modern media center.
Above: Amsterdam during the early 13th century. City archeologists are convinced that in 1995 they excavated foundations of the Amstel Castle depicted in this imaginary view.

Herons sometimes roost on bicycles.

Left: The *Batavia*, a reconstructed 17th century three-master, set sail on the IJ in Amsterdam harbor.

The Amstel Castle

In earley 1994 during excavations for a bank building and parking garage in a medieval section of the historical city center archealogists were on guard as the gigantic claws dug deep. When brick walls of a presumably large 13th century castle were uncovered, work was halted. Chills raced up the spines of those painstakingly cleaning the stones and recording the finds. Existence of the Amstel Castle had been a legend recounted for hundreds of years and dramatized in the poetic theatre piece of Holland's 17th century writer Vondel. This was stuff dreams were made of and there it was. Or was it? Experts are still fighting over the actual origin and significance of this major fortification in the inner city. Supposedly it should have been located under the Portuguese Jewish Cemetery in the outlying area of Ouderkerk. Or, it should be on the bank of IJ, as propagated by Vondel.

In the water by the castle's west wall, iron building tools, hammers and other utensils used in the construction were found, along with a pilgrim's pewter water flask engraved with a seated Maria on one side and a lion climbing on the other. These finds underscore the castle's existence in the early 13th century. City archeologist Johannes Baart theorizes that after Floris V was murdered in 1296, the castle might have been destroyed in reprisal, or this could have happened in 1304 when the Count of Holland ordered all of Amsterdam's fortifications to be destroyed.

Baart:'It probably was a four-sided castle measuring circa 27 by 23 meters. The exact building phases are not known, but Amsterdam's oldest earthen enclosing walls, which date from 1301 and were close to the castle, have also been dug up. It has a wealth of archeological treasures, including a gold coin, a so called *franc à pied*, and a fragment of a money weighing scale with weights clearly confirming the city's highly developed economy and trade. Radar is being used in the continuing studies and, in the future, the castle will be open to the public.'

Foundation walls of a 13th century fortress, believed to be the Castle of the Amstel. The location and age of the unearthed relics correspond with the archeologists' theories. Some historians are not convinced.

Insert: Johannes Baart, city archeologist, is certain the Castle of the Amstel has been found.

Archeological finds, reflecting Amsterdam's daily life over the past seven centuries, include a shoe, plate, tile, pipe head and a button.

and trading circa anno 1000. This led to Count Floris V's grant of a toll-free privilege in 1275 to 'the people living near the Dam', the spot where the mouth of the Amstel River empties into the Dam. This explains the city's earliest name, 'Aemstelledamme'. With this unfettered passage of goods through Holland's waters, the residents prospered to the point that expansion was necessary in 1380 to handle the increased population. At that time, the first two canals — the Oudezijds and Nieuwezijds Voorburgwal (Old and New Fore Walls) — and also the Achterburgwallen (Back Walls) were dug and fortified. The Singelgracht, now called the Stadhouderskade, was the enclosing moat on the southern side.

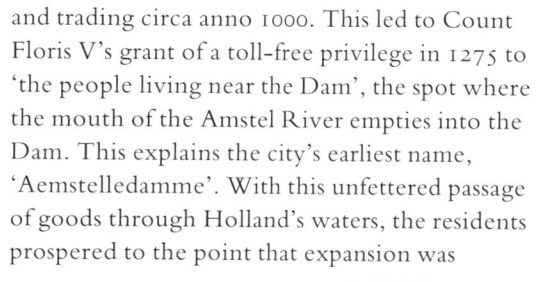

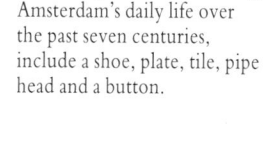

In the early part of the 17th century, expansion of the center had become an urgent necessity to meet desperate living space and warehousing shortages. The harbor had to be extended, the walled defense system needed strengthening. In 1611, excavation of the three major canals was begun. These set the pattern for Amsterdam life in the 17th century and left an unmatchable inheritance which still characterizes this city. Water even played an important role in house building through the ages. Since sea water regularly flooded this area in earlier days, a soft peat underground developed. Homes in the Middle Ages were constructed from wood to keep the weight to a minimum. When major fires in 1421 and 1452 levelled the city, including all the major municipal and church buildings, legislation was enacted requiring all construction in brick. This meant that home builders had to drive wooden piles of about some 12 meters in depth to reach a solid layer of sand to bear the heavy walls. When Amsterdam's ground water level drops, the wooden piles are exposed to oxygen and rot, explaining why some canal houses have sunk and lean sidewards. Today, office and apartment buildings rest on piles at a sand level of 60 meters.

Amsterdam remains for us, despite some of the unaesthetic intrusions, a virtually intact living museum of static, stately building styles reflecting the city's wealth and world power in the 17th and 18th centuries. The three great canals were dug, linking the inner city with the IJ river that flowed into the North Sea and onto world navigational routes. The Herengracht (Gentlemen's Canal) was named for the ruling regents, the Prinsengracht (Princes') for the Princes of Orange; the Keizersgracht (Emperor's) for Emperor Maximilian's crown in the city coat of arms. The concentric water web is lined with patricians' homes, which also served as warehouses for spices and silks brought from the East. Hooks and tows to lift the goods to the upper floors are still evident.

Amsterdam is a cityscape of contrasts: from two small wooden houses that survived fires in the

Toll privilege seal dating from the late 13th century.

Left: Boats of every size are moored on the canals.
Above: Wooden house, one of only two which survived the disastrous medieval fires that levelled the city, was moved to the Begijnhof. The other wooden house is still in place on the Zeedijk.

House boat, one man's dream of living in style, gently rocked by the waves.

Children's theater tram highlighting the Elbow Circus.

Oudezijds Voorburgwal. Painted bicycles leaning against bridge railings is a familiar Amsterdam sight.

Middle Ages to outlying Pentagon-like beehives built for 100,000 people. In between is the incomparable beauty of the inner city; a canal girdle lined with over 75,000 trees like a green ribbon along the rigid, bricked walls of the man-made waterways. When there is a deep water freeze, icebreakers keep the canals open to water traffic except for one part of the Keizersgracht which is left frozen to accommodate the traditional ice-skaters.

More than 7000 historic houses lining the canals make Amsterdam the largest antique center of any capital city on the Continent. It is a city of

houses and the spirit is best expressed by the language of these patrician houses. They were built by the wealthy merchant princes, world traders, who were inhibited by Calvinism from openly showing their affluence. Thus, while aristocrats of other lands built *châteaux*, the rich Amsterdammers built these outwardly austere houses during Holland's Golden Age when this seafaring nation ranked as the most powerful in the world. They were also proud of the swans on the canals until a city budget in 1673 eliminated the official swankeeper's position and the swans disappeared.

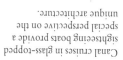

Canal cruises in glass-topped sightseeing boats provide a special perspective on the unique architecture.

Early day corruption characterized the digging of the three major canals. A pious Calvinist, Frans Oetgens, head of Public Works, had been given the responsibility for this major project. He had served for several terms as one of the city's four ruling mayors. Since Oetgens obtained early inside information on Amsterdam's impending expansion from 180 hectares to a greater center of 720 hectares, he bought up much of the needed land. After selling it back to the city, Oetgens quietly pocketed a profit of 112,000 guilders — a lot of money in those days. Despite Oetgen's corruption, the ruling oligarchy again appointed him burgemeester.

There is water, water everywhere. But, even with all the water from the river and canals — 100 canals are still flowing today — Amsterdammers never had wells or springs. They were always faced with a shortage of sweet drinking water. Rich Amsterdammers brought in spring water from outside the city by barge. The poor drank rainwater, or even sometimes canal water, with the inherent risk of cholera. Young and old drank beer since the water was polluted and the alcohol in the beer killed the bacteria. Well into the past century, city people used the canals for dumping from privies and pigsties, as well as for garbage disposal. Foreign visitors frequently commented on the canals' notorious stench. The locals did not seem to smell it. Sanitation improved with the centuries but the canals remain dirty. Despite city ordinances, Amsterdammers still dump refuse and unwanted objects into the waters.

One of the current canal plagues is the overabundance of houseboats and barges. There are nearly 3,000 — with almost 100 illegally moored. They block canal views from the canal houses, sometimes tap the water supply cables, damage sanitation lines and might be used for commercial purposes such as hippie hotels, prostitution or marijuana cultivation. One humane houseboat resident provides shelter for hundreds of stray cats. In all, there are some 7,000 vessels moored in Amsterdam, many of them boats used primarily on Queen's Day. The city has cracked down on unlicensed boats, especially those used by prostitutes, though bordellos on the canalsides are openly permitted and always have been. Boats can slip in during the dark of the night at several points where no bridge need be raised or lock opened.

Satirical print by Albert Hahn: greedy developers destroying rows of monument houses to build commercial properties.

Transportation is a centuries-old problem in water-laced Amsterdam. From as early as the 17th century, there were traffic jams caused by horse-drawn sleighs and carriages along the narrow canalsides. Even then, one-way directions had to be enacted on land and in the water for the heavy barge traffic. Public transportation evolved to horse-drawn trams in the last century, followed by steam-powered, and later, electric trams and buses. Many canals were dammed and filled in during the late 19th and early 20th centuries to handle increasing traffic problems. Some streets are now for pedestrians only.

Trams clanging over canal bridges are part of the city sounds, along with church bells tolling and barrel organs churning out their mechanical melodies. Spreading further into the suburbs, covering a network of 138 kilometers, 260 trams traverse the city at frequent intervals, annually transporting some 150 million passengers. Starting in the early seventies, construction of the first subway — called the Metro — met violent opposition and rioting since its trajectory ripped through the Nieuwmarkt (New Market) quarter taking most of the old homes in its wake. Metro expansion continued and three main lines now run from Central Station reaching into the suburbs, the RAI Congress Center, the World Trade Center and Amsterdam Schiphol Airport.

Bicycles and canals: spirit of Amsterdam. Canal bikes are a relatively new, popular phenomenon as visitors peddle amidst the sights of this city on the water.

which also has connecting rail links all over the country.

While the Metro now handles some 49 million passengers annually, the municipality hopes that the expanding subway, tram and bus networks, coupled with the elimination of streetside parking places and insufficient parking garages, will force automobiles out. Every day, some 215,000 cars weave their way through the narrowing traffic on the canalsides and narrow streets. Until the sixties a special fire department unit regularly dredged cars out of the canals. Only then was it realized that railings were necessary. A *burgemeester* had already proposed an 'iron rail' in the 18th century because horses and carriages frequently fell in the water — but the

city found his plan too expensive! As with the metro excavations, the city fathers had also been under critical fire in the late 19th century when they demolished buildings, hemming in the harbor to build three artificial islands as a base for the Central Station. Nine thousand piles were sunk 12 meters deep to a solid sand bank for a station big enough to accommodate the increased traffic resulting from the popularity of the steam locomotive. Steam power had ushered in a modest start of the Industrial Revolution around 1795. The country's first steam locomotive line was laid from Amsterdam to Haarlem in 1839. The railroad station, built by the architects Cuypers and Van Gendt between 1877 and 1885, is still

Realeneiland, a man-made 17th century island, has its picturesque 'Zandhoek' (Sand Corner), where the small houses have Dutch doors and views on the water.

resented today by some since it totally obliterates an open view of the harbor. Dr. Petrus Josephus Hubertus Cuypers had come to Amsterdam from the Catholic province Limburg and used ecclesiastic decorations on the Central Station. The reigning King Willem III swore that he would never set one foot in that 'Catholic' building. Cuypers also built the Rijksmuseum with a sisterly resemblance to the railway station.

Other artificial islands had already been created in the mid-17th century off the city's western and eastern coasts, and still bear their original names: Kattenburg, Wittenburg and Oostenburg in the eastern sphere and Prinseneiland, Realeneiland en Bickerseiland on the western side. The easterly islands were designed when Holland started the four wars against the British for supremacy of the seas. There were wharves for building warships, harbors and wide canals. These islands were perfect examples of 17th century town planning in capsule form. Houses, pubs and a church provided a self-contained life for the islanders. The East India Company built a shipyard on Oostenburg that was probably the largest global industrial complex of the time.

The westerly islands came into being for quite another purpose. They had the role of storing tar, oils, gunpowder and other inflammables, which the town fathers, fearful of fires, wanted well-isolated from the business and residential center. On these western islands were constructed the imposing and still-standing warehouses of the Dutch East India Company, whose ships circled the globe.

In the past, shipping and engineering were the island's driving forces. The chaotic mix of accommodation and workshops has always attracted lots of artists to the islands. Dutch impressionist George Breitner had a studio on Prinseneiland for eighteen years and the pioneering 19th century photographer, Jacob Olie Jacobzn, lived on Realeneiland.

Naturally, with all of Amsterdam's water, many bridges had to be built. In the first official city map drawn by Cornelis Anthoniszoon in 1544, 35 wooden bridges existed. By the beginning of this century, there were 350. Nowadays, Amsterdam claims to be a city of over 1,00 bridges. An engineer estimates there are nearly 1,200. Amsterdam supposedly has more bridges

Sun seeking, a Dutch pastime, on the expansive terrace of the Amstel Church, a 'temporary' building from the 17th century that survived long after its ignominious use as horse stables by Napoleon.

'Iron Railway' was a revolutionary accomplishment in 1839 when the first train link between Amsterdam and Haarlem was opened.

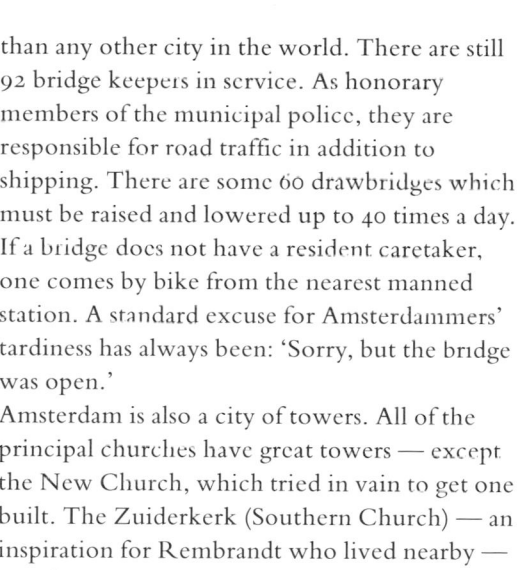

Art Deco sauna has authentic decoration salvaged in Paris.

Right: The Western Tower proudly bears Amsterdam's coat of arms and Emperor Maximilian's crown.

than any other city in the world. There are still 92 bridge keepers in service. As honorary members of the municipal police, they are responsible for road traffic in addition to shipping. There are some 60 drawbridges which must be raised and lowered up to 40 times a day. If a bridge does not have a resident caretaker, one comes by bike from the nearest manned station. A standard excuse for Amsterdammers' tardiness has always been: 'Sorry, but the bridge was open.'

Amsterdam is also a city of towers. All of the principal churches have great towers — except the New Church, which tried in vain to get one built. The Zuiderkerk (Southern Church) — an inspiration for Rembrandt who lived nearby — was the prototype used by Christopher Wren for his steeples in the City of London. This is one of the oldest and largest Protestant churches in the country, built between 1603 and 1611 by the famed city architect Hendrik de Keyser. Another tower of special significance is that of the Westerkerk (Western Church), consecrated in 1631. The city's highest, it was erected in memory of Maximilian, the Holy Roman Emperor who took Amsterdam under his protection in 1489 and offered his crown to adorn the city coat of arms. A gilded Emperor's crown is at the top of the tower.

Amsterdam, a walker's city, is a visual adventure. The city's rich architectural heritage was preserved, ironically, thanks to the early 19th century economic malaise after the French fled.

This resulted in passive protection. Starting in the early 20th century, mercenary contractors knocked down monumental buildings with disdain and filled in the gaping holes with Art Nouveau and Art Deco structures. Even worse, by the fifties and sixties, they put glass and steel-fronted 'modern' façades on new nondescript buildings. A screeching halt to the blight which, fortunately was relatively limited on the old

water web, came with the founding of the National Monuments Committee and strict control regulations.

Amsterdam is, more than anything else, a city with a heart — a social consciousness for the welfare of its citizens. After Amsterdam became Protestant with the Reformation in 1578, the cloisters were cleared out and these Catholic enclaves were converted by the newly Calvinist burghers to serve as hospitals, old people's homes, orphanages and prisons.

Amsterdam cares for its elderly, tired and sick, even law-breakers. Very progressive care for these people has been part of the city's pattern for hundreds of years. Amsterdam's 20th century social consciousness is evident in many reforms. Like all of the Netherlands, the city has been a European fore-runner in social amenities. Drug addicts and alcoholics are also pampered with professional care and guidance, which is often criticized as excessive.

One of the most appealing, picturesque and tranquil approaches for elderly citizens' housing, particularly women alone, is rooted in charitable acts from over 300 years back. Starting early in the 17th century, wealthy families founded alms houses to provide quarters where poor women of advanced age could live independently with dignity.

Amsterdam's most visually spectacular alms house is the Begijnhof. It was founded in the 14th century as a cloistered home for Catholic lay sisters. Tucked away behind high brick walls just off the busy Kalverstraat pedestrian shopping street, the Begijnhof is a large, enchanting square of 17th and 18th century houses grouped around the former Catholic church that became Protestant after the Reformation in 1578 swept over the Netherlands.

Happily, there is no real poverty anymore in Amsterdam since everyone is cared for under the far-reaching social welfare system. There is some substandard housing, but no slums in terms of other European countries and elsewhere in the world. Amsterdam is progressive in its approach to social work for all kinds of troubled individuals or groups.

Sign of the times: when inmates were moved to a modern Amsterdam penal facility from antiquated quarters in the downtown Leidseplein entertainment center, the old prison was renovated for shops, restaurants and housing. The new public square was fronted

with a pompous, pseudo-classical colonnaded front with Latin wisdom carved across the extended fronton: *Homo Sapiens Non Urinat In Ventum* ('A wise man does not urinate against the wind'). Amsterdam today!

Only the 17th century classical portal on the Heiligeweg (Holy Way) remains of the *rasphuis (rasp-house)* that has been there in a former cloister. Hendrick de Keyser was commissioned to create this entrance with a bas-relief showing a wagon driver whipping wild beasts pulling a load of hard wood. The inscription — *Virtutis Est Domare Quae Cuncti Pavent* — means 'It is

The Begijnhof, a quiet oasis of tiny 17th and 18th century houses for elderly women, just off the busy Kalverstraat pedestrian shopping street.

> City on the water. There's no better way to feel the true atmosphere of Amsterdam than from a boat gliding through the canals, with perspectives of the unique architecture and waterways framed by old bridges.

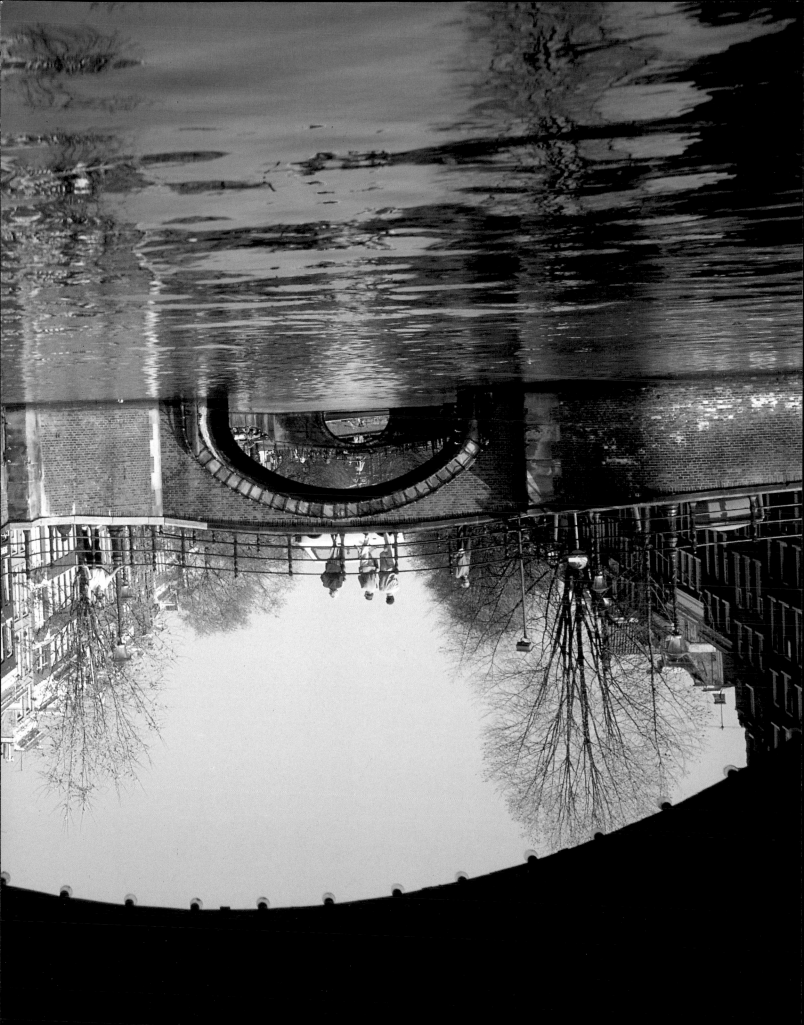

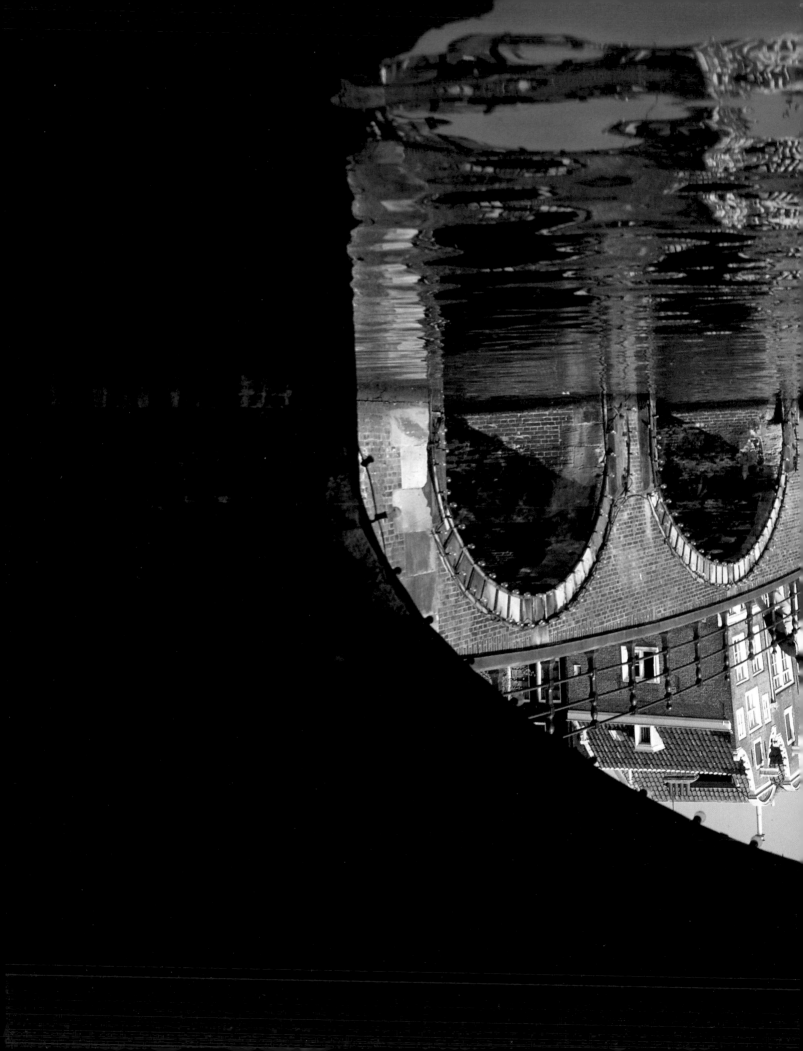

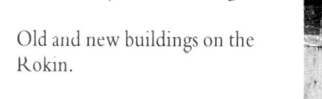

right to tame and master what the people fear'. Amsterdam feared criminals and idlers. They were tolerant with those who complied with their ground rules and work schedules — but medieval in punishment for those who did not. Shirkers were sent to a cell which could be filled with water. They could choose between using a pump or drowning. Or they ended up in the courtyard on the whipping block. Until recently, children happily skipped through that portal, unaware of the stern inscription, to the swimming pool that replaced the rasphuis, and which became in 1995 part of the Vendex complex, a shopping mall, with housing, parking and a police station.

Fortunately, that medieval form of justice had run its course by the end of the 18th century when a progressive approach to punishment

The New Market quarter with some of the remaining monument houses and many new buildings constructed after subway lines were dug.

Old and new buildings on the Rokin.

took its place. Today's prisons are very humane. They are often cited as a good example of a benevolent concept geared to minimum sentences and aiming at 'resocializing' law-breakers. They are showing offenders that society cares about them. Life is normalized as much as possible to prepare prisoners for a return to society. As a result, fewer and fewer people serve time, with a crime rate proportionally lower than in many other western countries.

Amsterdammers are universalist in the best sense. This is reflected in their attitudes and sympathy for events happening outside the city. There was a call in the City Council for an avenue to be named for the Russian dissident writer Alexander Solzhenitsyn soon after he was forced to leave his country. Coincidentally or not, the avenue selected was the Veluwelaan, where the Russian Consulate has been headquartered for years. A nearby Stalin Avenue had earlier been rebaptised the Freedom Avenue. Churchill and Roosevelt signposts remained, while the Rivierenlaan was renamed President Kennedy Avenue. In a western quarter there is a President Allende Avenue. After the Heineken brewery was demolished, plans were announced to name this new square in honor of Nelson Mandela, but the Commission for Naming Streets objected, pointing out that traditionally streets are not named for living, non-royal persons. As a result, the area honors the painter Marie Heineken, a niece of the brewery's founder.

Amsterdammers are openly sentimental about their city and everything connected with it. They can be outspokenly critical, but underneath the harshness there is an undying faithfulness. Real Amsterdammers, no matter how far they might travel or wherever else they may live, are always happy to be back in their place. They even treat St. Nicholas like their very own property. He is the city's patron saint as well as the protector of Amsterdam's children and fishermen. The Oude Kerk (Old Church), built around 1300, was named for him, but later that honor was transferred to a newer church on the Prins Hendrikkade near the wharf where he arrives by boat from Spain every November. Hardly anyone is too blasé to care and all Amsterdammers are like children who believe, at least for a few weeks, that the good saint has come to visit them. Architectural heritage marks the city and its

inhabitants. It's respected, while taken for granted. Amsterdam is vibrant, mondial, with-it, a city swinging in unexpected contrasts — and all in this incredible sphere where time could have stopped still, but didn't. There are wildly decorated discos in stately houses and disused churches. Restaurants and pubs, with their traditional brown smoke-stained color, continually spring up everywhere. There is the untranslatable *gezelligheid* (something like cosiness) everywhere.

Amsterdam is a youthscape, an explosion of attitudes, mores, habits (some bordering on illegality) and a *modus vivendi* that fits right into what could otherwise be a staid, stodgy Dutch city but is not — because it's Amsterdam. In this city, there seems to be room for everything, though it is physically small. A deeply-rooted Calvinist sternness is shaken off in keeping with the times. No one has heard of a generation gap. Solidly square burghers take their kids' break-outs in stride with an unflappable calm — even when young anarchists threaten to overthrow their well-patterned society. The streets, public squares and parks are staging grounds for the youth-in-motion that

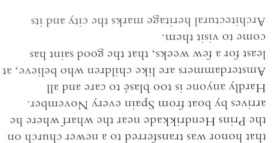

Max Euwe Square, honoring the late Dutch world champion chess player, has a pompous colonnaded entrance with the Latin legend: *Homo Sapiens Non Urinat In Ventum* (Wise men do not urinate against the wind).

Left: Classical 17th century entrance to a former penal institution. Its inscription proclaims: *Virtus Est Donare Quae Cuncti Parent* (It is right to tame and master what the people fear). This stone portal, on the Holy Way, was incorporated in the Vendex shopping mall.

'Het Lieverdje', sculpture of a mischievous street boy on the Spui square.

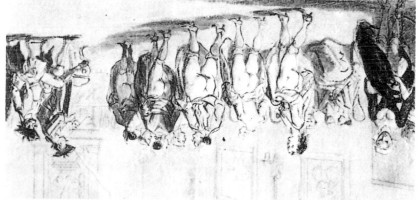

neither shocks nor upsets the Amsterdammers. They like to live and let live. Their mentality makes room for all kinds of people, many of whom do not fit any other Dutch mould. Their city has always been open for religious and political refugees. Young people come to escape the Establishment elsewhere in the Netherlands or abroad. The tolerance in the air makes it possible for individuals to be themselves, for protestors to take action, for prostitutes to openly ply their trade — in effect, for everyone to do his own thing.

There is the Prostitution Information Centre in the Narrow Church Alley providing assistance to prostitutes and their pimps on laws, taxes, insurance and condoms, as well as price indications for potential clients and curious tourists. Girls work in monuments in a quarter called the Walletjes, a name derived from the walls that hemmed in this oldest part of town. The red light in the windows clearly advertises the world's oldest profession. A carnival atmosphere persists as stolid Dutchmen and their

wives, foreign couples, and lots of single men with all kinds of accents jam the cobbled streets to window-shop and comment on the phosphorescent-lit wares sitting provocatively. The drug scene is surprisingly open. The municipality subsidizes several youth clubs like Paradiso (in an ex-church) and the Melkweg (in an abandoned milk factory), where soft drugs are openly peddled against a backdrop of live music. An overabundance of coffee shops openly serve a variety of soft drugs from printed menus. Homosexuals and lesbians have their own societies and clubs where they can drink, dance and flirt without fear of interruption or blackmail. These establishments, registered with the police, exist exclusively for members and

Above left: The Prostitution Information Center, neighboring the Old Church in the heart of the red light district, was initiated by Mariska Majoor, an ex-prostitute.

Above right: The Homo monument, at the foot of the Western Church on the Prinsengracht, was the world's first memorial to homosexual war victims.

Prostitution has been openly tolerated through the centuries. Historical print from the Rijksmuseum records the visit in 1722 by Prince Eugenius of Savoy and the British Consul to a Prinsengracht bordello.

Right: Night life is wild and varied in the clubs, such as ROXY party time.

their guests. The gay scene is very open in this city characterized by its tolerance. The 1998 Gay and Lesbian Games will take place in Amsterdam. The world's first 'homo monument' is on the plaza bordering the Westerkerk (Western Church).

Nowadays 25 percent of Amsterdammers are foreign born. The population, which is nearing 750,000, includes some 175 different nationalities, with the largest ethnic groups from Surinam, Turkey, Morocco and the Dutch Antilles. Amsterdam's tolerance was clearly evident when the Reformation forced Catholics to openly abandon their religion. The city's rulers allowed Catholics to hold services in clandestine 'hidden' churches, whose locations were open secrets.

Amsterdam society is open. It is physically evident in the homes with open-curtained windows for constant contact with street life, allowing everyone to look in. Supposedly this harks back to a Calvinist doctrine of 'not having anything to hide'. Daily open markets, including the one in the grotesquely impersonal Bijlmermeer housing project, are an integral part of city life. The Albert Cuyp in the multi-cultural De Pijp neighborhood, near the old Heineken brewery, is reputedly Europe's largest daily street market, with the city's most exotic foods, fruits and ingredients.

There is a riot of color, in all seasons, at the world-famed flower market, where growers sell their produce from permanent stalls on barges bobbing on the Singel. De Looier is an indoor antique market, while the old flea market on the Waterlooplein is amusing to scavenge through.

On Mondays, the Noordermarkt hawks fabrics and second-hand clothes, while farmers sell their cheese and vegetables on Saturdays. There are also open markets for books, postage stamps and many other specialized items.

Some of the aforegoing commentary was written when my adopted home city was celebrating her 700th official birthday. Though I have lived here as an American expatriate for several decades, before also becoming Dutch, my attitudes on this city's almost undefinable, conflicting charms have not changed. Amsterdammers are receptive to foreigners. Look at Heinrich Schliemann, the 19th century German archaeologist who gained world fame with his discovery of Troy and Mycenae, but actually got his start by chance in Amsterdam. He wrote: 'Amsterdam set me off on the road to my illustrious career; I have

Above left: Elaborate coach houses, which served the patricians on the Herengracht, have become restaurants with terraces in the formal gardens. Het Tuynhuys (Garden House) is one in this idyllic row.

Above: Flea market on the Waterloo Square, a daily mixed bag of second hand goods, spreads out behind the Town Hall and Opera.

Street theater in the parks, on street corners, everywhere one turns. Mimes who hold motionless poses are overabundant in the nineties.

The Amstel River in all its majesty flowing under the Thin Bridge into Amsterdam.

Albert Cuyp market, supposedly Europe's largest daily outdoor market, is an explosion of colors and tastes with food produce from all over the world.

Amsterdam to thank for everything that I know and have, which is why I feel deeply attracted to Amsterdam, and why I enthusiastically proclaim: Long Live Amsterdam!'
Amsterdammers are open to foreign ideas, welcoming new ideologies and ways of thinking.

This is a people's city. Monuments matter little except to honor men and their courage. Grandiose recollections of the past are practically non-existent. This is a city that quickly takes everyone to its heart and enraptures them with a spirit that is typically Amsterdam and not found in another Dutch city. While singing the praises of Paris and London, they chauvinistically choose for 'Geef mij maar Amsterdam' (... but give me Amsterdam).
Amsterdam's cityscape, especially in the old center, is an open showcase of past glory and living proof that Amsterdammers care about their heritage. They know what a special city they have. Back in the 15th century, when the Rotterdam philosopher Erasmus made a snide remark that Amsterdam inhabitants lived on the tops of trees like monkeys, no one really took offense. After all, they regarded building houses on wooden piles in marshlands as an early Amsterdam accomplishment. And, as all Amsterdammers, including this adopted son, will tell you, their city has been doing great things for more than 700 years.

The Dam

Vortex of the country

As always, throughout more than seven centuries of Amsterdam history, the Dam remains the heart and pulse of the capital and the nation. Everything that is happening seems to gravitate to this great square.

On a given day, one might see ecological activists distributing pamphlets, young people singing gospel songs, children licking their Italian ice cream cones and locals 'downing' onion-dipped herrings held by the tails. Bird lovers of all ages feed the pigeons and pose for pictures with them. Lines form at the entrance to Madame Tussaud Scenerama. Steps away, a small crowd is gathering at the little stage where Jan Klaassen, and his wife Katrijn, are performing in a Punch and Judy show, with the imposing Royal Palace as a backdrop.

In the mid-17th century, a real-life Jan Klaassen and Katrijn came to the Dam with their puppets as a satirical protest against the authorities' conduct of the war against England. The traditional characters have continued to play here for over 300 years, but their sharp political tongue has been tamed for light diversion. The message is now geared for the children who come to feed the pigeons, which are the town's fattest and most photographed.

On the other side of the huge Dam Square, split by the city's main traffic artery, three Caribbean music-makers are singing to their own Calypso beat. Uninhibited people are dancing under imaginary limbo poles that get lower and lower on the steps of the National War Monument. Higher on the steps, two French folk singers strum on their guitars, singing ballads.

When word of Amsterdam's traditional tolerance spread like wildfire around the world in the late sixties, the Dam became the meeting place, social center and bedroom for young people wanting to 'break out' from the commercial society and live without timetables, obligations or even money.

Amsterdammers regarded these free-wheeling nomads with *laissez faire* shoulder shrugging. This was freedom 20th century style. But lack of sanitary facilities eventually led to a rather messy situation. Protests from neighboring merchants brought action from the city government. The Dam merchants viewed the travellers on their doorsteps as detrimental to business. Besides, they were jamming their toilets every morning. So pressure was put on for their removal. One night, as dusk began to settle, police came along and hosed down the steps, washing away the youth and their backpacks. Later, stone flower planters were placed to break up the sleeping space and discourage overnighting. But during

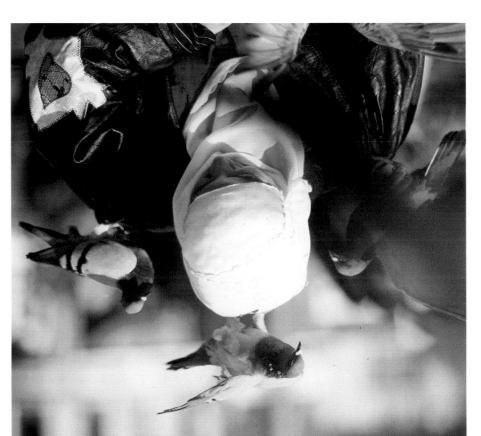

Pigeons on the Dam are extremely people-oriented.

the day, even now, you still see hordes of young people from all over the world snoozing in the sun, exchanging information on conditions in Nepal, North Africa or India and just relating to each other in their own free society.

Although the spirit of the Dam is essentially the same today as it has always been, with commercial bustle and local excitement, physically it is quite another place than the old square of even one century ago. In our times automobiles nose their insistent way to the nearby parking meters and car lots where water once flowed. All the open markets stocked with fish from the river, fresh produce from the surrounding fields, the stalls where textiles were measured and other goods weighed have disappeared to make room for department stores, banks and travel agencies. The gabled houses have been torn down. Not counting the over-fed pigeons, the only inhabitants sleeping on the Dam nowadays are hotel guests.

Still, the Dam remains De Plaetse (The Place), as it originally was called. When Amsterdam really began, in the marshy land where the Amstel river roared on its way to the IJ and the Zuiderzee, is lost in misty legends. Some insist that around the year 1000 fishermen dammed the river and settled there. (However, during subway excavations in the seventies, three Roman coins were found. This raised speculation that perhaps Amsterdam had, after all, been a Roman settlement like other neighboring Dutch places.)

Records do indicate that settlers built wooden houses along the river's eastern banks and were busy as fishermen, farmers and traders from at least the mid-13th century. A letter has been found which Gijsbrecht III of Amstel sent in 1240 to Lübeck asking for the release of a ship presumably belonging to an Amsterdam trader. More houses sprang up along the waters flowing into the harbor, and shipping quickened its pace in the search for new trading markets. The waters later took names which provided clues to the navigational rights of way. The two principal arteries leading from the Dam are the Damrak and the Rokin. Damrak was derived from rak, meaning sailing on the right coming from the IJ to the Dam. Rokin is a corruption of rak-in, also for bearing right along the route through the dam sluice.

Amsterdam probably received city rights in 1306 from Guy d'Avesnes, Bishop of Utrecht, and the burghers took great pride in their new status as citizens. But what really counted most for them, and still does, was the toll privilege Floris V granted them in 1275. This was the official start of the money game that Amsterdam has played so shrewdly for mercantile glory, power and wealth, unmatched by any other city in the Netherlands. Therefore

The Town Hall and New Church in the 17th century when the Dam was still accessible to ships sailing on the Damrak from the open harbor.

Freedom Festival celebration around the liberty tree, installed in 1795 on the Dam, baptized Square of the Revolution.

Above right: Jacob van Campen, architect of the Town Hall, now the Palace on the Dam.

Right: The Amsterdam Town Hall, built in the 17th century Town Hall was acclaimed as the 'eighth wonder of the world'. The grandeur of the Citizen's Hall was intended for the glorification of the ruling merchant princes rather than for the common man.

nothing could have been more logical for the ruling regents than to select the year 1275, and not the misty 1000 or the legal 1306, as the milestone when their commercial existence was given its first important impetus. 700 years of trading was celebrated in 1975.

The harbor on the Dam has disappeared, along with the waters that flowed from the Amstel in tributaries along the Rokin and Damrak. Both were filled in during the late 19th and early 20th centuries. The Middeldam is also no more, nor is the Vijgendam, where large supplies of spoiled figs were used as fill-in for foundations of the quays leading off the Dam. Even the names are gone, and the large area from the Palace to beyond the monument is now simply called the Dam.

While commercial demands, unfortunately, doomed most of the old buildings on the Dam, the New Church and the Royal Palace survived.

In keeping with Amsterdam's role as an international trade and commerce center, wood and grain staple market and dominant city in the most important global maritime country, the regents felt that their mercantile empire needed a glorious seat of government. The new Town Hall, in essence conceived as an aristocratic palace for the ruling classes, was finally completed in 1655 on 13,659 piles. ('This figure is drummed into Dutch school children's heads with: 'Put a 1 before and a 9 after, the number of days in the year.')

As the largest, most beautiful town hall in the whole world, it was called the 'Eighth Wonder of the World'. Its immense, 30-meter high Burgerzaal (Citizen's Hall) was intended more to glorify the merchant princes than serve the people.

On the large triangular marble pediment on the upper section of the building's rear façade, Amsterdam is personified by a female figure in the middle sitting on the edge of a medieval boat — the *koggeschip* (cockboat), an earlier symbol for the city. At her feet, two old men hold water jars representing the river Amstel and the river IJ, both with a central role in the city's history. These three figures are surrounded by people and animals from all over the known world — Africa, Europe, Asia and America (Australia was still uncharted territory). They pay hommage to the city might by offering gifts.

Quite befitting money-motivated Amsterdam, all of its earlier town halls were used not only for running the city, controlling trade and as an exchange for corn and textiles, but also as a money exchange to serve the merchants in their local and international commerce. The prosperous economy had grown out of the *stadhuis* (town hall) from the 14th century onward, and nothing was more logical than having a money exchange right in the Town Hall itself. For this exchange function, the Bank of Amsterdam was set up below the Council Chamber. The Amsterdam Bank system worked for almost 200 years, up to the French Revolution, with the city's *burgemeesters* (burgomasters) swearing to its accuracy and solidity.

In the same sense of running a well-regulated society, the regents also arranged for violators of civil or criminal law to be dealt with quickly, and often cruelly, right at the stadhuis. Town halls of the Middle Ages had special facilities for judging

start, it was always in the Town Hall that aristocratic burghers sat in council to create policies which would make them, and the city, richer. The first known Town Hall existed around 1395, when a house of the Order of St. Elizabeth Gasthuis was purchased at the corner of de Plaetse and the Gasthuissteeg. Besides being used for city meetings, there was a court (a 'justice has been done' sign was hung out each time someone had received gruesome punishment), as well as areas for business, such as the weavers' quality controllers. The big medieval fires damaged and then destroyed the Town Hall and all its records. City government continued on the Dam in makeshift town halls until Jacob van Campen, the well-known architect, was commissioned in 1648 to build a monumental structure.

Bloody justice symbol: the blood band embellished with the St. Andrew's cross, three Xs, from the city coat of arms.

Toll privilege granted by Count Floris V in 1275.

Even the most crass businessman could never have thought of tampering with these two institutions, both so significant in the events centered around the Dam throughout the centuries. Historic buildings situated on streets and canals surrounding the Dam were considered less commercially viable and thus survived intact.

Since Amsterdam life has been commercially-oriented by its merchant regents right from the

detachment of a lieutenant, three sergeants, a corporal, a drummer and twenty men kept the watch and there was a ceremonial changing of the guard every day between four and five p.m. Many foreigners unknowingly strolled into this forbidden area and were sternly reprimanded by the guard.

During the early 19th century French occupation, it was King Louis Napoleon who had put the ban on the stones after a baby was

t Oude Stadt Huys

The medieval Town Hall burned down and was replaced by the palatial 17th century structure.

left in a guard house one night and rumors flew around town and infants being left there nightly. He was shaken by the prospect of the foundling.

After the French left in 1813, the Dutch sovereign prince, who was later to become King Willem I, visited Amsterdam. In December of that year, he requested the Palace reversion to its role as Town Hall, with several suites for his use when in the capital. The city could not afford the conversion and placed the Palace at his disposal. There were outcries that the most important building in the life of the bustling commercial center was standing like a mummy, staring out with empty eyes. Nothing was done until 1935 when the Palace was sold to the State for 10 million guilders, despite protests from many civic groups. A spokesman for Amstelodamum, an organization dedicated to guarding the heritage of the old city, summed up the attitude, felt by many, that money always took precedence over history in such decisions. He quoted the 17th century Calvinist Bartens:

and punishing those convicted: a colonnaded *vierschaar*, a four sided area where the accused's sentence was rendered. As late as the 16th century, 'witches' were burned in front of the Town Hall. The last witch hunt victim, Volkje Hermans van Blokzijl, died of torture on the night before her scheduled death by burning on the Dam.

Since the Dam had already been the center of protests, Amsterdam's rulers, fearing riots getting out of hand, had the new Town Hall on Dam Square built like a fort, with very small entry gates and two canons that could sweep the whole square. Happily, those have never been used. Architect Jacob van Campen, presumably gave up a glorious main entrance to the Town Hall, placing instead seven unimposing little doors in order to simulate an outdoor tribunal as part of the front façade. This effect was achieved around the three middle doors which led up to one flight to the elaborately decorated vierschaar inside. There the magistrates sat on marble benches, amidst classical columns and massive sculptures, to pronounce the death sentences for crimes which would today get only light punishment. Each magistrate wore a blood sash embellished with the three Xs (St. Andrew cross) from the Amsterdam coat of arms, and held a rod of of justice.

The accused were kept in the long, damp cellar prison that was always found under the Town Hall and still exists under the present Palace. Torture, drownings and hangings were commonplace in those lower depths. Sometimes there were 'inside and outside' hangings. This meant death downstairs in the stadhuis, followed later by a simulated hanging on the Volewijk, on the other side of the IJ, so that in winter ice-skaters could enjoy their cookies and cup of soup while looking at the corpses.

A scaffold extended out from the corner of the stadhuis. As late as the 19th century, Amsterdammers came to the Dam to witness justice being done; it was always signaled with a *roede* (birch) hung out of a Town Hall window. An 1805 print shows a man standing on that scaffold with a sign around his neck: 'Two Wives'. Evidently bigamy was not considered such a serious crime since he was only on public view for fifteen minutes.

Until 1940, there was a statute on the city books prohibiting anyone from walking on the small stones paved in front of the Palace. A special

'The whore on the IJ can be bought with anyone's money
She serves Pope and heathen, Moor and Turk,
She cares not about God nor the dear fatherland,
She asks only for profit! Only for profit! Only for profit!

So the great building on the Dam still serves as a Royal Palace but is only used on important

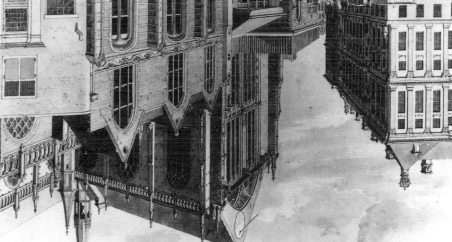

The Dam as it was in early days with a view of the New Church and the Town Hall which became the Palace.

Right: Admiral Michiel de Ruyter, 17th century naval hero, is honored with this elaborate tomb in the New Church.

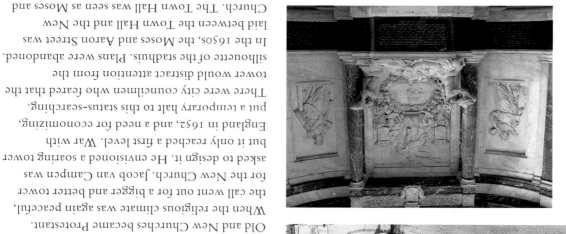

occasions and state visits. In recent years, Queen Beatrix and Prince Claus have received all their royal visitors and heads of state at the Dam Palace, which also serves as the official guest house. Neighboring the former stadhuis on the Dam is the imposing New Church, which started drawing worshippers around 1410. There were burials just outside the church in the

ellendigen (miserables) cemetery for suicides and people who had been sentenced to death. Ordinary burghers were interred in another cemetery. Prominent figures, statesmen and heroes like Admiral De Ruyter were buried inside the church.

From the beginning, there existed a rivalry for prestige between parishioners of the New Church and the Old Church, which had been completed around 1300. Since the big fires of 1421 and 1452 had destroyed the oldest part of the New Church, with each rebuilding the replacement structure and interior became more and more elaborately decorated. This brought competitive enlargements and embellishments at the Old Church as well. The status struggle between the two parishes was in full force. In the 16th century, the Old Church had 38 altars, more beautiful stained glass windows, a better organ and a tower was under construction. The New Church had only 36 altars, a better pulpit, larger windows, but no tower. In 1565, it was decided to build the New Church tower and even a carillon maker was hired to make bells. However, in the turbulent year that followed nothing came of it. The Statue Breaking of 1566 spared the New Church, but when Amsterdam went over into Calvinist hands in 1578 during the Reformation, all of the church decorators were dismissed. The Old and New Churches became Protestant. When the religious climate was again peaceful, the call went out for a bigger and better tower for the New Church. Jacob van Campen was asked to design it. He envisioned a soaring tower but it only reached a first level. War with England in 1652, and a need for economizing, put a temporary halt to this status-searching. There were city councilmen who feared that the tower would distract attention from the silhouette of the stadhuis. Plans were abandoned. In the 1650s, the Moses and Aaron Street was laid between the Town Hall and the New Church. The Town Hall was seen as Moses and the church as Aaron. Houses were knocked down on the Dam and the church now had its entrance and vista on the great square. Over the years, plans came up for new beautification but nothing significant was done. In 1849, a neo-Gothic steeple was added to the mini-tower, made even worse by further insensitive bungling in 1913. The church was restored to its former glory in the early nineties.

Maternal pride on Queen Beatrix's face as she guides Crown Prince Willem Alexander into the Dam Palace for his first attendance at a New Year's reception for the diplomatic corps. This was January 1995.

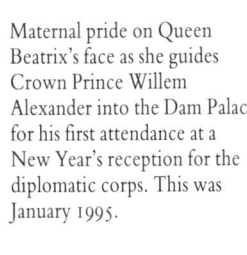
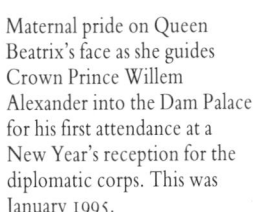

The Royal Palace on porcelain service.

Fun fair on the Dam attracts kids from all over the country.

The New Church has been used for royal inaugurations, from Willem I to Queen Beatrix. An indication of the democratization within the Royal House, and the easing of protocol rigidity, came on September 7, 1948, when Juliana arrived at the New Church for her inauguration. Although advised that she must precede Prince Bernhard, she pointedly took his arm saying: 'He is my husband.' They walked in together for the ceremony. Princess Beatrix would have been married in the New Church, but since it was being restored at that time (1966), her marriage to Prince Claus took place in the Western Church.

Starting in the early nineties, the National Foundation De Nieuwe Kerk has regularly used the cavernous Gothic New Church space, often in conjunction with Dutch and foreign musea, for blockbuster expositions which otherwise would not have been mounted in Amsterdam. Working through diplomatic and municipal channels, there have been extraordinary presentations, such as the *Treasures of San Marco*, *Rediscovering Pompeii*, *China's Distant Past*, *Lands of the Scythians*, *Royal Splendour in Gold and Silk*. Over the ages, the Dam, with the stately backdrop of the New Church and Royal Palace, has been witness to happenings both regal and repulsive, inspiring and degrading, cultural and

Dese Vertooninghen zyn t'Amsterdam (van doude Camer *in liefd bloeyende*) vertoont, op de vieringhe vant Bestand, den 5 Mey 1609.

ALDVS WAS HET TOONNEEL STAENDE OP DEN DAM, BY DE PAERDEN-STAL.

Liberation Day, marking the end of the World War II Nazi occupation, is celebrated on May 5th. Coincidentally, on May 5, 1609, there was great rejoicing on the Dam for the cease-fire after decades of fighting the Spanish in the 80-Year War.

commercial, festive and bloody.
Amsterdammers' aspirations, heroism, joys and sorrows, political and social drive, economic life, upheavals and change, protests and riots, search for greater power and wealth, world exploration, religion, corruption and greed, justice, pageantry and celebrations — all of these, and more, used the Dam as a stage from the very beginning. (see 'Protests').

If the Dam is the center of Amsterdam, the National Monument is the heart of the Dam. The monument consists of a soaring white column, gently sloping steps, and twelve urns, each filled with soil from one of the then eleven, now twelve, provinces. The twelfth urn contains earth from the fields of honor in Indonesia. It was erected after World War II, the money collected from the sale of 400,000 certificates entitling each owner to a symbolic share of the Dam. The monument was unveiled on May 4, 1956, the Dutch Memorial Day, honoring the dead of World War II. Each year on that day, Queen Beatrix and Prince Claus, accompanied

by Crown Prince Willem-Alexander, lay a wreath during a silent, emotional public service attended by thousands of Amsterdammers. On May 5, the Netherlands celebrate, now officially only once every five years, its liberation from World War II German occupation. Much of Amsterdam's festivity centers around the monument and the Dam. But few Amsterdammers know that a great celebration marking the cease-fire in another terrible war also took place on May 5 in 1609. The Twelve-Year Truce in the Eighty Years War (1568–1648) between Spain and the Netherlands was signed in April and on May 5 the Dam became the site for rejoicing. The Chamber of Rhetoric named *Blossoming in Love* performed allegorical pieces. The Dam stage, illuminated by torches, was decorated with carved dragons and Neptunes. Royalty, rioters, processions, strollers, shoppers and sleepers have always found their way to the Dam, the pulse and barometer of Amsterdam and Dutch life. For, as any Dam sitter will tell you: 'This is where it's really happening.'

Royal Link

Amsterdam/House of Orange, up & down relationship

Dutch monarchs, following legislation enacted in 1814, have all been inaugurated in Amsterdam's New Church. King Willem III's oath-taking in 1849.

Reigns of:
Queen Beatrix (1980-present)
Queen Juliana (1948-1980)
Queen Wilhelmina (1898-1948)
Queen-Regent Emma (1890-1898)

Since the late 16th century, the relationship between Amsterdam and the House of Orange-Nassau, the Dutch royal family, has not always been a very warm or happy one. There have been lots of ups and downs, incidents, easy and uneasy periods. With vacillating enthusiasm and aloofness, the reigning Prince of Orange was received in glorious processions or turned away with a cold shoulder. Amsterdam's rich, powerful merchants were convinced that their city politics, including making treaties, trading with the enemy and worshipping at a money altar, should take precedence over national interests. But the 'common man' was always pro-Orange and in bad times turned to the royal house for salvation as a counter-balance to selfish upper-class policies.

The ties between the House of Orange and the capital improved slightly after 1814 when a constitutional act provided that the inauguration of monarchs should take place within the walls of Amsterdam. But it was only in 1898 that the city became more openly Orange-minded when the eighteen-year-old Princess Wilhelmina ascended to the throne after the regency of her mother, Queen Emma. She won the Amsterdammers' hearts and never lost their fervent loyalty.

In an informal interview by this writer some years ago, Beatrix (then Crown Princess) and Prince Claus recounted their own affinity for the Dutch capital, while recalling the Amsterdammers' enthusiasm for the royal family. 'The people had a special affection for my grandmother, Queen Wilhelmina. She made it a point to live in Amsterdam for regular periods and felt a very close kinship with the Amsterdammers. On one occasion, she had been warned that due to some unrest in the working class Jordaan quarter, people would throw flowerpots at her. She set out in an open carriage. They threw flowers!'

Beatrix continued: 'Amsterdammers collected money to present Queen Wilhelmina with a gilded coach for her inauguration. She waited until her marriage in 1901 to Prince Hendrik to use it in their wedding procession in The Hague and then for their first official visit to Amsterdam.'

According to Beatrix: 'Queen Wilhelmina was proud of the Amsterdammers' behavior during the German occupation. This gave her strength during the war. The February 1941 dockworkers' strike to protest the deportation of

Jews epitomized their spirit in her eyes. Referring to the strike, she said: "For me, Amsterdam will always be the city where the people's resistance to the usurper first spread abroad like a flame." It was for this and other heroic resistance deeds that Queen Wilhelmina granted the city a device for its coat of arms. Beatrix explained that: 'My parents, Queen Juliana and Prince Bernhard, used to reside at the

Queen Juliana during her inauguration as sovereign, with Prince Bernhard at her side, in the New Church.

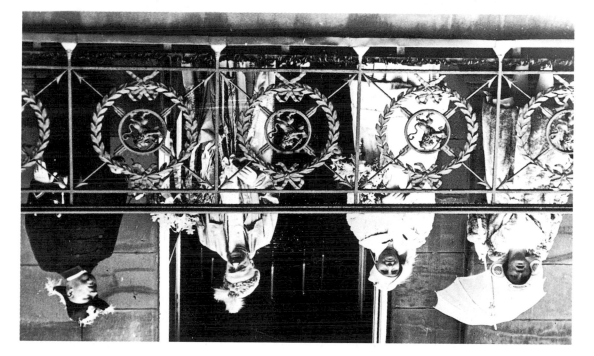

Dam Palace for given periods. But when the palace was closed for many years' restoration, they got away from that pattern. They subsequently used the palace for receiving state visits and diplomatic receptions.

Amsterdammers showed their affection for Juliana and Bernhard whenever they came to Amsterdam. Joyous occasions, such as Juliana's inauguration in 1948, and her silver anniversary on the throne in 1973, were enthusiastically celebrated. For their 50th wedding anniversary, there was a national gift and widespread rejoicing. But one of the most emotional ties between them and the city was the annual wreath-laying at the Dam war memorial. Each year on May 4, the royal couple came to Amsterdam for the national memorial service to Holland's war dead. Starting in 1980, Queen Beatrix and Prince Claus have participated in the ceremonial memorial service and observe the 'minute of silence'.

Beatrix and Claus have always been attracted to Amsterdam. They chose to be married in the capital in 1966. The burgomaster had warned them: 'Amsterdam is a difficult city, the Amsterdammers are difficult people.' The Provos, a rebellious anarchist movement, were threatening to disrupt the procession. To avoid succumbing to extremists' pressures, the wedding took place in Amsterdam. During the procession, the Provos threw smoke bombs, frightening the horses. But the carriages rolled

Their Royal Highnesses, Crown Princess Juliana, Queen Wilhelmina and Queen Mother Emma, during the celebrations in 1929 marking Emma's half century in the Netherlands. They greeted the rejoicing crowds from the Dam Palace balcony.

calmly on after the incident, as throngs along the route cheered the royal newlyweds.

Prince Claus said: 'We never regretted being married in Amsterdam, notwithstanding the difficulties. We felt that this was the place for the Crown Princess to be married. We understood the anti-German feelings of the Jewish community and others who suffered so much during the Nazi occupation. During our engagement, while touring Amsterdam by boat and car, there were banners of "Give my bike back" and other allusions to war-time German thefts and confiscations. I became the symbol of a hated enemy. In respect for the emotions that our wedding would awaken in Amsterdam, we were ready to change our plans, but the decision had already been taken for us. Now, in retrospect, we are both happy that our wedding did take place in Amsterdam since the city means so much to us.'

On April 30, 1988, after official Queen's Day visits to the provinces, Beatrix arrived unexpectedly by boat in the Jordaan. A boy, with his feet dangling on the canalside, spotted her and shouted: 'Hé, de Koningin!' ('Look, it's the Queen!'). Beatrix was greeted and applauded by the crowds and stall keepers who traditionally hawk motley offerings on this holiday in the so-called free market. She graciously accepted gifts as the masses opened up to welcome their sovereign. One brazen Jordaaner said: 'Meid, geef me een kus' ('Girl, give me a kiss'), in local dialect with an over-familiar directness. Many a monarch would have winced at such an affront and pulled back. Beatrix obligingly kissed him. After that, she could do no wrong. She had the Jordaan, and all of Amsterdam, in her hand.

Confetti was flying, signs proclaimed, 'Long Live Our New Queen', as throngs turned out on the Dam to celebrate Beatrix's ascension to the throne in 1980.

Her Majesty, Queen Beatrix, and His Royal Highness, Prince Claus.

Perhaps it was Beatrix's sweet revenge for Amsterdam's past rejections. Demonstrators had blocked the Music Theatre's main entrance in 1986 when she arrived for the official opening, obliging her to use the back staircases to her great annoyance. Six years before, her inauguration was disturbed by young anarchists. Amsterdam has always been an important part of the private as well as official lives of Beatrix and Claus. They often came to see artists in their

house for a chat, I got thrown out!'
Some years later, in March 1991, the entire Dutch royal family came by bus to the Western Church in the Jordaan for a special service in celebration of Beatrix and Claus' silver wedding anniversary. Minister Nico ter Linden, in his sermon directed at Her Majesty, clearly referred to the riots which disturbed the wedding procession, when he said: 'Exactly 25 years ago you were the bride. You were hurt but also

Her Majesty, Queen Beatrix, having arrived unexpectedly in the popular Jordaan quarter during Queen's Day celebrations, was asked for a kiss by a brazen local. The Queen obliged — to everyone's delight.

Right: Royal art subsidies recognize young Dutch talent. Queen Beatrix, in discussion with royal art subsidy winners during an exhibition of selected works in the Dam Palace. She is very involved in the artistic scene.

ateliers, to visit museums, go to art galleries, have dinner with friends in neighborhood restaurants, attend a party or shop. Claus — through personal charm, fluency in Dutch and a genuine interest in Amsterdam and the Amsterdammers — is accepted for himself. The early animosity has disappeared.

Beatrix's Amsterdam work pattern dates back to post-university days before her marriage. She studied various types of social work and went along with seasoned counsellors on home calls to the sick, visits to old people's homes and child care centers. On her program was also a period of participation in the activities of the Salvation Army.

Beatrix: 'Once I went along on the regular Wednesday program, which meant I sold the Army's newspaper, visited different kinds of cafés, talked to people on the streets and in their homes, discussed problems with youth in their centers and followed everything being done. Since the Salvation Army headquarters is right in the heart of the red-light district, it was interesting for me to see how various kinds of people in this mixed neighborhood were approached. But when I went into a prostitute's

embraced. Here in the Jordaan, I must say proudly. And it was here that one of our best sons of the Jordaan on Queen's Day asked for a kiss. Even though it was probably not intentional, he did this on behalf of all of us. That's why it was so good that you let him kiss you. We all know that love comes from two sides. But it must also be celebrated. And it was such a beautiful embrace.' To Prince Claus, he said: '25 years ago you left your country. This people shall become your people. After the smoke bombs cleared, you were taken up by the people.'

Through the years, Queen Beatrix and Prince Claus have continued to come often to Amsterdam for their own pleasure or as duty requires. They are in the Dam Palace for the Erasmus Prize ceremonies, the granting of royal subsidies for young artists, to host the New Year's reception for the diplomatic corps, but also when they invite a cross-section of the population for a special reception. The Queen, accompanied by Claus, inaugurates the annual Holland Festival, attends the Ballet Gala, Concertgebouw performances, opera premières, opens major exhibitions in the Amsterdam

H.R.H. Prince Willem-Alexander

When Crown Prince Willem-Alexander turned eighteen on April 27, 1985, he was entitled by law to start exercising his royal authority. His mother led him into a special session of the Council of State, the highest advisory board to the government. Her Majesty is Chairman of the Council.

The future King of the Netherlands celebrated his 21st birthday by coming to Amsterdam on his first official visit. The burgomaster's residence was the venue for the party attended by prominent Amsterdammers from all walks of life. Gifts included a pot of Amsterdam onions presented by a university student organization, while a *voetbal* player gave him an Ajax team shirt.

The mayor, who offered a silver scale model of the *koggeschip*, a symbol of the city, lightheartedly explained the legend, that 'in the 12th century such a vessel without oars was stranded on the rough Zuyder Zee shoreline. The surviving two men and a dog founded Amsterdam. It must be a biological miracle but from them have evolved over 700,000 Amsterdammers.' The burgomaster also reminded Willem-Alexander that Queen Wilhelmina, his great-grandmother, had received a golden coach from the Amsterdammers 90 years ago, but times had changed, as witnessed by all the incidents during royal weddings and visits. Ignoring the capital city's explosive reputation, the Crown Prince has often come unofficially and incognito in recent years, expressing a clear affinity for Amsterdam.

He now has official responsibilities, some shared with his mother and father and participates in many of the important ceremonies which take place in the Dutch capital.

More and more on his own in recent years, Prince Willem-Alexander is assuming a myriad of official obligations. He visited the Albert Cuyp boxing school in the low income de Pijp area, where his humorous exchanges won the hopeful pugilists' hearts and confidence. He attended the 'Lion King' première benefitting a childrens' rehabilitation center. When he inspected facilities for the homeless, to everyone's delight, he spontaneously remarked, 'Wat lullig voor u, dat u geen onderdak heeft' (tactfully translated: 'It's rotten for you that you don't have a place to live'). He has had his quota of button-pushing and ribbon-cutting, but he does the obligatory, routine handlings well-prepared and with genuine interest.

The newest, fourth sluice in the Amsterdam/Schellingwoude complex was ceremoniously opened by the young prince and took his name. He has discussed welfare assurances with a group of teenagers, using video and interactive computer programs at the Social Insurance Information Center. He triggered the functioning of the new commercial system of the Amsterdam Stock Exchange's modernized floor. On the cultural front, Willem-Alexander was presented with the first complete works of Multatuli, a famous late 19th century writer, ranked as the most important postwar Dutch literature publishing achievement.

Despite the paparazzi, the Prince leads a personal life. When he is in Amsterdam, like any young man on a night out in a concert hall, restaurant, café or disco, the average Amsterdammer might merely nod, or ignore him out of respect for his privacy. He is renowned for his good sense of humor and handling of impromptu situations. He has already made his mark among the difficult locals. Willem-Alexander is very active in sports. He skis, is an underwater diver, horseman, accomplished sailor and licensed pilot. He is often present when important ice-skating or soccer tournaments are being played. Proving his condition and endurance, he skated to the end of the strenuous Frisian eleven-city ice race and completed the New York Marathon. As an enthusiastic sportsman, he accepted the patron role for the Netherlands Olympic Committee and the Netherlands Sports Federation, together representing 89 sports associations with a total membership of 4.5 million. Willem-Alexander, who insisted on participation in

Crown Prince Willem Alexander bantering with some young hopefuls in the boxing school located in the Pijp working class neighborhood. Between the pugilists and the prince is Ruud van der Linden, volunteer trainer.

decision-making meetings, attends the most important sports events in the country and abroad. As the first Prince of Orange in well over a century, Willem-Alexander, with his mother's engaging smile, has become a popular, favored figure who will one day rule the country and assure continuation of the monarchy.

'this is the first time,' Horowitz wrote in the program book. 'I'll be back when the tulips bloom.' The Queen reacted: 'If you come back, I'll be there.' When the renowned performer reappeared the following spring, the Queen and Prince Claus were there, despite their return the night before from a tiring state visit to Sweden. 'I had promised, so I'm here,' said the Queen, as she visited the maestro's makeshift dressing room.

Extremely sensitive to underprivileged and minority groups, the royal couple have opened experimental homes for the handicapped, attended services in the Portuguese Synagogue marking the 350th anniversary of the Jewish settlement and enjoyed the Moroccan/Dutch puppet theatre in the underground theatre of the Royal Tropical Institute.

musea, is present at Dutch film charity benefits, celebrates anniversaries of social, educational and cultural institutions, and participates in many international congresses with themes varying from 'Realization of Human Rights of Children' to 'Trauma and Tragedy'.

The Queen's intense interest in classical music and great performers was exemplified by her anxiousness to attend the octogenarian American pianist Wladimir Horowitz' performance in the Concertgebouw. At last minute notice, contrary to protocol, Her Majesty and Prince Claus were invited for the concert. When the royal couple met the great maestro afterwards, the Queen handed him her program book with a request for an inscription. The pianist, known for his humor, asked: 'Do you always ask for autographs?' 'No,' replied the Dutch monarch,

Queen's day brings out performers of all ages and skills.

Queen Day's crowds choke the parks, canals and streets. Everyone is out for fun in a Mardi Gras atmosphere.

Traditionally children sold old toys and books. Now, adult entrepreneurs hawk everything imaginable amidst the food stalls and music stands.

Monument Life

Amidst unique historical inheritance

T he wonderful thing about living in the heart of Amsterdam is the rich inheritance of the past in the former home of a grand aristocrat or a simple craftsman, with centuries-old stones, history, legends, warmth and heart. The city has some 7650 classified monuments — the largest concentration on the Continent. If these were placed side by side, they would form an unbroken line some 55 kilometers long. Against this remarkable backdrop, one walks, breathes, experiences the past wealth that moulded the center. Besides the official monument protection offices, many individuals and private associations actively safeguard this invaluable heritage by financing restorations, registering endangered monuments and aggressively opposing any political or commercial plans which could infringe on the unique monumental cityscape. The 17th century brick canal houses had gradually evolved with a varied number of gable tops. Besides the traditional stepped ornamentation, there came the pilaster, neck, curved neck and cornice gables. In the 18th century, austere rows of uniform façades, usually with cornice gables, appeared as unbroken fronts on canals and streets, without seeming to be separate homes. This harmonious urban decor was heightened by the use of black and brown tones. The 19th century saw some minor modifications in windows and interiors. Calvinist sobriety had imposed itself on the way of life and architectural style from the late 16th century on. Outward ostentation was frowned upon. The houses' façades were for the most part not elaborate, conforming in scale and line to all others along the canal. Some of the great patrician houses later followed Italianate or French influences, which came into favor with ornamentation on the gables and statuary on the roofs. Thus, many houses are much older than their fronts reveal.

The patrician houses built among the major canals had gablestones embedded on their façades as identification and addresses. These façades reflected the owner's imagination, religious fervor, occupation or place of origin. But this picturesque and artistic address system was abolished when French forces occupied the city in 1795 since they could not understand the legends or the language of the *gevelsteen* (gablestones). When the French divided the city into districts for the election of representatives, the more prosaic system of house numbering was imposed on Amsterdam.

Amsterdam gablestones first came into use after many of the city's wooden houses were destroyed by fire in 1452 and regulations were enacted obliging rebuilding in brick. *Uithangborden* (sign boards) — which included African and Indian figures for tobacco dealers, boots for shoemakers and wine kegs for the spirits merchants — were partly replaced by

Monument houses, more than 7,000 registered in the center, are a unique inheritance unmatched in any other European city. Amsterdammers live in modest craftsmen's houses, elegant canal houses, grand patrician palaces, old warehouses and barracks.

Gable decorations lighten sober façades. Gable stones often reveal a house builder's beliefs. Decorations on top might be ostentatious. Open-mouthed gapers were early advertising symbols.

DE DRIE FLESCHJES

16 07

T WAPE VAN VENETIEN

1 6 26

D CORENDRAGER

these stone plaques on the houses, which also contained shops, business space and storage areas for goods, or had adjoining warehouses.

Today's Amsterdammers live, work and play in the canal houses, sometimes in ways undreamed of by their ancestors. Some have been turned into museums, others into art galleries, boutiques, bank offices and restaurants. A few still house wealthy families. Many more have been cut up into rooms or small apartments for artists and students. Large canal houses have been split into handsome apartments, which are eagerly snapped up by young families in the clear return trend to the canals.

Even 17th century warehouses, many of which once stored exotic goods from the East, have been converted into dwellings. The large concentration of warehouses on the picturesque Brouwersgracht, and over 80 historic warehouses on the Entrepot docks, were transformed into housing.

Façades are protected by law against outward change, but inside the monuments people can do what they want in keeping with their 20th century life-style. And they do some imaginative, modern-day decorating, revert to traditional decors, go Bohemian, or really far out. Amsterdammers are not in awe of their monuments.

There are houses with St. Michael slaying a dragon, elephants, serpents and other unexpected decorations on the façades. Each has its story, as do hundreds of other houses which must be explored beyond the gable for legendary links with mythology and history.

There is the story of a one-window wide house at Kloveniersburgwal 26. This was built by the Tripp brothers for one of their servants who was overheard wishing for a house as wide as the masters' front door. It is across the canal from their ostentatious mansion at Kloveniersburgwal 29. Seeking prestige and acceptance in Amsterdam society, the Tripps had commissioned their double mansion to outshine the pompous Coymans House and as a one-upmanship over their arch rival in arms dealing Louys de Geer, who occupied the House with

Warehouses, which once stored spices, silks and other exotic goods from around the globe, have been converted into comfortable apartments on the canals and islands.

Oude Schans seems unchanged through the centuries in the historic center.

An old church, which was last used as an auction house, means soaring space for gracious living.

Right: Decorative inheritances from the Golden Age enrich life style for 20th century canal house inhabitants.

the Heads (see '... and the world').

There are houses which still bear the name of the original resident and are now intimate museums or memorials, like the Rembrandt House, the Fodor House (contemporary art), the Descartes House (used by the People's University to teach foreigners Dutch) and the Anne Frank House.

At Prinsengracht 263, the Anne Frank House is a grim reminder of the desperate World War II years. In this small warehouse, the Franks hid in an attic from their Nazi German pursuers until their betrayal shortly before the end of the war. The Franks, and other Jews undercover with them, were hauled off to the concentration camps and no one survived except Anne's father. Amidst the rubble cleaned out of the attic, the diary of the schoolgirl Anne Frank survived as a poignant personal account of Amsterdam's terrible occupation days. The Anne Frank House was restored to its wartime state as a moving monument to those who disappeared from Amsterdam life.

A number of stately homes have been saved by foundations which were created to assure preservation of these monuments and their historic collections. Salvation came in that manner to the gracious home of Jonkheer Jan Six van Hillegom, whose ancestral paintings by Rembrandt still hang in the front room. Another is that of Jonkheer Maurits van Loon.

who now lives in former service quarters in the attic, while the family's heirlooms are exhibited in the house functioning as a museum. The identical house next door had been used as a drug and alcohol rehabilitation center until its recent conversion into luxury apartments.

Jonkheer Maurits van Loon

The aristocrat traces his lineage to the village of Loon, in Brabant, where family history was recorded from 1390. The Van Loons, Protestants, fled by boat to Amsterdam around 1600 when the Catholic Spanish occupied the country's southern provinces. They were among the 17 founders of the East India Company in 1602 and added two Moors to the family crest to reflect the slave trade. The Van Loons were prominent in the city's economic and civic life from the early 17th century until after World War II, when democratization meant retrenching to more modest living patterns. The Van Loons in Amsterdam reflected a monumental way of life enjoyed by the privileged oligarchy, a small group of merchant princes who ruled the capital city and exerted a disproportionate influence on the running of the nation. They kept this power in their own hands through co-optation, a system in which councilmen were not publicly elected. Instead they themselves would choose a new member every time one of them died. With strong family

ties, a few aristocratic families held a monopoly on all municipal offices.

Jonkheer van Loon: 'When our family arrived in Amsterdam, the city was like a little republic. There was a power struggle between the moneyed ruling class and the Prince of Orange, who had popular support, and this continued until the end of the 18th century. Through inter-marriage and the ground rules of co-optation, the family kept the wealth and power in their own hands. Early in the Golden Age, a Van Loon married a burgomaster's daughter, and there was a succession of eight Van Loons in the law-making municipal council well through the next century.

'The family continued as merchants of the East India Company until that came to an end in 1795 with the French occupation. Most of the prominent families experienced a big come-down under the French. The girls had one black dress and pinned white lace on as cuffs and bodice when guests came to call. After the French occupation, the patrician families hoped for a comeback, but the Prince of Orange became king and bought them off by giving them titles. From 1815 to 1848, we still had political weight through seats in the House of Lords, but after that date it became a paper nobility of empty titles without power.

'My great-grandfather bought this house as a wedding present for my grandmother and her husband and she lived in it until her death in 1946. But since there was such a postwar housing shortage, the building was requisitioned by the city and homeless people were quartered here until 1962. I inherited the house in 1949 upon my father's death, but realized that even after these people had found other shelter I could no longer use the entire building as a personal residence. Since this is one of the few stately homes with original interiors and ancestral paintings intact, the Van Loon Foundation was established and the house was restored to its late 18th/early 19th century state. While I am the main director of the foundation, in the tradition of co-optation, I hope that my daughter, Philippa, will some day follow me and keep the house in the family.

'Of course I was aware of social changes that had taken place during the intervening decades in Amsterdam. In 1914, the city had been riddled with tuberculosis. Families with thirteen children lived in one room in dark alleys. Sewers opened right into the canals, which were not drained regularly like they are now. The big houses were a major source of employment for the so-called lower classes. Twenty people worked in a house like this.

'Look at Amsterdam now. A great social revolution has taken place, which I think has brought liberation, even for people like me. We were always on stage, required to play a role, dispensing generosity around us. Now we can lead a normal life without having continually to appraise how much a person would need to live on. When my father died, I inherited the responsibility for the pension fund for former servants and their widows. Some of them had worked for my great-grandfather who had died in 1901.

'It's ironical because ours was one of the five most powerful families in Amsterdam in the 17th and 18th century. And even in 1940, three out of four Amsterdammers could tell you where the Van Loons lived. Grandmother went around in a horse and carriage and she was the best known woman in town after Queen Wilhelmina. Grandmother was *dame du palais* to the Queen and often went abroad with her. My wife, Martine, is now Mistress of the Robes to Her Majesty, Queen Beatrix.

'As for our life in the monumental house, we have adopted a schizophrenic attitude. The foundation and house bear our name and we live in part of it, albeit only the renovated attic, but

Willem van Loon was one of the 17 merchants who founded the East India Company in 1602. Moors, added to the family coat of arms, reflected the company's slave trading.

Under the centuries-old beams of canal houses one finds surprising interiors decorated with antiques and modern accessories.

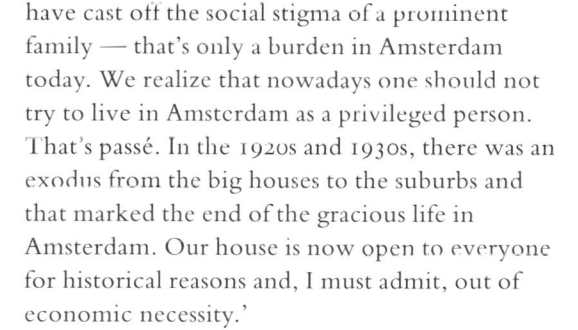

Jonkheer Maurits van Loon,
20th century patrician.

Van Loon garden room.

Van Loon formal French
garden with garden house.

have cast off the social stigma of a prominent family — that's only a burden in Amsterdam today. We realize that nowadays one should not try to live in Amsterdam as a privileged person. That's passé. In the 1920s and 1930s, there was an exodus from the big houses to the suburbs and that marked the end of the gracious life in Amsterdam. Our house is now open to everyone for historical reasons and, I must admit, out of economic necessity.'

Jordaan

Customs, humor, music, idiomatic language

Breitner, a turn-of-the century painter, recorded Jordaan scenes such as the bucolic Lauriergracht in the snow.

The working class Jordaan quarter — traditionally home to the real Amsterdammers with their own dialect, customs and music — was officially called the 'Nieuwe Werck' (New Work) when development by regents and speculators was started in 1614. In sharp contrast to their own carefully measured ample plots in a well-regulated pattern along the main canals, these privileged merchants exploited the growth of the Jordaan in a haphazard manner. The long, narrow plots fronted by drainage ditches became miserly land allotments for miniscule houses. Paths were widened to become streets, while ditches were deepened to become canals. Expansion continued, without any town masterplan, at an uncontrolled, slower pace than around the main canals. This reached its motley saturation point in 1640 when every available square meter had been built on, with many houses constructed for the waves of immigrants fleeing religious persecution elsewhere.

Likewise, land was designated for factories, whose noise and smell, danger of fire and pollution were considered undesirable in other developing quarters. Tanneries were assigned parcels near three canals — the Looiersgracht, Elandsgracht and the Passeerdersgracht. A number of dye works were moved from the inner city to a canal which took the name of the Verversgracht (Dyers' canal). Since the municipality owned much former Catholic property, including cloisters, creating these industrial zones was no problem.

Because many streets and canals are named after flowers, some say the Jordaan is a corruption of *jardin* (garden), originated by French Huguenot refugees who settled in the developing quarter. Another theory claims as the source the Jordanne, a river in the Auvergne, from where the Protestants fled Catholic persecution to seek a safe haven in Amsterdam. Others believe the Prinsengracht water was called the Jordaan, the

Dutch equivalent of the Jordaan River flowing through the Holy Land. In the early 17th century, the quarter was popularly referred to 'being over the Jordaan'.

Although there are conflicting feelings about the exact borders of the Jordaan, it's generally accepted that the Singelgracht (now the Nassaukade), dug to replace the old city walls, marks the western limit. The maze of narrow streets, with only four canals of the original eleven still existing, extends over 26 hectares, to the canal web to the west. This former marshland is 1¼ kilometers from north to south and 450 meters from east to west. The Rozengracht cuts the Jordaan into northern and southern parts.

The northern Jordaan has remained the most authentic, while the southern part has undergone many changes. The Noordermarkt (Northern Market) square has been the site of fairs since 1627. Nowadays, besides the flea market, stalls are set up to hawk textiles, clothing, small birds or organic produce sold by the growers. Around a thousand small businesses, many of which are run by old style craftsmen, function in the compact oblong area bordered by the Brouwersgracht, Passeerdersgracht, Lijnbaansgracht and the Prinsengracht. While some wealthy merchants built gracious houses in the Jordaan at the outset, the quarter

was already stamped as working class in the 17th century when hordes of laborers and craftsmen arrived, as did religious and political refugees, including the Huguenots, who took menial work in the tanneries and other factories and hawked on the streets. The French immigrants also went into the textile trade. Things got progressively worse and more congested in the Jordaan with passing time. In 1800, 24 percent of Amsterdam's total population lived in the Jordaan, with more people in every house than anywhere else in the city.

While this deprived area was a closely-knit neighborhood by the nature of the situation, it simultaneously became the city's most destitute residential area. One-room dwellings were common, just as sanitation was scarce. Families with ten to twelve children lived on top of each other. They jammed into one room or moved into basements. Backyards were built over to create more industrial spaces. People worked in the neighborhood — in sugar refineries, cloth weaving, dye works, tanneries, glue manufacturing, toy making, printing and small craft industries. They never had enough to eat.

Poverty was a hallmark of the Jordaan from the Golden Age until a few decades ago. Jordanese often pawned shoes or clothing at the municipal loan bank, popularly called 'Ome Jan' (uncle

Cabaret with home-grown performers, some of whom went on to national fame, is still a big draw in the local cafés. A half century celebration of Jordaan cabaret was held in 1995.

Right: Kitch as can be characterizes many Jordaan homes and cafés, such as the popular Café Nol. Over-done, but warm and welcoming.

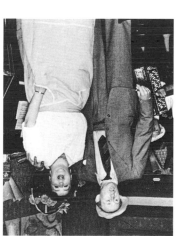

Jan), to survive until their meager weekly paycheck came in.

This poverty and inadequate housing welded the Jordaanese into one big family. No one was a stranger in the Jordaan. The children called adults aunt and uncle. They shared what little they had and helped each other in cases of sickness, accidents or death. Birthdays and wedding celebrations spilled out onto the canalsides. Music came naturally to many of them, with home-grown talent of singers, cabaret and big neighborhood drum and bugle bands. The Jordaanese had their own way of communicating. The area evolved into a closed realm of Amsterdammers, comparable to London's East End cockneys, with their own slang, down-to-earth humor, love for opera, over-sentimental songs and dancing on the streets around barrel organs. The Jordaanese also became pigeon trainers and anglers, interests supposedly inherited from the French immigrants.

By 1860, though new districts had emerged beyond the western ramparts, the Jordaan remained a no-man's land cut off from the main surrounding streets and public transportation. They had to wait until 1908 for a bus line linking

The Jordaan Festival, a street party with beer drinking, entertainment and group singing, has been an exciting neighborhood folk event for almost 20 years.

Under left: Big emerging talent like Peter Beense drew emotional ovations from the huge crowds moved by his romantic ballads.

Under: The Northern market, the square in front of the Northern Church, has regular open air sales of second hand goods, fabrics, farm-grown vegetables and clothes.

the area with the center, but the locals' outspoken criticism of exhaust fumes soiling their wash drying outside led to a suspension of the service. It was only in 1924 that an electrified tram service was effected.

The Jordaanese, proudly calling themselves monarchists, are actually anarchists at heart. Revolts against the authorities have characterized this quarter through the centuries, with the Eel Riot of 1886 and the Protest of 1934 among the bloodiest encounters. When the City Council proposed the levelling of the district's dilapidated housing to be replaced by tall tower buildings in 1969, the locals' loud protests forced the planners to back down. In 1973, a compromise was accepted with some

Blonde Sientje

Amsterdam's brown cafés with the most local color atmosphere are found in the Jordaan. One of the best-known to Dutchmen and foreigners is Rooie Nelis, a landmark meeting place for almost 60 years, which has inspired national television series, countless broadcasts and welcomed guests varying from Japanese tourists to Dutch royalty. The current female captain is known as Blonde Sientje (Little Blonde Sien), though officially she is Sien Blommers-Ruwaard in her late sixties.

Blonde Sientje followed her mother, Rooie Sien (Red Sien), who had founded the café with her

was called Sien Schellevis (Sien Shellfish) since she hawked her fresh fish in the streets. This wasn't insulting. It's typical of our humor and the way we use words which other people do not understand. 'The café keeps my father's name alive, as well as the memory of my first husband, an underground worker executed with three comrades on "Crazy Tuesday" in 1944. Many people know the terrible story and are attracted to the photo of them on the back wall. The caption says, "Four Loyal Friends". When we had our 50th anniversary, over 1,000 people came to celebrate. There were bands,

husband, Rooie Nelis (Red Nelis). Sien explained 'that everyone in the Jordaan had a nickname. My grandfather was called Zwarte Nelis (Black Nelis), maybe because he was always covered in coal dust. He peddled coal until just before he died at age 90 but it took him three days to earn enough to buy meat. He was an alcoholic who fathered 23 children, of whom six survived. My grandmother

flowers, serenades and I was told that Willem-Alexander, our future king, was among the guests. I wish I had seen him since I'm very fond and respectful of our royal family, especially Queen Beatrix. She has been in our café twice during working visits in the Jordaan. Once I spoke to her at great length as one working woman to another. My mother had taught me that we had nothing to

be ashamed of and could always talk to a queen. 'Things used to be really hard here. Kids were warned not to touch the bread during the day — it was measured with a rope as control. The young were sent to work and often remained illiterate. But everyone was happy with very little. There was a family feeling and everyone pulled together to help. You know that the Jordaanese are good people when you see the children who came out of this poor neighborhood. Locals never went much further than their own streets. My grandmother never got to the beach at Zandvoort, only 15 miles away, in her lifetime.

'People used to lean on their window sills to sing opera, argue, curse or fight, but everything came out. It was all part of the street life. They danced in the streets and sang in the cafés. That's all changed. Old-timers were chased away with expensive renovations and high rents. If they didn't return within ten years, they had no claim on social housing. This is such a pity since these Jordaanese wanted to come back to their roots. New buildings have entrances like prisons and no window sills, so everybody is locked inside.

'Now people go away for weekends and summers in their caravans. They'r just back from one trip when they start bragging about where they're going next year. Sure, everything is now much better but with the new buildings not adapted to the old Jordaan blocks and the new people who move in, the neighborhood is losing its special character. 'However, the Jordaanese are so proud of their origins and tradition that a certain nostalgia hangs in the air, despite all the modern changes. Since I feel Jordaanese right down to my toes, I wrote memoirs of much that I've seen happen in the Jordaan during all my years. I called my book, just for the fun, *Red Nelis' Jaw and Other Stories.*

demolition and spacing out new buildings. Neighborhood action groups are fighting to regain livability in the quarter. Oversized wooden buckets, planted with trees and flowers, keep the curbs clear of illegal parkers. The city sent in gardeners, appropriately named Groen and Moss (Green and Moss), to create small parks in holes left by the bulldozers. Playgrounds were built and ugly blind walls decorated with frescoes by local people.

The calm broke again in 1995. Eight Jordaanese women, dressed in traditional costumes, had gotten official permission to submit their grievance — and, for the first time ever — an action group was allowed to sing their protest in limerick style at an urban renewal meeting. After a school had been demolished, there were plans for more buildings, including several national monuments and others with architectural styles typical of the quarter, to be destroyed. The Jordaanese continue their vigil against municipal blueprints for massive levelling in the city's western section, including large areas of the Jordaan, arguing that this will again chase out many of the natives, who will be unable to purchase the new housing, never to return.

Though only a small number of historical façades, with their characteristic gable stones, have survived from the 17th and 18th centuries, there are over 800 residential blocks from the

past century which are now protected as monuments. These stand in handsome contrast to the clusters of uninspired new architecture. The Jordaan has always appealed to writers and intellectuals, just as it now attracts painters, photographers, writers and the inevitable yuppies, though real gentrification has not occurred.

Among the 17th century residents, there was Rembrandt, whose last home was at Rozengracht 184 and, not far away on the Lauriergracht, the painter Govert Flinck, a follower of Rembrandt. The Czech humanist and philosopher Amos Comenius was also a Lauriergracht resident over 350 years ago, like George Hendrick Breitner, the Amsterdam Impressionist, in the last century.

Three generations of the Blaeu family, among the world's most famous map makers in the 16th and 17th centuries, lived and sold their cartography at Bloemgracht 74 and 76 (Flower canal), mockingly referred to as the 'Jordaan Herengracht'.

Ruud Gullit, the great soccer player, was born in 1962 on the Bloemgracht. He rose through the ranks of Dutch teams before being bought in 1987 by the Italian club AC Milano for 17 million guilders, at the time the highest price any club had paid for a soccer player. Gullit was called *Il Tulipo Nero* (Black Tulip) in Italy, when

Willy Alberti, a Neapolitan tenor who gained national acclaim and is remembered with a plaque on the Western Church tower. In his Jordaan kitchen in 1954 with his wife and daughter Willeke, now a popular singing star.

Wash day in the Jordaan, 1951.

> Brown cafés are everywhere in the city, each with its own decor and special public. Regulars come to drink beer or *jenever* (gin), play cards or just seek companionship in the traditional pubs' warmth.

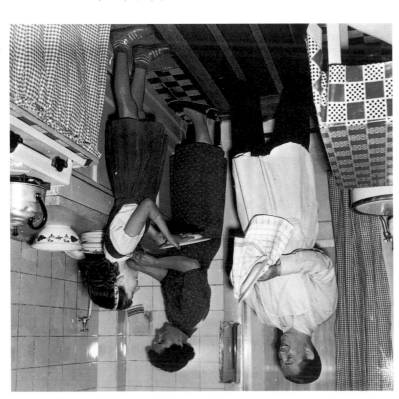

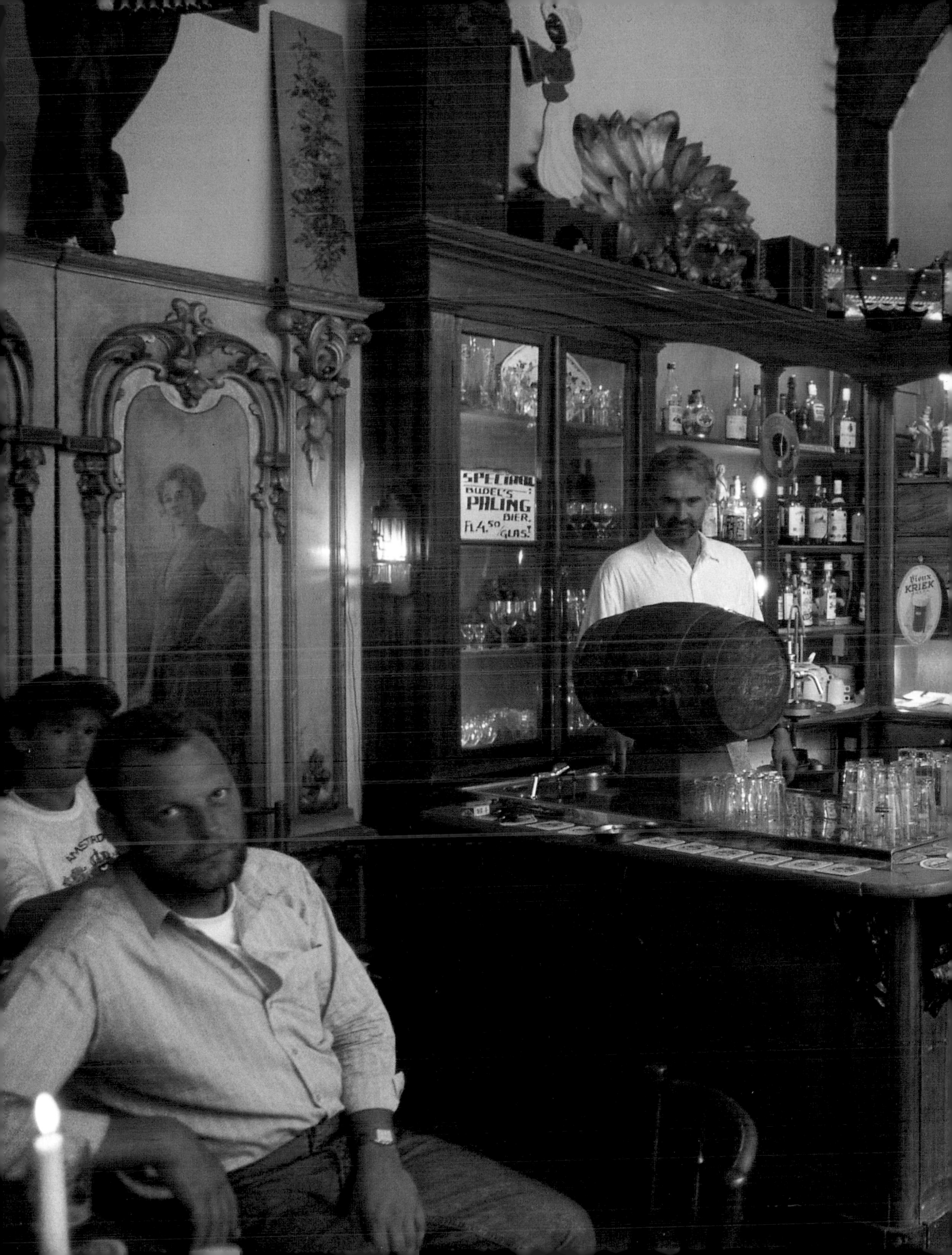

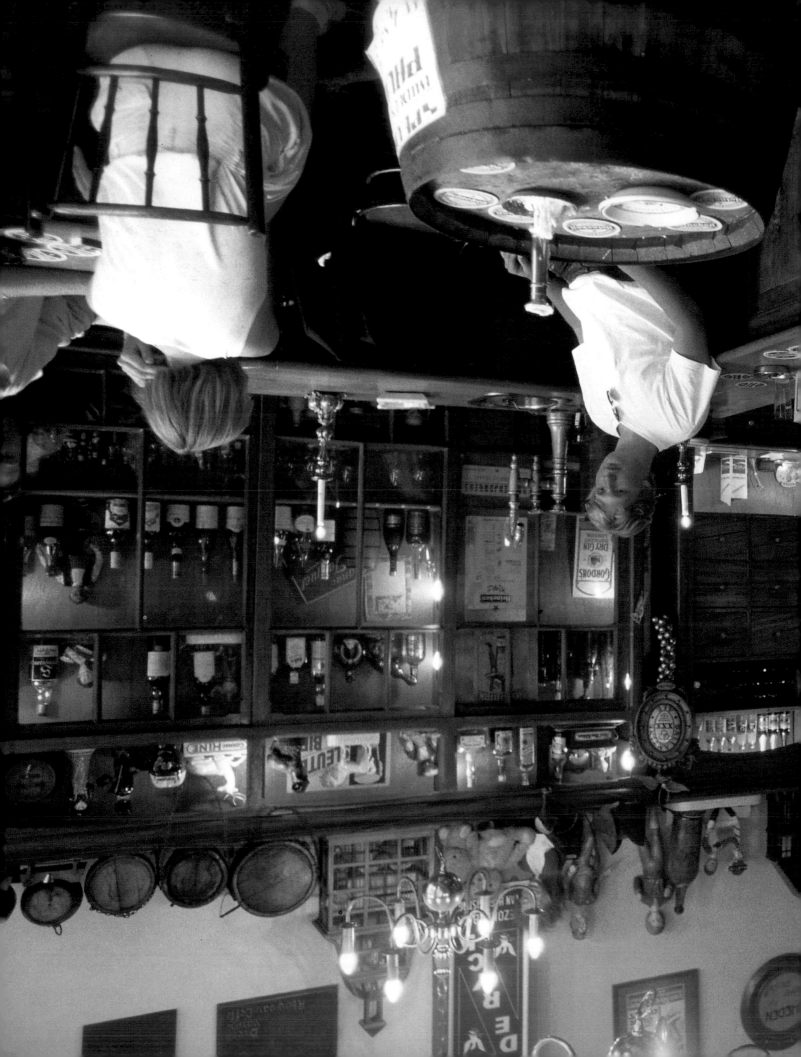

he lived there. Frank Rijkaard, another Jordaanese who learned street soccer with Gullit, also ranked among Holland's top players.

A stretch of the Prinsengracht has housed a number of typical cafés which sprung up in the days when the old potato market was held here. Licensed to serve from four in the morning when the market opened, these cafés catered to the locals who unloaded the barges and received their wages in gin. They bore amusing nicknames like Piet Narigheid (Pete Misery), Dove Manus (Deaf Manus), Bram Halve Zool (Abe Half Sole), Jan Iep (John Elm Tree) and De Perenplukker ('The Pear Plucker').

Every September, the Jordaan Festival is a colorful street party with lots of beer and gin drinking, dancing, singing and rejoicing. Some homegrown singers emerged from these festivals to become nationally known recording stars like Johnny Jordaan (alias Jan van Musscher), Tante Leen, Piet Römer and Willy Alberti. Johnny and Tante Leen have been immortalized by their neighbors with statues on a square at the corner of the Elandsgracht and the Prinsengracht. Willy Alberti baptized the Johnny Jordaanplein. Willy Alberti, whose songs included an ode to the Westerkerk

(Western Church), was commemorated with a bronze plaque embedded into the church tower 'honoring Willy Alberti, our Amsterdam Neapolitan tenor'.

In recent times, much has changed. Street life has given way to television. The authentic old Jordaanese are dying off, being replaced by students, artists and photographers. Fashion boutiques, antique shops, foreign restaurants, macrobiotic eating houses and other manifestations have appeared, making this quarter into a kind of Dutch Chelsea. Cars choke narrow streets where canal waters once flowed. The Jordaan is experiencing a traumatic existence as new styles are imposed, old-timers are forced out, newcomers buy in and only a small number of Jordaanese trickle back to their roots.

Folk heros Johnny Jordaan and Tante Leen, interpreters of sentimental local ballads, were enshrined with sculptures on the Elandsgracht.

Two Swans café is the most renowned in the Jordaan for tear-jerker sing-alongs.

Mokum

Jewish refugees' imprint on local life

For over four centuries, Amsterdam has been known as 'New Jerusalem' or 'Jerusalem of the West' with good cause. Jewish refugees fleeing persecution in other European countries found a tolerant haven, religious freedom and friendly acceptance in the Dutch capital city. The Jews also called the city Makom, from the Hebrew *Makum aleph*, 'the best city of all', or 'the Place'. Amsterdammers made it into Mokum and call themselves Mokummers.

The first Sephardis (from Sepharad, Hebrew for Spain), Jewish refugees from the Iberian Peninsula, arrived in Amsterdam around 1590, while Rhineland Jews, Askenazis (from Ashkenaz, Hebrew for Germany), came around 1630. Marranos (Spanish for swine) were Jews who professed conversion to Christianity to avoid persecution in the blood-letting of the Inquisition, when Ferdinand of Arragon and Isabella of Castille, the Catholic rulers of Spain, issued an edict in 1492 expelling all Jews from their territory. The Portuguese King Manuel I obliged Jews to convert *en masse* or face immediate expulsion in 1497. Iberian Sephardis, known as Portuguese Jews in Amsterdam, included Spaniards who had first gone to Portugal. They continued their flight via Bayonne, Bordeaux, Hamburg and Antwerp, fleeing in 1585 after the Spanish conquest. By 1597, Sephardis in the Dutch capital felt secure enough to file applications to purchase citizenship. A year later, a burgomaster told a group of applicants that rights would be sold, but no public religious services could be held. The Jews knew that unofficially they could pray in private. The Union of Utrecht (1579) had assured no persecution for religious beliefs. (The only restrictions for Jews were not converting Christians to Judaism or sleeping with Christian servant girls).

In September 1603, when Portuguese Jews were

at prayer in a house on the eve of Yom Kippur (Day of Atonement), the Amsterdam sheriff and his men raided the congregation expecting to find a Papist meeting. Those were sensitive times — it was less than twenty years since the Reformation had changed Catholic Amsterdam to Protestantism. They searched for crucifixes and holy wafers. On finding none, they asked the Jews to include the Magistrate of Amsterdam in their prayers.

The Portuguese synagogue, supposedly patterned after King Solomon's temple, with interior view painted by Emmanuel de Witte in the 17th century.

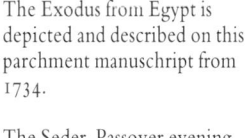

The Exodus from Egypt is depicted and described on this parchment manuschript from 1734.

The Seder, Passover evening in a Portuguese Jewish household depicted by Picart in 1725.

Burial in the Portuguese cemetery in Ouderkerk. The body of the deceased was brought by boat since internment for Jews was forbidden in Amsterdam. This religious ceremony is recorded in an etching by Romeyn de Hooghe, circa 1680.

Burial in Muidenberg in the present day.

By 1609, when Spain's domination of the Lowlands had been broken, scores of Marranos flooded in and brought with them their wide experience in foreign commerce plus a worldly culture. From the outset, the Jewish immigrants had been immediately welcomed into Dutch life. They became stock holders in the globe-spanning Dutch West and East India Companies, helping develop trade with North Africa, the Near East and Italy, and influencing the first Jewish settlement in the New World.

A petition filed in 1654 through the Dutch West India Company to Peter Stuyvesant, then governor of Nieuw Amsterdam (later to become New York), resulted in permission for 23 Jewish refugees to come from Dutch Brazil after it had been recaptured by Portugal.

A house synagogue was built in Amsterdam in

Jewish Historical Museum

The first Jewish Historical Museum, which functioned from 1923 in two little rooms in the Waag (Weighing House), a medieval city gate (now used as a Media Center focused on new communication technology and its effect on society), was closed when war broke out in 1940. The collection, entrusted to the Stedelijk Museum for safekeeping, was confiscated in 1943 and taken to Offenbach, Germany. Of the 738 items catalogued in 1937, only 20 percent had been recovered by the time the museum reopened in 1955 on the Waag's upper floor.

The official dedication date of the present Jewish Historical Museum was on the 3rd of May, the day before Holland's Memorial Day, in 1987. This day links the past and present, as a permanent reminder of the dark chapter in the Amsterdam Jews' history and culture during World War II. In 1989, the prestigious Religious Council of Europe 'Museum Prize' was awarded for the collection's presentation and outer appearance of the four 17th and 18th century synagogues linked via the narrow old Shulgass (synagogue alley). This creative architecture made the museum truly distinctive and unique. 'Seeing leads to remembering, remembering leads to the doing' (Babylonian Talmud) has been the museum's underlying philosophy to provide insight and understanding of Jewish religion, culture and history in the Netherlands. *Tzedakah* (justice and righteousness), as a Jewish historical concept, is a recurring theme in exhibitions.

Holy ark with torah in an old synagogue incorporated into the Jewish Historical Museum.

Esther roll, parchment and silk, with cut-out figures and hand-written texts, dated between 1700 and 1800.

1612, despite the protests of the Reformed Church and the Spanish Ambassador, who claimed discrimination against the Catholics. This was possible through a loophole in the law, whereby the Jews did not own the building, but rented it from a member of the municipal council. For weddings in the synagogue, they paid a double tax to the city. People were profiting from their tolerance! In 1616, Amsterdam's municipal authorities officially sanctioned the Jewish settlement of their city and referred to members of the Jewish Nation.

When these Sephardis settled in Amsterdam, they tried immediately to buy suitable burial ground within the city, but were refused. Finally, the small group found land available in Groet, near Alkmaar, about 32 kilometers from the capital. The first burial there was held in 1602 for Garcia Pimentel, brother of Manuel Pimentel (alias Isaac Abeniacar), a favorite of King Henri IV of France.

But the journey to Groet was long. Jews were obliged to pay a tax to every church passed by the funeral procession en route from Amsterdam — and there were many churches! (That law stayed on the books until 1721). The Portuguese Jews petitioned once again on June 19, 1605, to the burgomasters of Amsterdam for burial grounds within the city. They were again refused, possibly since the local tradition was for Christian burials under the churches or, sometimes, in enclosed churchyards.

In 1614, two of the three Sephardic communities joined together and purchased at a cost of 2,700 guilders a tract of land for burial ground in Ouderkerk. The remains of some 100 persons interred in Groet were moved to the cemetery in this village on the Amstel river. For almost 400 years, Portuguese and Spanish Jews have been buried here, including many great rabbis and the parents of the philosopher Baruch de Espinoza, better known as Spinoza. Since he had been excommunicated for teachings considered heretical at the time, Spinoza could not be buried in the cemetery.

The Sephardis brought a rich literary, artistic and cultural tradition, which was meshed into the Dutch capital's life through the ensuing centuries. Their religious schools became a model of scholarship for other Jewish

Rembrandt lived among the Jews and used his neighbors as models, especially for Biblical subjects. His *Jewish Bride* is a top Rijksmuseum attraction.

... communities on the Continent. Amsterdam became known all over the world for Hebrew and Yiddish works. The first Hebrew book was printed in 1627. The first Jewish newspaper, the Spanish language *Gazeta de Amsterdam*, appeared in 1675, followed later by a Yiddish bi-weekly, the *Kurant*. The Hebrew printing press attracted Jewish authors to the city. During the 17th and first half of the 18th centuries, many non-Jewish financiers sponsored Hebrew book printings.

In 1679, Jekoetiël Blitz translated the complete Tenach (Old Testament) into Yiddish. This was published by Phoebus ha Levi, who had received approval from not only the Askenazi and Sephardic rabbis in Amsterdam but also from German and Polish rabbis. With this publication went a ten-year ban on any reprints. More strangely, Johan III, King of Poland, issued a decree in Latin forbidding any reprinting within twenty years, with a penalty of confiscation and

View on those synagogues depicted in the old prints as they now appear after their incorporation into the Jewish Historical Museum.

payment of twenty marks in fine gold. Background of this bizarre ban by a Polish king of a Yiddish language bible was that two non-Jewish Amsterdam patricians, Willem Blaeu and Laurentius Baeck, had backed the publishing venture. The king was protecting their investments. The influence of the rich regents extended far beyond Amsterdam.

Protestant ministers and scholars, interested in the Old Testament, maintained contacts with learned Jews and read the books printed by the first Dutch press under Rabbi Menasseh ben Israel, including a Torah (bible). They profited in percentages of sales and received quantities of the books. Thus it was not unusual for Hebrew books to come up at Amsterdam auctions from Christian sources. These books were sold in Poland, France, Germany, Italy and as far as North Africa and Cochin, China.

Even Rembrandt van Rijn, who lived among the Jews, was involved in the Sephardis' publishing ventures. In 1655, he produced four book etchings, a rare departure in his artistic oeuvre, to illustrate *La Piedra Gloriosa*. The book was written by his good friend, Rabbi Menasseh ben Israel, who was also a printer and diplomat. Rembrandt used his Sephardic neighbors as models for biblical paintings while he created his greatest masterpieces at home from 1639 to 1659. Simon Schama, in *The Embarrassment of Riches*, wrote, '... Rembrandt gives us not only a David but a St. Matthew and a Jesus with the features of his Jewish neighbors on the Breestraat.'

In 1675 on the Jonas Daniël Meyerplein (a square named for the first Jewish lawyer in the Netherlands), in the heart of the old Jewish quarter, the Sephardis built a magnificent, classical style synagogue.

An early 18th century etching shows the complex of Portuguese and High German synagogues, circa 1710. The New Synagogue was only built in 1752.

J.C.E. Belinfante

Judith C.E. Belinfante, Director of the Jewish Historical Museum since 1976, actualized the approach and moulded the institutions's character during the past two decades, especially after expansion into the new quarters.

'Jewish life in our exhibition is always reflected against a backdrop of Dutch culture. We illustrate Jewish history in the Netherlands with Dutch symbols like mills, water and boats as subtle references. The woods honoring Wilhelmina, Juliana and Beatrix form a recognizable link when we feature tree planting in Israel. We were the first Jewish museum in Europe to relate our presentation with an identifiable national character. Research underscores our universal appeal: 40 percent of the visitors are non-Jews, many of them Germans. We always have a young German volunteer assigned by a German church organization on staff.

'Our changing exhibitions often have international themes, such as the Sephardic Diaspora, Jews of

Russia, photo reportages from New York and Lithuania, bonds with Israel, Jews under Islam and experiences of the Shoah. Among our greatest

draws have been Chagall's graphics and Dutch Golden Age painting. Spiegelman's *Maus*, his comic strip personnages from the Holocaust, drew record crowds. Our exposure of lesser known aspects, such as the pre-war, dire poverty level of many Amsterdam Jews, was highlighted in the Council of Europe "Museum Prize" citation.

'Her Majesty, Queen Beatrix, with Prince Claus, officially opened our new complex. The German Ambassador inaugurated the painting exhibition of Felix Nussbaum, an exiled German artist, who had died in the Auschwitz gas chambers. International visitors have included Gorbachov, Chaim Herzog, Eli Wiesel, Teddy Kolleck, Chaim Potok and Art Spiegelman. Steven Spielberg asked the museum for advice and assistance in his worldwide major project to video survivors' personal experiences. The Jewish Historical Museum, while fulfilling its special role, has assumed its rightful place among Amsterdam's most prestigious musea.'

Considered among the world's most stately Jewish houses of worship, this synagogue was patterned after King Solomon's Temple and faces southeast toward Jerusalem. Services are still conducted by candlelight from more than 300 candles in four immense and 22 smaller 17th century copper candelabra.

Since a number of the congregation members were influential, the municipality and Royal House were very solicitous and tolerant. Francisco Lopez Suasso financed 2 million guilders for the ruling Dutch Stadholder Willem III's crossing with Mary to claim the English throne in 1688. The Portuguese Synagogue's close relationship with the House of Orange has remained until today. Prayers in Portuguese for

Street vendors, such as this herring cart man and wife, were in dire poverty, struggling for survival in pre-war days.

the royal family are part of every service. Dutch rulers, starting with Willem III in 1690, have visited the synagogue on special occasions throughout the ensuing centuries. Jews from Central Europe, Askenazis, fled to Amsterdam as the Thirty Years' War (1618-1648) resulted in intensified, bloody pogroms. These Askenazis spoke Yiddish, their language since the Middle Ages, in contrast to the Sephardis who spoke Spanish and Portuguese

Market men around 1910 eked out a meagre living and always existed on the fringes of starvation.

among themselves. Through the 17th and 18th centuries, thousands more came from Germany and eastern Europe, outnumbering the Portuguese. They formed their own congregations, including the Great Synagogue built in 1671 and the New Synagogue opened in 1752.

In general, the Spanish and Portuguese Jews had been accepted by the ruling regents. Attacks on these Jews came primarily from the Reformed Church in the area of religion and from the guilds in economic matters. Despite special by-laws enacted against them, which remained in effect until the fall of the Republic in 1795, these Jews experienced relative freedom, unparalleled by conditions elsewhere in Europe at the time. The very poor German and Polish Jews were the frequent targets of Christian attack, with complaints about their street vending. As late as 1755, a Christian group had petitioned the municipality to establish a ghetto. The liberal magistrate refused. Amsterdam Jews never suffered the degradation of such confinement. It

was explicitly forbidden to wear special Jewish identification, such as the Jews' hat or Jews' cloth, then customary in other European countries. The yellow Star of David only became mandatory on all outer clothing during Hitler's occupation.

Though the municipality remained very fair in its judging of civil pleas brought by the Jews, tough economic limitations were exerted on them. Only Jewish merchants had to register and pay a fee for insurance policies because they supposedly took greater trading risks than others. Jews were banned from almost all of the guilds which controlled the city's commercial life. The guilds of the brokers, surgeons and book dealers allowed a few Jews into their ranks. Since the St. Peter's guild of fish-sellers was open to them, the bustling fish market on Dam Square was largely a Jewish affair for several centuries. Earlier constraints had forced Jews to resort to trade for income, though the vast majority eked out a livelihood as peddlers. They continued to seek work in the traditional sectors which limited them to money and stock markets, printing, textiles, metal, livestock, food and diamonds. From 1796 to 1940, Jewish enterprises developed as limitations fell. In the wake of industrialization in the second half of the 19th century, they set up factories.

When Louis-Napoleon became King in 1806, he took steps toward integrating Jews into the Dutch population. He ordered Jonas Daniël Meyer to carry out a study of the Jewish community in Amsterdam, which revealed great poverty. He also obliged Jewish teachers to use the Old Testament translated into Dutch. If convicted of using a Yiddish or Hebrew version, they faced six months' dismissal for the first offense, permanent dismissal for the second. After King Louis was deposed by his brother before the acts could be enforced, the first Dutch monarch, Willem I, put his predecessor's political ruling into effect. In 1817, there was a royal decree that Jewish education was not to be given in Yiddish but in Hebrew or Dutch, with an implicit preference for Dutch.

With Amsterdam as a safe haven, the Jewish community had multiplied. A population census in 1796, the first recording Jews separately, revealed 23,335 in the city. Except for a few rich Sephardic families, there was a growing Portuguese Jewish proletariat due to the economic crises of 1763 and 1772-1773. The

recession of that period had impoverished this community more than the Christians because the Stock Exchange was the mainstay of the Sephardis. The Askenazis' economic position had always been much poorer than the Amsterdam average.

Against a backdrop of total religious freedom, the Jewish community thrived and their contributions to Amsterdam — and Dutch — intellectual and business life were many. On September 2, 1796, the Netherlands was the second European nation (after France) to grant Jews equality with other citizens. In 1797, a group of young Amsterdam Jews organized Europe's first Reformed Judaic congregation with the Dutch language used in the simplified services.

While the Jewish population had reached 54,479 by 1889, the Jewish quarter was a virtual slum with its impoverished inhabitants trying to subsist at market stands selling fish, fruit, second-hand clothing and rags. The Jews lived on top of one another in the city's most deplorable housing conditions. The educated and the illiterate, the working class and the higher social class inhabited the same streets. They gravitated together to share a Jewish life based on their language, sabbath, food rituals and religious observances. Some were wealthy patricians but most Jews were unbelievably poor and on the brink of starvation.

In the years before World War II, Christians were attracted to the Sunday market in the Jewish quarter, enjoying the vendors hawking their goods with a sprinkling of Yiddish humor thrown in with the pitch. Amsterdammers regarded Jews as a strange, different kind of people choosing to live in their own society within the greater Christian city. The Jews, with all their misery and suffering, added a colorful, exotic accent to the staid capital. They introduced cabaret around 1840 and were prominent in the Amsterdam entertainment

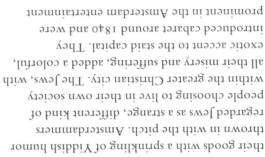

Pesach celebrated with family and friends in an Amsterdam household.

Under left: Service in a modern synagogue.

Under: Torah decorative finials were inspired by the Western Tower in the 17th century.

Diamond Trade

Around 1585, the Sephardic settlers introduced a new product in Amsterdam: the rough diamond. With centuries of experience in diamond trading, they established this industry classified as a 'free' profession without a restraining guild. They engaged fellow Jews, boycotted by most guilds, to cut and polish the stones for trading. It became and remained until today a primarily Jewish affair, though there has always been a gentile minority. During the first half of the 18th century, 300

Diamond workers engaged in the tedious routine.

Right: Diamond polishing depicted in a 19th century etching.

Christian diamond workers went on strike to protest cheap Jewish labor. In 1748, they petitioned the city to require exams for Jews already employed, to prevent the hiring of any more Jews and to forbid Jews from working on Sunday. They demanded the formation of a diamond guild to which Jews would be taxed for membership but not entitled to any advantages. The city refused on the grounds that the Jews had started the diamond industry.

After great poverty in Amsterdam during the

French era, the diamond trade experienced a revival around 1820. The first diamond polishers' factories were generally in filthy, drafty and dilapidated attics. This caused much sickness and many accidents. The diamond cleavers and cutters worked in their own homes or in their patrons' residences.

In 1822, a group of jewellers founded a 'horse

Diamantslijperij van de firma M. E. Coster, te Amsterdam.

factory', replacing the women mill-turners in their back-breaking work by horses. The first steam-powered polishing factory was opened in 1840. Ten years later, there were 560 so-called 'mills', with a jewellers' combination owning 520 of them and monopolizing the business.

Large diamond finds in Brazil in 1844 led to the expansion of the diamond industry. Apprentice numbers grew. Diamond cutting became one of Amsterdam's leading industries. But with the cut-back in Brazilian production and intervening wars

(especially the Crimean War), there was a severe economic depression among Amsterdam's diamond workers. A slight upswing improved matters until the French-German War of 1870 disrupted things, resulting in a new bitter poverty. The legendary finds in South Africa around 1869, coupled with peace in Europe, brought a boom. Many more non-Jews came into the trade around the 'Cape period'. This discovery of diamond reserves also prompted jewellers like Asscher, Coster, Van Moppes and Boas to build large diamond factories. World War II was a grim period when more than 2000 Jewish diamond workers were dragged off to the German extermination camps and most never returned. Though revival of the diamond industry after the war seemed impossible, the few hundred workers who survived managed to re-establish the trade with retrieved material, foreign assistance and government support. Four years after the liberation, the diamond trade had sufficiently recovered and staged an exhibition in the Diamond Exchange which attracted 100,000 visitors. Though highly sensitive to world tension, Amsterdam's diamond trade continued to grow and again became one of the city's most important industries.

The 'Amsterdam cut' has long been synonymous worldwide with perfect craftsmanship. In 1908, the oversized 3,024 carat *Cullinan*, the largest diamond ever found, was entrusted to Joseph Asscher for cleaving and cutting. The most important of these stones were used in the crown and sceptre of the British crown jewels. Back in 1852, the *Koh-I-Noor* had also been cut in Amsterdam and added to the treasures in the Tower of London. Today there are some twenty diamond factories, as well as Europe's only diamond sorting school, founded over 50 years ago. From a tradition started in the late 16th century, when refugee Jews brought this trade with them, Amsterdam has remained a city of diamonds.

world a century long. From the Polish and German immigrants, many Yiddish words came into Amsterdam Dutch usage like *goochem, mazzel, sjofel, gannef, majem, jajem* and *bajes*. Amsterdammers still say '*Daar ga je*' (here you go), which is a corruption of *le hajim* (here's to health).

By 1940, Jews in the capital city participated importantly in the arts, business and social life. The Jewish imprint on Dutch literature, humor and even the language were natural developments in this traditionally liberal, tolerant country. But the war years of Nazi occupation took its grim toll despite the heroism

Above: Rembrandt on the front steps of his house with his Jewish neighbors in the 17th century.

Nazis closed off the Jewish quarter, including the Rembrandt House. Most of these people never returned from the extermination camps.

The Jewish quarter bustled with push cart selling which attracted Amsterdammers to this colorful street life.

of the Dutch underground.

The Portuguese Synagogue, placed in 1940 on the national monuments list, was for some bizarre reason respected by the German occupiers. Its 72 high arched windows, too large to be blacked out, also saved the synagogue from becoming a deportation center.

The complex of four Ashkenazi synagogues – two large, the Grote (Great) Sjoel and the Nieuwe (New) Sjoel – and two smaller ones – the Obene (Upper) and the Dritt – (Third) were stripped of all their treasures and used as stables by the Germans. The buildings have been restored and now house in the Joods Historisch Museum (Jewish Historical Museum).

Remembrance of Amsterdam Jews lost to Nazi oppression is very poignant. The Anne Frank House, the Verzet (Resistance) Museum and the Hollandsche Schouwburg (Theatre) have educational functions related to the Nazi persecution and extermination of Amsterdam's Jews. The Jewish Historical Museum is also concerned with the war situation, while tracing Jewish culture, tradition and history in a specific relationship in the Netherlands.

During the 20th century, Amsterdam's Jewish population has increased steadily, especially with the inflow of thousands of German Jews arriving

in the 30s when Hitler's Third Reich became more menacing. By the time the Nazis came goose-stepping into the Netherlands in 1940, there were 86,000 Jews in Amsterdam, 10 percent of the local population, with a total of 140,000 Jews in the country. Jews were systematically rounded up for deportation, first herded into the Hollandsche Schouwburg, then brought to the Dutch internment camp at

Westerbork, en route to the gas chambers in Poland.

Amsterdammers resisted the Nazis' brutality to 'our Jews' but were soon suppressed by superior forces. Symbolic of the numerous heroic acts was the dock workers' revolt with bare hands against the heavily-armed German soldiers during a round-up of 400 young Jews. There was an active underground network and Jews were also hidden. After the war, with births and returnees, there were 13,000 Jews registered in Amsterdam. Unlike the Dutch, who tallied their war dead, the Jews counted those who were alive.

Of the 5,000 in the Portuguese Synagogue congregation before the Occupation, there were about 500 left. Today there are some 600 members.

Ironically, Franco became a savior for Sephardis who could reach the Spanish border. He had publicly announced their protection if they proved their Spanish origin. A small number survived thanks to the dictator's humanitarian decree.

Nowadays, when Amsterdammers talk of Mokum in nostalgic terms, they recall memories of street markets and merriment. The ghosts of those carted off to the gas chambers would probably understand. For, despite their struggle for life, they were free and happy in Amsterdam, their Makom, the Place where they felt nothing could ever happen to them.

Under: Book case entrance to the hiding place of Anne Frank and her family.

Right: The Hollandsche Schouwburg, a former Jewish theater, was used by the Nazis for round-ups. Victims by name are remembered in a memorial. The stark, empty building is used for school visits to inform youth about the atrocities.

Once-Holy Place

Amsterdam Miracle, religious upheavals

I n the Middle Ages, the 'Amsterdam Miracle' took place. Catholic pilgrims came from all over Europe after official church proclamations recognized this miracle and designated Amsterdam as the Holy Place.

It all started in March 1345 after a priest gave the last rites to a man dying in his Kalverstraat home. The man did not die, but vomited. A woman caring for him threw the vomit in the hearth, only to discover that it had taken the same shape as of the wafer given by the priest during the Holy Sacrament. She reached into the fire and without burning her hand removed the unscarred, cool 'wafer'. She placed it in a house shrine and ran for the priest, who took it to his church.

Mysterious things occurred. The 'wafer' reappeared in the house shrine. That and other inexplicable incidents created a sensation in town. In a great procession, the 'wafer' was carried to the Old Church. People prayed before it, attributing wondrous healing powers to the white object. But, on the next day, the 'wafer'

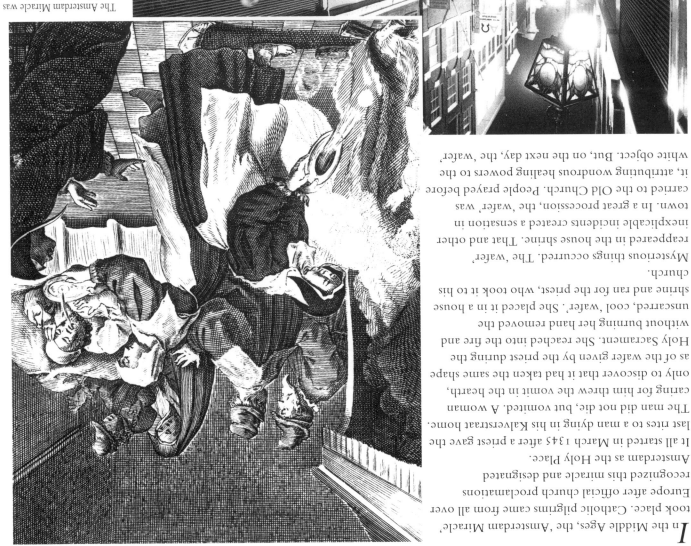

The Amsterdam Miracle was proclaimed when a dying man's vomit, which became a wafer, mysteriously kept reappearing in the house altar after it had been carried in a great procession to the Old Church.

Left: The 'Silent Procession' annually draws pious believers, including foreign groups, to commemorate the Amsterdam Miracle.

Amsterdam procession drew hordes of the faithful.

When the city went over to the Protestant Prince of Orange's side in 1578, the Silent Procession was forbidden. In the meantime, some three centuries later, the procession again gained impetus. The Beginhof Church replaced the demolished chapel for services commemorating the 'wafer miracle' and became the procession's starting point. Nowadays, due to the inner city's traffic congestion, the procession takes place at night. The number of Catholic believers who walk in the procession has dwindled enormously. No pilgrims come anymore to the once-holy place.

Amsterdam had remained Catholic until the 16th century. There was a surface tolerance tempered by 'everyone knowing his place'. As long as non-believers in the official religion were not blatant in following their faith, they were left alone. But the status quo was threatened by the upcoming Protestant movement. A fanatic Anabaptist sect mobilized forces in March 1534 for a mass march to Munster, heart of their reform movement. Five of the organizers, in full enthusiasm, ran through the streets at night shouting, 'The day of the Lord has come'. The five Anabaptists were seized and beheaded on the Dam. They were punished not for heresy but for tampering with law and order. Before that, the Anabaptists were just considered nuisances and given light sentences. A number of succeeding incidents also brought harsh punishment, including burning at the stake, 'execution by water', decapitation and cutting hearts out.

The following year, the Anabaptists plotted a revolutionary take-over of Amsterdam, convinced that this was the Holy Place. During one night of frenzied preaching and praying, a 'prophet' envisioned the Garden of Eden and threw his clothes into an open fire, commanding his brethren to follow. The men and women obeyed and the resulting smell brought down the landlady. She soon joined them and they all ran out to the Dam crying: 'Woe, woe, the wrath of God.' The Stadholder had the men decapitated. Their heads were set up like trophies on a tollgate's spikes. The women were drowned, while the landlady was hung in her own doorway.

Thus, February 11, 1535 became a strange footnote in Amsterdam history: the night of the

was back in the house shrine.

In 1347, the man's house was demolished to build the Chapel of the Holy Place (*Locus Sacer*), also known as the New Side Chapel. A Silent Procession became an annual tradition on the first Wednesday after March 12, the day of Saint Gregorius.

In 1486, when Maximilian I of Austria, later to become a Holy Roman Emperor, fell deathly ill in the South of Holland, he swore that if he

recovered he would make a pilgrimage to the chapel. Maximilian visited Amsterdam two years later and dedicated a stained glass window and presented embroidered cushions. In 1489, he gave Amsterdam the crown of the Holy Roman Empire, since it is not adorned with a coat of arms such as it ought to have'. Charles V, King of Spain and a Holy Roman Emperor, came in 1532. Word of these kings walking in the

Right: Playful students, who streaked in 1974, ended up with their pictures on the newspapers' front pages.

Streaking across the Dam in the mid-16th century, fanatic Anabaptists (Mennonites) believed they were in the Garden of Eden. They ended up on the executioner's block and lost their heads.

naked runners. These saintly streakers, over four and a half centuries ago, were the forerunners of the seventies craze!

The Anabaptist incidents shook up the otherwise complacent city councilmen who were previously so tolerant in religious matters. This minor revolt made them all strongly Catholic. Charles V's edicts were put into force. Any Protestants, even idealistic passivists like the Mennonites, were severely persecuted.

In September 1549, Catholic Amsterdam set up a gate of honor on the Dam. A large allegorical painting, bearing the legend 'Faith Holds Down Error and Heresy', welcomed the 22-year-old fervently Catholic Crown Prince Philip of Spain. He arrived on a royal barge in the Damrak, while gun salutes were fired and the city bells rung. He was coming to be officially installed as Count of Holland. The city fathers wanted to assure him how Catholic they and official Amsterdam were. Since the stall keepers on the Dam had to make room for the procession and all the decorations set up for the royal visitor, they were compensated with 2 guilders if they could prove resulting loss of income.

In 1578, an agreement was negotiated with the Protestants. It gave them permission to worship outside the walls and bury their dead inside the city in unconsecrated ground. The Protestants, given a finger, wanted a hand. On February 28, they overthrew the city government. When five Protestant representatives were received at the Town Hall, ostensibly to discuss burial ground difficulties, a 'coup' took place. Monks and regents who were dragged to the Dam, expecting to be beheaded, were simply transported by boat to a dike outside the walls. They were left to settle their own future. Most of the evicted regents set up a prosperous life elsewhere.

This marked the beginning of Protestant Amsterdam. A new non-Catholic Council was appointed. In true Amsterdam tradition, the new Council kept enough of the old to insure painless and profitable continuity. The empty cloisters were put to excellent use as hospitals, factories, warehouses, old people's homes, orphanages and prisons. The St. Cecilia cloister on the Oude Zijds Voorburgwal became the Prinsenhof, and was later converted into the Town Hall.

Prince William of Orange arrived in Amsterdam in March 1580 and the 'Reformation' was complete. Calvinism not only became the official Amsterdam religion, but marked the character of the total population. It is often said that, regardless of their religion, all Dutchmen are Calvinists at heart.

Freedom for other faiths was allowed but the Dutch Reformed Church was strongly favored in financial support for its needy and public office for its wealthy members. Until well into the 17th century only the Dutch Reformed Church was permitted to build new churches and to hold public services. Other groups had to worship in private or clandestinely.

Even several break-away Protestant sects had to construct churches hidden behind patrician residence facades. The Catholics went underground with their clandestine churches and by 1658 there were 26 hidden houses of prayer in Amsterdam. The Portuguese and Spanish Jews, who started arriving in the last decades of the 16th century, also benefited from the religious freedom. They congregated in house synagogues. Officials knew about these places of worship but turned their heads.

Today the most splendid surviving clandestine Catholic church is 'Our Lord in the Attic', situated in a 17th century wealthy burgher's home, on the Oude Zijds Voorburgwal, in the heart of the red-light district. It is open as a

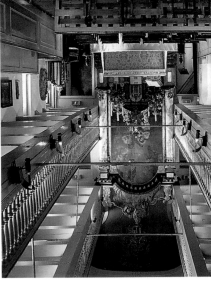

This Church on Kalverstraat lures shoppers with posters advertising 'a quarter of an hour for God'. This is the site of a former hidden church.

Our Lord in the Attic, a 'hidden' Catholic church dating from the Reformation, has an elaborate altar wall on wheels which could be turned to a plain side when civic control was feared. Actually all the clandestine churches were an open secret.

The Old Church stained glass windows.

The Western Church, its tower with the Amsterdam coat of arms, bears the crown of Emperor Maximilian of Austria. Seventeenth century print indicates first service was held in 1631.

St. Olof's Chapel, dating from around 1440, was converted over 550 years later by the Golden Tulip Barbizon Palace Hotel into a conference venue. An underground tunnel links the old church and the modern hotel.

museum and used sporadically for services.

With the 'Reformation', all of Amsterdam's Catholic churches became Protestant. These included the Old Church, New Church, St. Olof's Chapel and the New Side Chapel. A former cloister became the Walloon Church. Though the lay sisters of the Beghinhof were put out of their church, they could conduct Catholic services in a Beghinhof courtyard house within view of their old church. During the 17th century, imposing Protestant churches were built: the East, West, North and South Churches, as well as the Old Lutheran and Round Lutheran Churches. Likewise, the Portuguese and Askenazi Synagogues were erected in this era.

Also constructed was the Amstel Church, called a shed church because of its provisional wooden structure. It was later nicknamed the stable church after Napoleon supposedly stalled his horses there during Amsterdam's French occupation in the early 19th century. The picturesque 'temporary' house of worship has survived to become, after restoration, a cultural center with a restaurant, municipal monument architects' offices and a Third World shop.

At the end of the 18th century, the first official Catholic church after the 'Reformation' was built, replacing a hidden church called the Pigeon. Most hidden churches functioned until the early 19th century, when they were demolished to make room for large, imposing Catholic churches built on the same sites. This 'Pigeon' Church, occupied by squatters in the seventies, now holds services and doubles as a youth club at night.

There was renewed interest in churches for non-religious use. One church became Paradiso, a municipally-sponsored youth club, with rock music and soft drugs as the order of the day. Churches are used as a weaving center, carpet showroom, offices and exhibition space. One, functioning as an auditorium for university lectures, is also used on Sundays for services. This is a typical Amsterdam phenomenon — science, commerce and worship all under one roof.

Two impressive old churches were deconsecrated to become unusual cultural and congress centers. One is the St. Olof's Chapel on the Zeedijk, built around 1440, in a pure Gothic style unique among Amsterdam's churches, by a Norwegian seamen's guild who were engaged in

a flourishing trade with Holland. It was named after an 11th century Norwegian king elevated to sainthood for championing the Christian faith. It served as the first precursor of the current Stock Exchange, then became a Protestant church, later was home to the cheese trade and, during World War II, as a soup kitchen. In the sixties, there were some limited cultural manifestations before it was boarded up

Under: The Amstel Church, a temporary wooden structure from the 17th century, also organizes exhibitions.

The 17th century Round Lutheran Church is used by the Renaissance Hotel as a congress and cultural center. A meticulous restoration was completed in 1995 after a raging fire had destroyed the landmark dome and much of the interior.

The Lutheran swan, gilded and restored after the fire, again roosts over the church and Amsterdam's rooftops.

to prevent further decay. In the early nineties the Golden Tulip Barbizon Palace Hotel, situated around the corner, undertook a complete restoration, built in state-of-the-art technical equipment and excavated an underground passage to link the modern hotel with the mid-15th century monumental St. Olof's Chapel. There was a good precedent for a hotel-cum-church. The landmark Round Lutheran Church, built in 1671, had been deconsecrated in 1935 by the Lutheran community. Rented out for years as a camping goods showroom, it got a new lease onlife when the Sonesta (now Renaissance) Hotel took a 99-year contract and assured its complete restoration and maintenance. Timed for the hotel's opening in 1975, this soaring space had a complete face-lift, kitchens were incorporated and modern facilities added to serve congresses and cultural events. There are Sunday morning coffee concerts in the Renaissance Congress and Cultural Center which reopened in 1995 after a disastrous fire, like the one in 1883 which had destroyed its graceful dome covered by copper presented by the King of Sweden over 300 years ago.

Among the city's four other great Protestant churches built in the early 17th century based on Hendrik de Keyser's designs, with inspiration from Christopher Wren's steeples, the Westerkerk has the strongest pattern of regular services, supplemented by cultural use. In the Noorderkerk, with several side wings used for city archaeological expositions, there are

Right: The Vondel Church became an office building.

Right: The New church on the Dam is the venue for major international exhibitions.

The Church of England on the Groenburgwal.

Pilgrims' Icons

When Johannes M. Baart was an archaeology student at the University of Amsterdam, he went along with construction crews sinking foundations for a subway system in the early seventies. As a dedicated buff, he feared the workmen would be blind to any precious relics that the soggy earth underneath the city's pilings might reveal. He was right. Medieval utensils, leather shoes, pottery, a ship's frame, rare pilgrims' icons and many pilgrim badges were uncovered. In the mid-seventies Baart, was appointed as the first official archaeologist in Amsterdam's 700 year history.

According to Baart: 'Amsterdam was one of a trio of cities which experienced "wafer wonders" and attracted faithful hordes by the thousands during the Middle Ages. The other two were Wilsnach and Blomberg, both in Germany. Pilgrims, tourists of their day, travelled the 650-mile route between the three cities. A pilgrim's icon was dug up intact and in perfect condition during the Zwanenburgwal excavations near the 15th century fortified walls. It was probably dropped by an Amsterdammer returning from a pilgrimage since it was found close to a former city gate. This simple church-shaped pine plank had the pewter insignias of Wilsnach and Blomberg nailed to it when the dredgers' giant claws freed it from five centuries of mud. This was the first complete pilgrim's icon ever found in Europe. It was custom to embark on religious missions for one's own salvation, or as punishment

Rare pilgrim's icon excavated when the subway was being built. These were carried as identification by believers travelling between the "wonder wafer" cities. This assured lodgings in cloisters along the route.

for a crime, and then return with insignias — the holy badges — as proof of the pilgrimage. Whereas today's tourists buy souvenirs and stickers, the pilgrims picked up icons and attached the insignias purchased in the holy cities. We knew about these icons from medieval literature but none had ever been found here before. The pilgrims hung these icons around their necks, wore a cloak and carried a staff. With this identification, they could eat and sleep without charge in all the cloisters along the holy route. And it protected them against arrest as vagabonds within the walls of strange cities.

'Other specimens of only three badges, representing the three hosts of Wilsnach, with scenes from the life of Christ, had been uncovered. We dug up ten sets of the badges, including five during subway building. Many others have come to the surface in France, England and other countries. But the insignia of Blomberg — a "witch" throwing 45 holy wafers into a well — had never been known before. Finding these badges mounted on the original plank, was quite exciting.

'On our icon, which is now in the collection of the Amsterdam Historical Museum, you can read *corp christi blomhb* under the rose of Lippe on the Blomberg insignia. (Bernhard VII of Lippe was an ancestor of H.R.H. Bernhard, Prince of the Netherlands.) The "witch" has a benign smile as she leans over her wafers, watching them descend into the well. She is framed in a Gothic architectural motif. We have definitely dated this insignia, and thus the entire icon, in the last quarter of the 15th century. The other insignia recalls through its three medallions the "miracle" of 1383 when a fire destroyed the entire village of Wilsnach and only the three wafers remained unscarred. In the "Amsterdam Miracle" there was one wafer.

'In many places the pilgrims' souvenirs were openly burned by Reformation leaders. So it's a kind of miracle that our icon survived. We still hope to dig up an Amsterdam insignia some day' (see 'Monument Life').

Left: Unused churches are deconsecrated, sold off for other use, or demolished.

Right: The Paradiso youth club, venue for pop concerts, is in a former church.

occasional services. The Zuiderkerk has become the permanent project showcase with models and blueprints of the Department of Urban Planning. The Oosterkerk is used as a cultural center with expositions and free coffee concerts. This century's changing religious times and an exodus to outlying areas meant that churches were closed, sold, given another function or demolished. Still, Amsterdam has some 150 churches of various denominations with many changing to suit incoming refugees and new congregations. The St. Nicholas Church, located opposite the Central Station, mainly serves ex-Yugoslav workers. Two icon painters, a Slav and a Dutchman, worked on the decoration. A Dutch choir sings old Slavic hymns. There are regular services in the Parrot, once a secret Catholic church, situated in the bustling pedestrian shopping street, de Kalverstraat. Disciples of Eastern religious sects like the Guru Ram Das and the Hari Krishna have set up temples in city houses.

Since there is no longer religious registration in Amsterdam, estimated affiliation figures are not accurate. Today's general trend away from organized religion is most evident in Amsterdam's center, but non-affiliation was already an issue in the early 19th century. King Louis-Napoleon issued frequent memos to his ministers demanding reports on the 17,000 Amsterdammers who appeared to be without religion.

Muslims are among the fastest growing religious group, with well over 60,000 in Amsterdam, due to the waves of immigrant workers starting in the sixties. This is in sharp contrast to the seven Muslims who had come in 1889 from the former Dutch colony, now Indonesia. Even by 1960, there were only 154 Muslims. Hindus and Buddhists together now number some 8,000 to 10,000 souls in the capital and are growing forces in non-Christian religious circles.

After establishing mosques in unused buildings, as early as 1971 in the center of Amsterdam, a large mosque was built in the Amsterdam Bijlmer area. Opened in 1985, it caters to the religious needs of Surinam and Pakistani Muslims. Shaped like a white cube with a small turquoise dome and four minarets, this mosque called the Taibah is surrounded by an enormous subway overpass and the towering apartment buildings which dominate this outlying residential section.

Amsterdam is no longer the really holy place it once was for Catholics, Protestants and Jews. Many practising Catholics seek anti-Rome directions under the guidance of jeans-clad, ostracized priests. Protestants have modernized their liturgy. Holocaust survivors and their offspring attend synagogue services in smaller numbers, with many integrated or shying away from organized religion. There is tolerance in the air. Amsterdam has shed its Calvinistic mantle. Church-goers and the faithful are proportionately fewer in number here than elsewhere in the country. While small groups still follow the traditional path, Amsterdam has largely turned its back on the church. The most dedicated allegiance is evident among recent refugees, most visibly among the Muslims, Hindus and Buddhists. The once-holy city has taken a new turn.

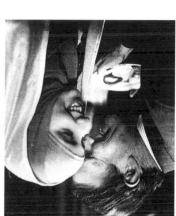

Above: The Mosque, the Taibah, was built in Amsterdam Bijlmermeer to serve residents from Suriname, Pakistan and other countries.

Under: Amsterdam burgomaster Patijn in conversation with a university student during the sugar festival held in the Town Hall to mark the end of Ramadan.

French Accent

Napoleonic occupation to current Gallic presence

hen Emperor Napoleon Bonaparte arrived in Amsterdam in September 1811 to visit the 'third city' of his Empire, he was received under an arch of glory built in his honor and inscribed. Napoléon Empireur (sic).

Amsterdam's burgomaster Willem Joseph van Brienen van de Groote Lindt added still another *faux pas*, in fractured French, with his poetic greeting:

Napoléon n'a pas fait de sottise
en se mariant avec Marie-Louise.

In an attempt at clever rhyming, the city father said 'Napoleon wasn't foolish in marrying Marie-Louise'. Napoleon, stung to the core,

Louis Napoleon's arrival in Amsterdam in 1808 to take up residence on the Dam as King of the Netherlands. Passing the Portuguese and High German synagogues, he was welcomed by jubilant crowds.

quickly sought his snuff box as a diplomatic distraction.

Those were still the days when French was widely spoken by the Netherlands' upper classes. It was, in fact, Dutch world influence through the 16th and 18th centuries that propagated French as the diplomatic language since no one understood Dutch outside of the small republic. In the 17th century, after Louis XIV had revoked the Edict of Nantes guaranteeing a certain degree of protection to the French Protestants, the Huguenots were persecuted for their religion and thinking men for their writings. The Huguenots fled in great numbers to the Netherlands, especially to Amsterdam. Besides their culture, they brought with them capital and

La Fontaine found their way onto Amsterdam printing presses, later ending up in France. Huguenot refugees retained their native tongue in Amsterdam. Under their influence, many French words came into the daily vocabulary. Even today, Amsterdam newspapers have obituary notices where, under old Huguenot names, there are biblical quotations in French. Some 15 to 20 percent of the contemporary Dutch language is of French origin. The regent class snobbishly used French at home. It is well known that in 1584, when Prince William the Silent was dying in Delft from an assassin's bullet, he uttered: 'Mon Dieu, ayez pitié de moi et de mon pauvre peuple.' ('My God have pity on me and my poor people.') Few people know that Queen Wilhelmina, fervently devoted to the Huguenot sect, uttered a final prayer in French just before her death in 1962. Walloon Protestants had started arriving in Amsterdam as religious exiles in 1540, a century before the Huguenots. In 1586, the municipality gave these refugees the last remnant of a medieval convent as a place of worship.

An Amsterdam cultural group, called Nil Volentibus Arduum ('Nothing is difficult for the willing'), was started in 1669 to promote French classical writers like Molière, Corneille and Racine. In the regents' houses, there was more French than Dutch literature on tables. The stately Felix Meritis ('Happy through Merit') building was opened on the Keizersgracht in 1787 as a lofty center of Enlightenment, through art, science and commerce. Elegant apartments were decorated in French style. Works by Voltaire and Rousseau were presented in the upstairs theatre. After a fastidious restoration, the Felix Meritis Foundation now uses its halls for theatre, dance, music and lectures.

French was in the Amsterdam air centuries before the French hussars came as conquerors in 1795, putting an end to the Republic of Seven United Netherlands Provinces. The Republic had existed since the 16th century with Amsterdam as its most powerful and influential city. Parisian fashions and wigs had long been copied by the Amsterdam aristocrats. French furniture and interior decoration was de rigueur inside the great patrician houses along the canals. French architecture influenced the refacing with stone, ornate carvings and statuary of the canal houses' austere brick façades. When the hussars arrived on the Dam, the

a highly developed know-how in textiles. Many became French tutors and governesses to the children of the rich, thus further projecting the French influence.

In the Dutch capital, French bibles and critical essays were printed. Later, Descartes, Voltaire, Montesquieu, Diderot and Rousseau escaped French censorship when their manuscripts were published here and smuggled back. A French 'underground' newspaper and the erotic fables of

Right: The Weigh House on the Dam which King Louis had demolished since it blocked his view.
Under: Lottery for conscription in Napoleon's Grande Armée took place in the Amstel Church. Young Dutchmen were obliged to comply.

Maison Descartes, French cultural center, was named in honor of the philosopher who resided in Amsterdam. The amusing sign alerts passers-by to the good french kitchen inside the complex

mercantile city was at an economic low. In the last decade of the 18th century, the West and East India Companies had gone bankrupt. The Exchange Bank of Amsterdam could no longer meet its obligations. In 1795, the French were welcomed as liberators. On March 4, the anniversary of the French Revolution was celebrated on the Dam, which became the Square of the Revolution. The French tri-colors flew from all the buildings.

Liberté, Egalité, Fraternité was the official policy, but in reality the burghers suffered under France. With the French 'liberation', Amsterdam was reduced to equality with all the other cities. Liberty was submission to Paris. And fraternity meant accepting the French soldiers, themselves brothers in need who had to be clothed and fed. And worst of all, the Amsterdammers had to manage with the almost-worthless French *assignats* circulated as the only valid currency and help pay France's war debt of 100 million guilders!

After a few years of faltering French control, Napoleon Bonaparte, self-appointed Emperor, offered the country a choice of annexation or the acceptance of his younger brother, Louis-Napoleon, as king. In Paris, Louis prepared for his new role by taking a cram course in Dutch. Upon his arrival in The Hague in 1806, he announced to the ministers' great consternation, in heavily accented Dutch, 'Ik ben de konijn van Holland' (I am the rabbit of Holland), confusing the Dutch word for king (*koning*) with rabbit (*konijn*). He later moved his throne to Utrecht before deciding to reign from 'the country's most important city', Amsterdam. Official word was conveyed to King Louis in February 1808 that 'the decision to convert the Town Hall into a palace and royal residence shall resound throughout Europe and will warm all the Amsterdammers' hearts'. The city assumed the central governmental role and King Louis-Napoleon was enthusiastically welcomed.

King Louis took his responsibilities seriously. Through benevolence and understanding, he sought to endear himself to the people, in contrast to his stern brother's plans. He worked for national unity; improved financial and economic conditions, which included disbanding the guilds; established the Royal Library, the Royal Museum (now the Rijksmuseum), the Academy of Art, Royal Institute of Sciences, Letters and Art and the

Emperor Napoleon's arrival in Amsterdam in 1811. He was greeted in fractured French by the burgomaster.

Napoleon was welcomed by cheering throngs on the Dam, which had been renamed Place Napoléon. The French tri-colors were flying from the palace and the New Church.

King Louis knocked down the old Weighing Tower in the middle of the Dam for a better view from his windows of the boats unloading. He was concerned about the Amsterdam dikes, which were in his opinion too low for the city's safety. He disapproved the Hope Bank's consideration of a loan to Spain and contraband trade flourishing with England, while recognizing that trade with the enemy was an old Amsterdam custom. He worked at being a good national ruler. In essence, he prepared the 250-year-old Republic for its first Dutch King. The sickly King Louis, who limped and was

mockingly called Lamme Louie, also had domestic problems. His pedantic wife, Hortense de Beauharnais, did not move into the palace until two years later in April 1810. She preferred mondaine Paris to Amsterdam's rigidity. Disenchanted with her husband's elaborate conversion and refurbishing of the Town Hall as a palace, Hortense also objected to the exterior smells and stifling air. She wrote: 'My salon, earlier as a criminal court, has a frieze of black and white skulls. They didn't want to destroy this highly esteemed decoration. The halls are somber. My suite directly faces the church. When one opens windows, only stale air and sulphuric fumes come in from the canals.' Hortense held out for exactly 27 days before leaving the lamentable Louis in May 1810. (The

'skulls' she despised never actually existed!) She took their child, Napoleon-Louis, with her to the Emperor's headquarters in Paris. The king's letters pleading for visits by his son went unanswered. Hortense wanted no further contact with her estranged husband. Nor did the Emperor wish his successor to become 'so Dutch' like his father. King Louis' only solace was Tiel, his dedicated, fox-colored dog. The name came from the Dutch city where, during the king's visit, the mongrel jumped on his lap. Perhaps King Louis also sought distraction in the former Town Hall's cellar prison, which he had converted into a cave. The wine reserves were posted on each cell door, such as *primeur caveau du roy, vin diff. qualités, vin de Tokay, vins ordinaires*. Wine and liqueur labels are still on the doors.

Napoleon was continually critical of his brother's reign. He showed his displeasure by humiliating him and undermining his authority. King Louis fled, with Tiel in his arms, during the night of July 1, 1810, just two months after Hortense had deserted him for the Parisian high life. The Netherlands was annexed to France on July 10. The Code Napoleon was put into effect. Dutchmen were drafted into the French Army. Censorship and police control came into effect. In a grand gesture, Napoleon added the guilded bee to the Amsterdam coat of arms but no one cared. (It was later abandoned!)

The merchant city of Amsterdam suffered under Napoleon's rule as never before. Whereas 2,500 ships had called at the port in 1805, four years later (after the illegal American contraband

Palace wine cellar initiated by King Louis Napoleon to store his *vins ordinaires, vin de Tokay, vin diff. qualités and primeur caveau du roy.*

Geleidebiljet voor een leverantie van likeur der firma WIJNAND FOCKINK te Amsterdam aan Z. M. Keizer Napoleon I te St. Cloud op 4 November 1812.

Emperor Napoleon's liqueur receipt for his purchase at Wijnand Fockink. The old distillery still maintains a 17th century tasting pub near the Dam, hidden in an alley behind the Krasnapolsky Hotel.

KLEEDING EN GEWOONTEN.

carrying trade had been eliminated), the number had dropped to a little over 300. By 1811, not one ship came in. Dockworkers' numbers had fallen from 3000 in 1806 to around 350 in 1811. Almost one third of the Amsterdam population was on relief in 1808.

But Napoleon's wobbly empire in the Netherlands went on, with surface gaiety at the Théâtre Français and a rich social life among the French colony and Dutch court followers. On March 20, 1811, a son was born to Napoleon and his young wife, Marie-Louise. This occasion was wildly celebrated in Amsterdam. In September of that year, news came from Paris that the Emperor and his Empress would come to the Netherlands and stay in Amsterdam on Place Napoléon (the Dam).

When Napoleon entered Amsterdam on his white stallion, closely followed by his militia, he was presented the key to the city as a token of the 'inestimable honor and happiness since the Amsterdammers felt privileged to welcome their majesties within their walls'. The people of Amsterdam turned out in unprecedented numbers. The palace blazed with great festivity. Amsterdam aristocrats outdid themselves in welcoming the Emperor and his entourage when they came by royal barge to visit. They threw their most precious personal carpets on the cobblestones for the party to walk on from the quays to their houses.

Soon afterwards, Napoleon departed on inspection tours of other parts of this Dutch kingdom, leaving Marie-Louise alone to occupy herself with touristic distractions, although she was not amused. She confessed to the Duke of Montebello that she would die of boredom if she lived here. When Marie-Louise and her ladies-in-waiting explored Amsterdam, they were intrigued by the luxurious oak and mahogany coffins displayed on the street of the coffin makers en route to the Théâtre Français; the bridges numbering almost 300; the linguistic facility of the educated class; and the Portuguese Jews, among whom they found the most distinguished and refined people of Amsterdam, with the most beautiful women. Amazed at the debauchery in the music halls, they were shocked when a bordello owner, Madame de Nicolai, audaciously appeared at the palace one day to promote her establishment. They found Dutch women well-dressed by Parisian standards, but the men rude in the guise of being

frank. They were amused by the beds built into the wall and the massive feathery down covers. They found Amsterdammers' habit of eating apples, pears, nuts, dried dab (an European flat fish), and smoking in the theatre to be very repulsive and reminiscent of lowly French taverns.

The Amsterdammers accepted the French until 1813, when many local sons died fighting in Napoleon's Grande Armée on the Russian front and in other disastrous Bonaparte defeats. Unrest started to set in. Continuing their contraband business with the English enemy, they were affronted when the unyielding Emperor burned their confiscated goods on the eastern end of the Herengracht. What couldn't be burned was dumped into the water. The mercantile

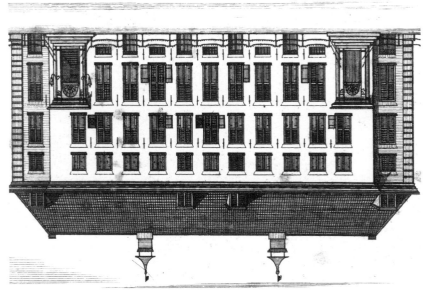

The Wallon orphanage, 17th century view. Maison Descartes is now housed here.

Amsterdammers would have preferred seeing their illegal goods given to the poor, or even used by the military, instead of this obvious waste.

It was during this period, for the first time in years, that 'Up with the House of Orange' was heard from the royalist underground movement. French customs officers, with stones around their necks, were thrown into the canals. The detested tax collector's Rokin office was ransacked, records burned and large amounts of money thrown into the canal. Many French officials were attacked and beaten up.

After Napoleon was defeated at Leipzig, Amsterdam's opposition and resistance to French rule became more intense. House of Orange colors were flying everywhere. In 1813, the

French quickly retreated and on November 17, 1813, Dutch independence was proclaimed. At the end of that month, Prince William of Orange returned from exile in London. On December 2, he arrived triumphantly in Amsterdam. The Prince of Orange remained only a few hours, just long enough to receive city officials and be proclaimed sovereign Prince of the Netherlands. Though he offered to return the Dam Palace to the city, this was placed at his disposal as an

The Dictionary of the French Academy was published in Amsterdam during the 17th century by the underground press and smuggled into France.

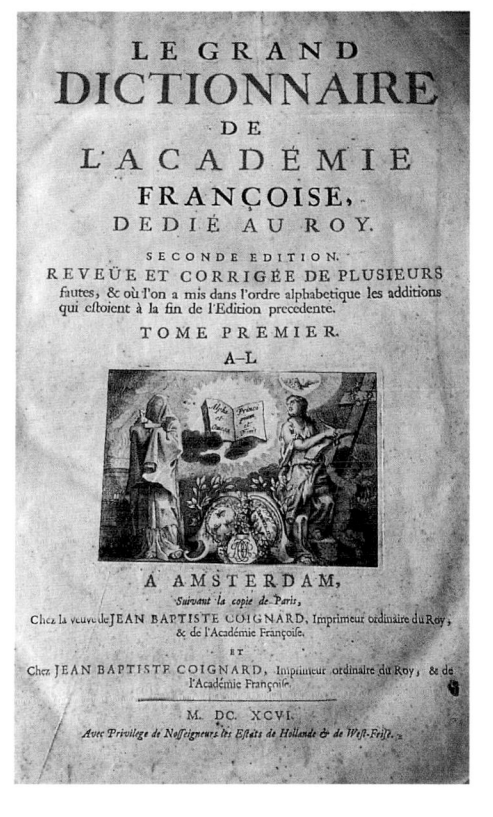

official residence. On March 29, 1814, in the New Church, an assembly voted for new laws to govern the nation. The next day, in the same church, the Prince of Orange took the oath. In May 1815, he became Willem I, King of the Netherlands (which included Belgium). The French occupation was over but French remained chic in the court and among the upper classes.

Over the centuries, many Frenchmen described Amsterdam with Gallic perception in their letters and travel diaries. The mathematician and philosopher René Descartes, who found Amsterdam an ideal place for his metaphysical reflections, lived here with his Dutch wife from 1629 to 1635, on the Kalverstraat, the Dam and finally at Westermarkt 6. He wrote in 1631 to his friend, the poet Jean-Louis Guez de Balzac: 'I

suggest Amsterdam for your retirement ... it is preferable to all the monasteries. A country house may be very well run, but there are always all sorts of things missing which can only be obtained in a town and even the solitude you are hoping for is never total ... Whereas in this great city everybody except me is in business and so absorbed by profit making that I could spend my entire life here without being noticed by a soul. I go for a walk every day in the Babel of a great thoroughfare as freely and restfully as you stroll in your garden.'

Voltaire, who visited several times starting in 1713, wrote: 'The Dutch are silent and frigid. Their women do not escape these faults. The habits, the simplicity, the equality are the same in Amsterdam as Sparta. Likewise for mediocrity ... There are no jobless, no fops, no aggressive people.' When Voltaire left Holland he wrote: *'Adieu, canaux, canards, canailles. Je n'ai rien vu chez vous qui vaille.'* ('Goodbye canals, ducks, scum. I've seen nothing here that's worth anything.')

Montesquieu, in a 1729 letter, wrote: '... The city of Amsterdam is aristocratic, with an aristocracy that is extremely sensitive. The people are governed by a small number of persons, not *jure hereditario*, but elected. There are four ruling burgomasters who share the responsibilities.'

The Marquis de Sade, who came in 1769, commented on the city and its population in a chauvinistic letter: '... As far as company is concerned, this city is in a sorry state. Whenever you are invited for dinner, it's solely to eat. As soon as you have left the table, your host will disappear into his office. You can either depart or join his ladies, who are usually rather ugly and on the whole absolutely boring because of their narrow-mindedness ...

... On the whole they seem to be good people, completely taken up by obtaining new riches all the time, and only interested in the means to obtain them. Nevertheless, they are quite prepared to be of service, as long as it doesn't cost them any money. They are phlegmatic, cold and rather disinclined to show an interest in anything that cannot be turned into a profit. As the men determine the women's characters, it is rather obvious that they are not very lovely. They could be much more lovely, but one cannot blame them for this. One sees very few slim waists. They are rather white, devoid of

personality.' In 1990, there was a de Sade sequel. A fifth generation descendant, the young Marquis Thibault de Sade, came to Amsterdam to hype a champagne bearing his libertine ancestor's name on the étiquette illustrated with a chained woman.

In the mid-20th century, Albert Camus was in Amsterdam for an entire day and full night observing street life, especially on the seedy Zeedijk, which swarmed with prostitutes, pimps, drunken sailors and underworld figures. In monologue form, Camus recounts his Mexico City bar impressions in *La Chute* (1956): '... Well, the gentlemen you see here live from the work of those ladies over there. Men as well as women are notoriously common beings and they usually only come here because of their mythomania or stupidity. This boils down to one and the same thing. On one hand they fantasize too much and, on the other, they lack every conceivable power of imagination. Now and then the men play with a knife or a gun, but don't think for a second they enjoy it. They are more or less obliged to do so, that's all, but they are half scared to death when they fire their last bullets.'

Through the centuries, Amsterdam has maintained interest in the French language and culture, which has been further stimulated by the Maison Descartes since 1933. The French government purchased the expansive Hospice Wallon in 1966 to provide a truly French showcase in a prestigious setting for the Maison Descartes. Michèle van Hasselt-Guibert, Director of the Amsterdam-based French Chamber of Commerce, reports on business interests, 'There are some 50 French firms based in Amsterdam, employing over 6000 persons in the production and service sectors. Throughout the Netherlands, there are circa 350 French establishments, representing 250 companies, with 21,000 personnel. Total investment is around 100 billion French francs or 32 billion Dutch guilders. Two out of five cars driven here are of French manufacture. Our active French business club, "Le Pot Mensuel", regularly brings together some hundred French and Dutch chief executives.'

Felix Meritis, a late 18th century center of enlightenment, was elegantly decorated in French style. Molière, Corneille and Racine were discussed. Now it is used for international theater, dance and the Amsterdam summer university.

Voltaire relied on Amsterdam to get his works published when they were banned in France. These were smuggled back into his homeland via underground channels. Voltaire visited Amsterdam in 1713.

Americana

Historical, architectural, cultural inheritances

Almost 400 years ago, the Dutch were already in that part of the New World now popularly called America. In 1602, they fished off Cape Cod and collected pelts on the island of Mannahatannk.

In 1602, three small, competitive companies were merged into the Verenigde Oostindische Compagnie, voc, (United East India Company), with a monopoly granted for all trade and

shipping east of the Cape of Good Hope. The Englishman Henry Hudson was dispatched by the voc on April 4, 1609, to find an ice-free, shorter route north of Russia to the East. He departed on this exploratory voyage from the Tower of Tears, erected in 1482 on the city's harbor. Still standing, it has a memorial plaque placed in 1927 by the Greenwich Historical Society of New York. (see '... and the World'). When his vessel, the *Half Moon*, was blocked by ice in the Arctic, Hudson changed course and accidentally became the first European to land

on the island that would become New York. Hudson also explored the river flowing north which later took his name, expanding trade opportunities for the Amsterdam-based company in that valley region.

English Separatists arrived in Amsterdam in 1608 during their Dutch exile. The City Council gave this sturdy band of religious exiles, later known as the Pilgrim Fathers, use of a small, 14th century church which had been empty for twenty years after a Calvinist coup. That house of worship, in the medieval, walled-in enclave of the Begijnhof courtyard, is still known today as the English Church. A plaque on the tower and a stained glass window commemorate the Pilgrims' prayers and passage. In 1620, they departed on their long tortuous return route to Southampton for embarkation on the *Mayflower* to sail to the New World.

There was Nieuw Amsterdam before New York. The Nieuw Nederland colony, founded in 1625, purchased the island a year later from the Indians for ten shirts, 80 pairs of socks, ten muskets, 30 bullets, 30 pounds of gunpowder, 30 axes, 30 cooking pots and a copper frying pan. Americans today are still amused at the bartering exchange which had been used by the Dutch, who were the only people buying land rather than usurping land like other foreign colonizers. The official purchase document from Peter Schagen, a Company delegate, indicates: 'Our people have purchased the island of Manhattan from the Indians for the value of 60 guilders. It is 11,000 *morgens* in size.'

In the 1970s, New York legislators proposed an official resolution to correct the founding date and give credit due to the Dutch: 'The flag, the seal and other official insignia of the City of New York erroneously bear the date of 1664, rather than 1625, as the date of our origin. New York City recognizes its ties with the early

Nieuw Amsterdam after its surrender to the English and the name change to New York in 1664.

colonists and their heritage by the orange, white and blue flag of the City and the seal of the city of New York includes the arms of the city of Amsterdam, the windmills of Holland, the beaver and wampum denoting the original trade of the Netherlands in North America.' The resolution was not passed.

Though recognition would have been appreciated, it's known that the traders had established official commercial relations between the Dutch Republic, primarily Amsterdam, and America soon after Hudson's landing. Settlers had gone over in increasing numbers right from the start. The handful of earliest pioneers, more secure after Fort Amsterdam was built in 1625, grew with the arrivals to about 10,000 in 1664. Even after Holland lost to the British three years later, the city, then baptised New York, remained the focus of Dutch trade to America. Nowadays, the Netherlands is among the largest foreign investors in the United States. Some 15 million Americans have Dutch roots, while currently 11,000 Americans reside in the Netherlands, of which some 4000 in Amsterdam. Amsterdam's most prominent monuments indelibly linked with America are the West India

House, called the 'cradle of New York', on the Haarlemmerstraat, and the West India Company warehouses, including the impressive complex on the Prince Hendrikkade/'s-Gravenhekje, where beaver skins from Manhattan were stored.

In the West India House courtyard, there is a bronze statue of Stuyvesant seemingly staring angrily at the boardroom, where the directors called the Gentlemen XIX, who voted for the establishment of Nieuw Amsterdam, had ordered him to capitulate to the Duke of York and return for reporting. Despite the surrender, the company continued to play an important role in the history of the American colonies. More than 350 years' Dutch/American history was almost extinguished in 1979 during a blaze caused by fireworks which destroyed roofs and damaged the old interiors of the West India House. Lovingly restored to its early 17th century state, the house now provides offices and lecture rooms for the John Adams Institute, named in honor of the diplomat and statesman who lived in Amsterdam, established close ties with the Netherlands and became the second president of the United States. Among the Institute's programs is the much lauded

Peter Stuyvesant, in the courtyard of the West India Company building, seems to be glaring up at the meeting room of the directors who ordered him to surrender Nieuw Amsterdam to the Duke of York and return home.

West India Company Headquarters, built in 1623, as it now appears after restoration to its original state. It is called the 'Cradle of New York'.

Insert: Exterior view when it was built, in 1623.

SIGILLUM civitatis

ANTIQUUS HABITUS

Domus Societatis Indiae Occidentalis condita anno 1623.

Het West-Indische Huys ghel.icht in't jaer 1623.

'American Literature Today' lecture series which has brought literary giants like Saul Bellow, Gore Vidal, Joseph Brodsky, John Irving, John Updike and many others to Amsterdam.

Over two centuries before the world-famed writers who came to the Dutch capital, men who were making history in the struggle for freedom arrived and were warmly welcomed by Dutch sympathizers. When the American admiral John Paul Jones showed up in Amsterdam in 1779, he received a hero's welcome, much to the dismay of the British enemy who considered him a renegade pirate. A popular song from those days is still sung today:

Daar komt Pauwel Jonas aan
'T is zo 'n aardig ventje
[Here comes Paul Jones
He is such a nice fellow]

John Adams, a Revolution leader, arrived in the Netherlands in 1780, seeking loans and recognition of the new nation. After a few weeks, he wrote to his wife Abigail: 'I am very much pleased with Holland. It is a singular country. It is like no other. It is all the effect of industry and the work of art. The frugality, industry, cleanliness, etc. here deserve the imitation of my countrymen.'

His Amsterdam home for one year was at Keizersgracht 529, where he supposedly had a warm relationship with his landlady. Starting in 1781, he brought over his two eldest sons, John Quincy, also to later become an American president, was rough-minded like his father. Charles was homesick and missed his mother. Both boys first attended the Latin school in Amsterdam and later the University of Leiden. John Quincy stayed on, but Charles returned home before completing his studies.

Adams was successful in securing loans at the banking offices of the Van Staphort Brothers at Singel 460 in the elegant Odeon building which was virtually destroyed by fire in 1990, subsequently restored and is now a discotheque. In 1782, three Amsterdam banks granted an early kind of 'Marshall Aid' to the fledgling United States of America. John Adams, America's foreign minister, received the country's first loan of 2 million dollars and by 1794 nearly 12 million dollars had been borrowed. Adams became the first United States ambassador to the Netherlands and the Treaty of Amity and Commerce was signed, formalizing the friendly relations between the two republics. In that year, Adams wrote: 'I love the people where I am. They have faults, but they have deep wisdom and great virtues and they love America ...' The New York Historical Society has a painting showing the American war vessel, *The Constitution*, setting sail with a cargo of coins for the American government's repayment of interest on the loan by Hope & Co., presently

John Paul Jones, the American admiral, was called a pirate by the British but the Amsterdammers took him to their hearts with receptions and songs in his honor.

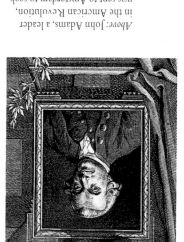

Above: John Adams, a leader in the American Revolution, was sent to Amsterdam to seek recognition and secure loans for the fledgling country. *Right:* Letter by John Adams to his wife Abigail, in which he writes, 'Oh! Oh! Oh! That you were here to do the Honour of the United States.'

Right: John Adams lived here. An etching from Caspar Philips' *Canal Book* (1771) shows the Keizersgracht 529 as the future American president knew it when he moved in.

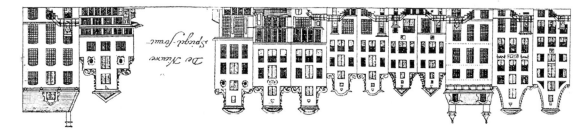

De Nieuwe Spiegel-straat

Above/under left: The American Hotel was built on the bustling Leidseplein at the turn of the century. Its landmark café has retained its pure Art Deco style.

Left: A woman breast-feeding her baby, an old man, figures staring into the unknown future are insurance symbols on the façade of the New York Building completed in 1891.

> Gabled houses, more than 7,000 protected as monuments, line the concentric web of canals dug over three centuries ago. Light filtering through the trees in the changing seasons projects new dimensions on the decorated façades.

Mees Pierson. The painting illustrates Amsterdam's pivotal role in the development of the United States.

Around the turn of the 19th century, the Dutch merchant bankers Hope and Co. and the British Baring bank had heard rumors of the pending sale of Louisiana by France to America. They managed to arrange a contract for 15 million dollars but, because war broke out between France and England, Baring was blocked and all financial arrangements for the Louisiana purchase had to be completed in the Amsterdam offices of Hope & Co. Ironically, in 1995, almost 200 years later, Baring — banker to the British royal family — was virtually ruined by managerial manipulations. The saviors, who took over the devastated Baring reins and brought them to Holland, was an Amsterdam-based bank, the ING Group.

Besides the sometimes flagrant American presence in hamburger and other fast food emporiums, there are numerous earlier, historical and architectural references to the New World. Amsterdam's Maritime Museum has a map of Nieuw Nederland with the oldest known view of the island that would become New York. In the floor of the Citizens Hall in the Palace on the Dam, the Western Hemisphere is depicted with California still seen as an island. On the tympan on the back side of the Palace, the four known continents (Australia had not yet been discovered) bid their symbolic fruit and produce to the Amsterdam City Maiden. America, then still relatively unimportant, is

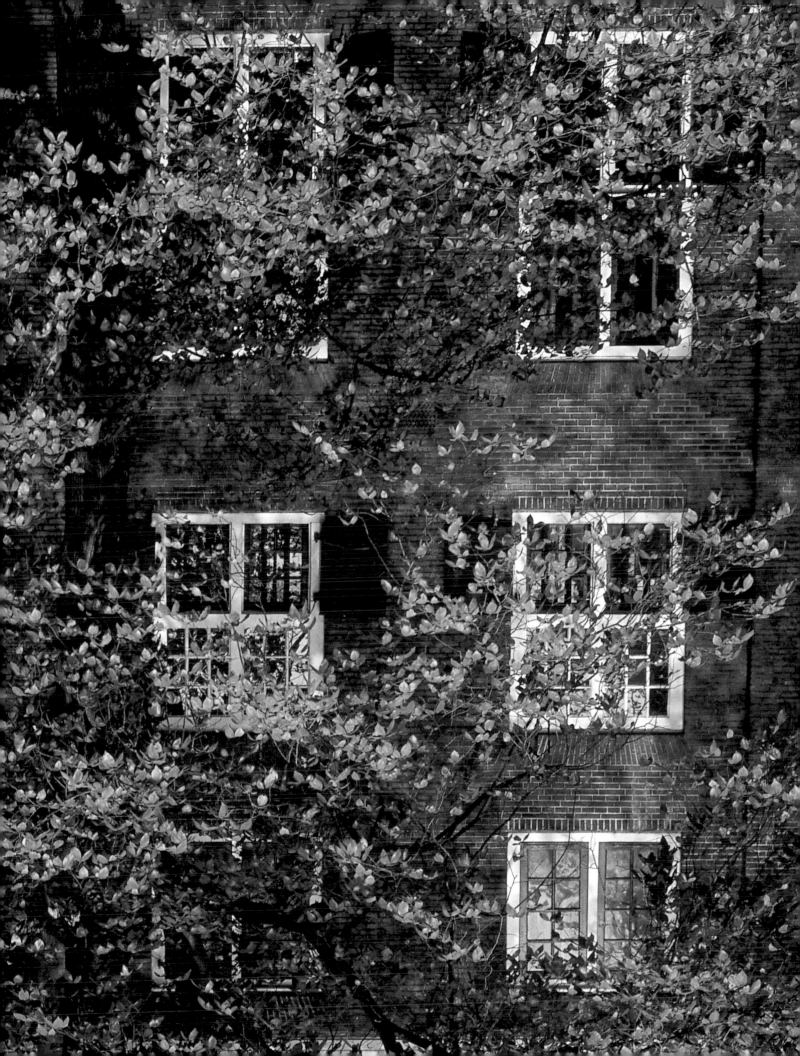

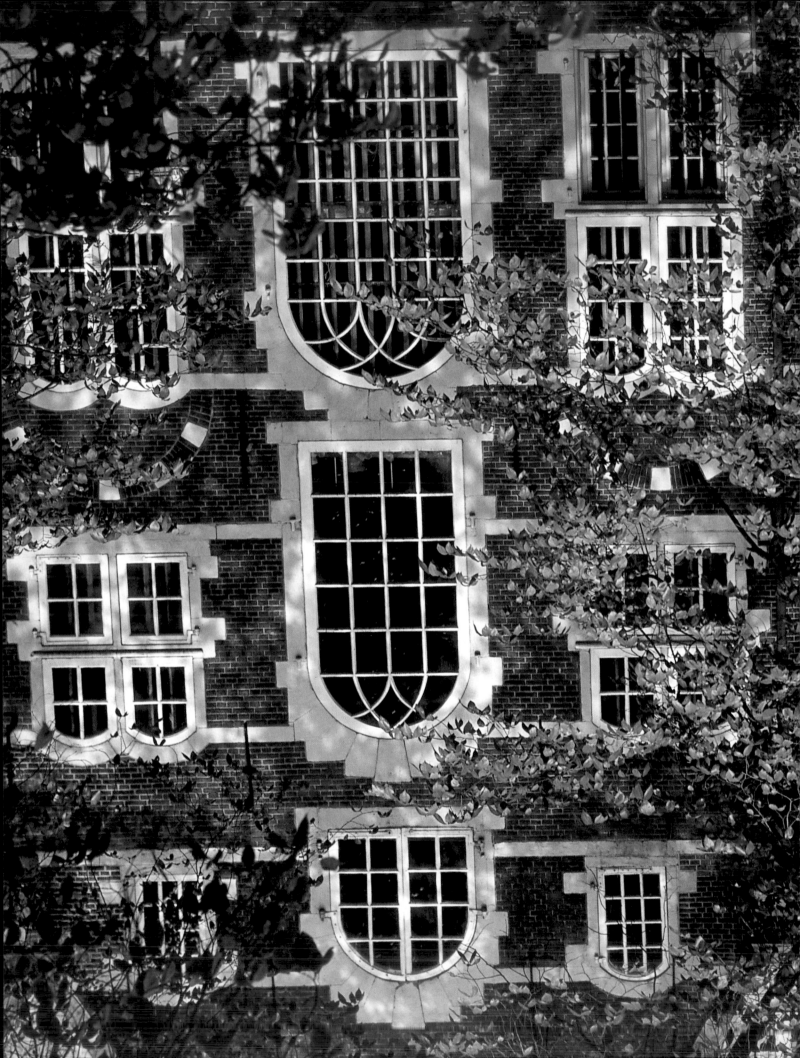

B.C. Alexander

PRESIDENT, AMERICAN CHAMBER OF
COMMERCE IN THE NETHERLANDS

Buford Alexander, who is Director of McKinsey in his professional life, commented:
'Americans who have worked and lived here for a longer term have a secret they are not very anxious to spread and thus spoil the special, surprising quality of life in the city — rather village — of Amsterdam. While the Dutch capital suffered from an image as a mecca for free-living youth in the 1960s and 1970s, the truth today is quite different. There has been a complete turnaround. The hysteria has gone. Things are again normalized. As a matter of fact, it's safer than most U.S. cities.
'There is nothing like Amsterdam on a Saturday morning. It is then truly a village at its best, full of helpful neighbors, all of whom know each other. It's a time for cycling or strolling through narrow streets crossing the canals, to browse in a myriad of shops specialized in everything imaginable, a

cornucopia of curiosities you don't find easily in many other cities.
'There are hundreds of cafés and restaurants with their inimitable Amsterdam ambiance and charm, where you stop for a glass of gin or beer, or a good meal. As soon as the proprietor or guests hear a slight accent in your reasonably fluent Dutch, they talk to you in good English. Admittedly, they want to show off their linguistic ability, but at the same

time they want to make you feel at home. It's no wonder that so many Americans have restored canal houses and have become part of the local scene.
'Like American individuals, American companies find it easy to establish here and integrate effortlessly into Dutch business life. The American Chamber of Commerce epitomizes this rewarding balance, since roughly half of the 1,000 member companies are Dutch. American companies provide 150,000 jobs, which is highly appreciated by the Dutch Government. This is continually underscored by the open dialogue between senior officials of the Government and the Chamber and its members.
'We've found that when American companies consider investing in the Netherlands, the factor that really tips the balance for a favorable decision is the lifestyle of American executives and their families in and around Amsterdam. We've all experienced this firsthand and don't want to shout our secret from the rooftops.'

Peter Pulitzer bought and restored 32 adjoining historic houses and warehouses on the Prinsengracht and Keizersgracht to create an unusual hotel. There are inner courtyards and gardens beyond the old monuments.

represented on the lower right side with three Indians recognizable by their feather headdress. In the heart of Amsterdam, on the bustling Leidseplein, a Dutchman who had become an American returned and built in 1881 the wonderful *fin-de-siècle* American Hotel. The façade was renovated in 1902. The stylish Art Nouveau café was opened, now unmissable on the Amsterdam scene.

A decade later, the New York Life Insurance Company constructed Amsterdam's tallest private building at that time on the corner of the Keizersgracht and the Leidsestraat. The letters 'N' and 'Y' are visible above the main entrance. An eagle holding the American flag is suspended from the top floor. This handsome building is now used by Metz & Co., one of the capital city's smart shops.

Peter Pulitzer, grandson of the newspaper publisher whose newspaper will established the famed journalistic prize, decided to open a hotel in Amsterdam in 1968. His courageous undertaking involved the renovation and restoration of 32 historical homes, warehouses, industrial premises and shops stretched along the Princes' and Emperors' canals. The maze of public spaces, inner gardens and rooms were created for the delightful, unorthodox Pulitzer Hotel.

Americans have always had an affinity for Amsterdam and have happily come to visit. There have been countless artists who work, marry, stay, build careers and enjoy the quality of life. There have been countless artists in residence, dancers with the ballet companies, classical musicians in the great large and small orchestras, jazz musicians in the clubs, writers, translators, free-wheelers who finally felt at home here and so many more very individualistic Yankees who became Amsterdammers during the course of time. Entrepreneurs have pioneered in establishing the European Options Exchange and many trade, consumer, financial and cultural undertakings which have been successfully absorbed into the Amsterdam scene. Diplomats and businessmen assigned by the multinationals often come back to establish a viable venture on their own with a *pied à terre* in their beloved Amsterdam. The city holds a certain magic.

The Amsterdam region is home to over 320 subsidiary companies — about 25 percent of the total number of American firms in the Netherlands. These Amsterdam area companies directly employ some 30,000 people. Household names include AT&T, Allen-Bradley, American Express, Bank of America, Bell Helicopter, Citibank, Coca-Cola, Colgate, Palmolive, Federal Express, Honeywell, IBM, LA Gear, Levi Strauss, Merril Lynch, McKinsey & Co, Microsoft, Mobil Oil, Rank Xerox, Raytheon, Time Warner, Unisys and Warner-Lambert.

Unquestionably, the fastest growing American firm is the newcomer Morton Automotive Safety Products Amsterdam. They set up shop in Amsterdam in October 1994 with eight employees. In October 1995, there were 165 on staff, with planned growth in the ensuing four to five years to reach a level of 700 personnel to meet existing orders. This market leader in airbag systems has contracts from European, U.S. and Japanese car manufacturers. Production space capacity was geared for this expansion. Jay Stewart, Chairman and CEO, Morton International Inc., indicated the choice of Amsterdam was based on 'central location, excellent infrastructure and multilingual population'.

The International School of Amsterdam (ISA), with its 550 students, serves a diverse expatriate community with families of 38 nationalities. American students — the second largest group in the school — comprise 25 percent of the ISA enrollment.

The newest rage of the mid-nineties is American football. The local Amsterdam Admirals have been sweeping a championship route across Europe, with an increasing number of Dutch fans, supporting them at all matches. They will be playing regularly in the new Amsterdam Arena.

The Amsterdam Admirals have attracted growing numbers of fans with their rough American football. Crowds are amused by the cheerleaders included in the colorful spectacle. Future games will be played in the Amsterdam Arena.

Nippon on the Amstel

Japanese business community life

*T*he commercial link, initiated by the Dutch in 1598 when they became the only Western traders allowed to remain in the country during Japan's long isolation, has now come full circle with 20th century Japanese businessmen settling in Amsterdam and its suburbs in increasing numbers.

Unlike the early Dutch, who were restricted in their movements and confined to a limited area, today's Japanese choose the Dutch capital for its facilities but voluntarily remain among themselves. Though their ancestors' hilarious misconceptions about the Dutch (see '… and the World'), have been forgotten, they remain confused about the 'Dutch wife', originally used in English and Japanese for a bamboo leg rest in the Dutch East Indies. Nowadays in Japan it's a life-size inflatable woman, while a shrewd Tokyo manufacturer also produces a 'Dutch boy'. Both bed partners sell for 1,200 guilders in Japan. Aside from this pejorative reference, the Japanese language incorporates widespread references to Western culture and scientific knowledge taught by the Dutch *sensei* (teachers). Curiously, perhaps as a sign of the times after centuries' frustrated starts, a new Dutch/Japanese dictionary was published in late 1994 simultaneously in Japan and the Netherlands. Nishi Zenzaburo made the first attempt around 1760 but died after completing only the letters A, B and C. The Dutchman Hendrik Droef went further in 1810, but the

Japanese/Dutch dictionary title page, 1810.

Right: Dutchmen in Nagasaki as seen through Japanese eyes.

Left: Karaoke club fun when young Japanese sing out without inhibition.

Japanese school class learning rules of a ball game.

newest publication, compiled by the Japan-Netherlands Institute in Leiden, is the most comprehensive to date — and should facilitate clearer communication.

In 1862, fifteen of the 38-strong first Japanese delegation to the Netherlands spent four days in Amsterdam seeking companies as suppliers for Japan. The burgomaster and railway authorities ceremoniously welcomed them. Crowds of curious Amsterdammers lined the streets as the Oriental visitors were pulled in horse-drawn carriages along the Haarlemmerdijk, Keizersgracht, Leidsestraat, Herengracht and Reguliersgracht to Brack's Doelen Hotel. Following the lunch served on antique Japanese porcelain, the group visited Coster's diamond cutting factory, the Diaconie orphanage and the Rijksmuseum (at that time in the Trippenhuis). After dinner, there was a tour of the Royal Palace and the Old Church.

The next day had a maritime theme, with visits to the Entrepotdok (docks), Zeemanhuis (seamen's hostel), the steam kettle factory of Van Vlissingen and Van Heel and the Marinewerf (naval wharf). That evening a garden party was given in their honor by the Nederlandsche Handel-Maatschappij, then located on the corner of the Herengracht and the Nieuwe

Spiegelstraat. The building was lavishly decorated with an arch, through which a painting of the Edo Palace could be seen on a Japanese pavillion erected in the garden. Unfortunately, this lavish reception reaped no commercial benefit for Amsterdam. When the delegates returned to Japan, they encountered political upheaval and were immediately dismissed.

From 1863 until 1866, a number of Japanese studied in the Netherlands, including naval officers who had already learned the language during the Dutch marine detachment's posting in Nagasaki from 1855 to 1859. Their stay coincided with the construction of the *Kaiyo-maru*, a warship commission from the Imperial Japanese Navy, initiated by Van Vlissingen en Van Heel, suppliers of the steam kettles. One of the group, blacksmith and machine builder Ookuwa Kitaroo, died in Amsterdam at the age of 33 in September 1865, later recognized as one of the fifteen founders of modern Japanese industry, was buried in a second-class grave in the Westerbegraafplaats with ten countrymen at the interment. He was reburied in a first-class grave one year later with a commemorative column ordered for 160 guilders. This monument disappeared when the

Oude Westerbegraafplaats was cleared in 1956 for removal to the new cemetery. Renewed Japanese interest in him, stimulated by a Mr. Katsuyama's research in 1982, resulted in a replica of the monument being placed at the new burial site, the Nieuwe Oosterbegraafplaats. The first Japanese officially registered as an

Sony Netherlands headquarters, a new building on the main Amsterdam–Schiphol Airport highway, has a welcoming entrance between the two office towers which at the top form a 'skybox', with a panoramic view. There is a soaring atrium.

Amsterdam resident was naval officer Akamatsu Disaburo, who chose to remain when all the Japanese returned home. He lived at Amstel Y 93 (now Amstel 180) from February 1866 until November 1868, while working in the city's naval shipyard. It's known from his diaries, published only in Japanese, that he arranged a Handel-Maatschappij credit for the Shogun's brother when he visited the Paris World's Fair in 1867.

Nowadays, there are some 2000 Japanese living in the Amsterdam area, with 1300 in suburban Amstelveen. In all, 5000 Japanese reside in the Netherlands. One hundred fifty Japanese companies (many with European headquarters) are based in Amsterdam, accounting for 50 percent of all Japanese companies in the Netherlands. Of these, 63 percent are in management, 32 percent in wholesale and 5 percent in service and repair sectors. Among the companies: Nissan Europe (European distribution center), Canon Europe, Sony Nederland, Takenaka Netherlands (with 90 percent of all Japanese building contracts), Epson Europe, Yamaha Motor (European distribution center), Yakult, Dai-Ichi Kangyo

Mr. T. Shirai

PRESIDENT OF NISSAN EUROPE
N.V.(AMSTERDAM) AND MANAGING DIRECTOR &
MEMBER OF THE BOARD OF NISSAN MOTOR CO. LTD
(JAPAN)

Mr. Tadahiro Shirai reiterated Nissan Europe's decision to locate in amsterdam:
'Our 300 man personnel are responsible for developing and coordinating corporate, marketing, sales and after-sales strategies for Nissan in Europe. They monitor business and political trends, handle product planning and analyse market data.
'We selected Amsterdam in order to efficiently provide a high service level to circa 5 million Nissan owners in Europe, as well as our extensive network of distributors and dealers.

'Amsterdam offers a stable political and economic environment for international companies requiring a European coordination center. The education level is generally high, with English spoken well as a second language. Its "Three Mainport" concept of international airport, seaport and teleport is unquestionably the city's unique selling point. This advanced infrastructure means easy access by land, sea, air and satellite, precisely the vital links required by our company in providing goods and services to a broad customer base.'

Bank (world's largest bank), Fuji Bank and Bank of Tokyo. Mitsubishi Europe, strongly represented here, has five production factories, its own bank, trading and holding companies. Nissin Foods, market leader in Japan's multi-million dollar instant noodle market, set up headquarters close to Schiphol Airport for its strategic push into Europe. The company is targeting Benelux, United Kingdom and German markets with two instant noodle products in four flavors manufactured from pure wheat flour in their Dutch factory. Another Japanese food manufacturer, Yakult Honsha, is marketing a revolutionary health drink from its offices in suburban Amstelveen.

All Japanese firms in the Amsterdam region are run by Japanese directors in contrast to one American in every seven American firms. Sony is an exception. Operating as a subsidiary company of Sony Corporation, Sony Nederland B.V. has an all-Dutch management in its majestic 'Sony City' headquarters (opened in 1993) on the road leading from Amsterdam to Schiphol Airport. Gerard ten Velden is Managing Director, while Deputy Director, Jan van Grondelle, is responsible for Corporate Communications. The complex was designed by the architectural firm of Van den Oever, Zaaijer, Roodbeen & Partners with two metallic silver office wings joined on the highest floor with a 'Skybox' offering a panoramic view over Amsterdam and the airport. Design and placement on the site

allows ample space for future expansion. Also housed here are representatives of Audio Europe, Video Europe, both holding company divisions with Japanese management.
The Japanese Chamber of Commerce, Amsterdam–Japan Club, Japan Trade Club and JETRO (Japan External Trade Organization) are all based here.
In Japan the economy revolves around so-called *keiretsus*, a number of large industrial groups usually centered around a bank. An example of such a powerful network of companies linked through share holdings includes Mitsubishi, Sumitomo and Fuji, all locally operative. But this far from Japan, contacts are looser than in

Meidi-Ya on the Beethovenstraat is always crowded as Japanese residents shop for food specialties from home.

of Limburg, is sold in the Okura.

Incidentally, the 23-story Okura, the city's tallest hotel, a virtual skyscraper by Amsterdam standards, provides another service for its Japanese clientele who might not understand the Dutch TV weather news. When the Netherlands' largest barometer shows a blue-lit roof, one can expect a sunny day; A transparent roof means changeable weather ahead. If the roof is green, take an umbrella.

The Japanese School of Amsterdam, founded in 1979 with a primary and junior high school curriculum for an initial 42 students, now has circa 350 pupils and serves two thirds of all the Japanese in the Netherlands. The parents are primarily businessmen, educators and diplomats. Since an understanding of local culture is considered essential, Dutch language classes are mandatory for the first 5 grades. An exchange program assures interaction with a Dutch 'sister school' in Sneek. Organized trips give students practical insight to various aspects of Dutch society, like farms, newspaper offices and old people's homes. At the International School of Amsterdam, four out of ten pupils are Japanese. Most pupils return to Japan to complete their high school and university education.

In a recent survey among Japanese in the Netherlands, an interviewee summed up a general attitude: 'The stay in the Netherlands is addictive. Life is very cheap here and everybody gets used to drinking a good glass of wine with their meal. We all have a much higher living standard here than we could ever afford in Japan.'

Akio Hirata, who resigned after six years as Casio Europe's Vice-President when he was called back to Tokyo, is one of a growing number of Japanese who prefer Amsterdam life. Hirata set up a consulting office for small Japanese firms coming into the European market. This was doubly remarkable since Hirata not only left his employer, contrary to customary lifetime allegiance, but began his own business outside of Japan. Hirata commented: 'The houses here are much bigger. Everyone understands English. My wife can buy everything we want to eat on the Beethovenstraat. There are Japanese and international schools for the children. I travel much quicker to my work here than in Tokyo and can spend more time with my family.' Japanese women are involved in their husbands'

the mother country. The Dai-Ichi Kangyo Bank regularly organizes client get-togethers here.

For Nissan (formerly known as Datsun), Japan's second largest car manufacturer, Amsterdam came out head and shoulders above all other Continental candidates for European headquarters during a seven month comparative study. Geographical advantages of Amsterdam's 'gateway' location in northwestern Europe, the local work-force's English fluency and the

Sake ceremony honored Japan Airlines' anniversaries and inauguration on the Amsterdam-Tokyo direct service. Participating at the time were the Japanese ambassador, Management and Jaap Rost Onnes (second from right), Honorary Consul-General of Japan in Amsterdam.

'Three Mainport' concept were among the decisive factors for Nissan Europe n.v. setting up on the main road leading from the capital's center to Schiphol Airport.

The Japanese community in Amsterdam is a tightly-knit one, a *habatsu* (Japanese for 'clique'). They live and work together and buy from each other in Amsterdam's Japanese shops. These include a green grocer, butcher, the Meidi-Ya deli, all located on the Beethovenstraat, a Japanese take-out restaurant and a supermarket. Japanese can relax at home with rentals from the Japanese video shop, show up at a private (Japanese only) karaoke club called 'Yume' to unwind in raucous group sing-alongs, play a Go game or attend cultural events in the Go Centre. The Okura Hotel is their home away from home with Japanese restaurants, a Japanese barber, a Japanese food store, *shiatsu* masseurs and the only Japanese bookstore in the Netherlands. The European edition of the *Nikkei Sangyo Shimbun* newspaper, published in the southern province

representative functions in sharp contrast to their relegation to the back room back home. They are invited to dinners and official receptions and respectfully introduced as the executive's wife. Going home for Japanese is traumatic after their westernized, liberal life pattern in the Netherlands. Often there is jealousy and suspicion. One Japanese manager, who became a wine connoisseur in Amsterdam, refused to even examine a wine label in Tokyo, fearing ostracization as a snob.

A Dutchman who has long been responsible for an extremely smooth relationship with the capital's Japanese business community, as well as top diplomatic and commercial contacts in the Netherlands and Japan, is ABN AMRO Bank Senior Executive Jaap Rost Onnes, Japan's Honorary Consul in Amsterdam. He, more than anyone

Above: Okura Hotel by night: many lights on the high rise hotel with its panoramic view over Amsterdam.

Right above: Nissan Europe headquarters, a large-scale steel frame building, has the Presidential Office, a cantilevered 'cockpit', on the 9th floor. Before construction could commence, 187 piles had to be driven 20 meters below sea level onto a sand layer.

Left: Management and two senior managers of Dai-Ichi Kangyo Bank Nederland n.v. at the entrance of the Amsterdam-based office on the Apollolaan.

Under: Japanese businessmen arrival at the Central Station.

over 150 canal-laced hectares also close to Scheduled for completion in 1997, spreading project called Holland Village/Huis ten Bosch. architecture and culture — is the 2 billion dollar compliment for Japanese admiration of Dutch Building on that success — an even grander attracted more than 2 million visitors annually. the Bay of Nagasaki, which since 1983 has Dutch is the Oranda Mura (Holland Village) on Evidence of the great Japanese admiration for the friendship with their oldest European relation. 2000 being planned by Japan to mark 400 years' during the mammoth celebrations in the year to remain here will feel even more at home The increasing number of Japanese who choose annual *Sinterklaas* (St. Nicholas) celebration. to Dutch culture and customs, including the which regularly introduces Japanese businessmen initiated the popular Amsterdam-Japan Club, diamond factory owner Edward Asscher, Municipal Director of Economic Affairs, and Rost Onnes who, with Harry Grosveld, bridge between the Japanese and Dutch. It was else, has personified the business and social

Nagasaki Omura Bay, this duplication of the royal palace, Huis ten Bosch, plus the most characteristic Dutch cathedrals, houses, waterways, streets and markets is bigger than life. An Amsterdammer entering the elegant Hotel de l'Europe would feel transplanted. Streets and canalsides are being paved with Dutch bricks. Amsterdam gables appear everywhere in this Japanese composite, reflecting the Japanese developer's admiration for the way Holland integrates past and present. Included in this displaced Dutch setting are look-a-likes of Amsterdam's East India Company headquarters, Maritime Museum, as well as waterways lifted from the Amstel and Keizersgracht. Amsterdam architect Fred Hofman is coordinating building, while former Rijksmuseum director, Dr. Simon Levie, has assumed responsibility for the historical accuracy of the Queen's palace. Dutch artist Rob Scholte was commissioned to paint a mammoth fresco on the palace ceiling. Its images reflect Amsterdam waterways and bridges, with a sensitivity for the Japanese aesthetic.

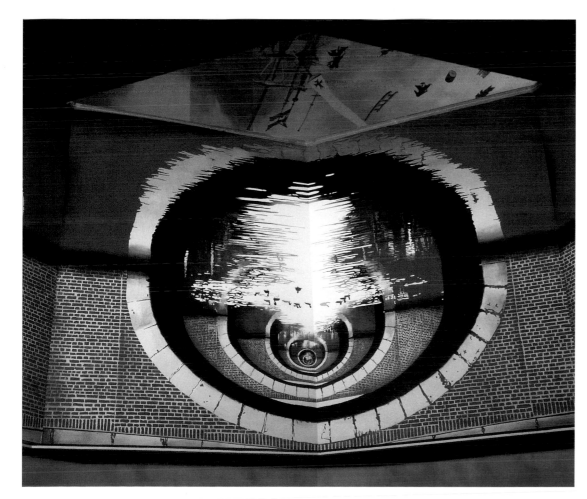

Holland Village/Huis ten Bosch, a 2 billion dollar project to be completed in 1997, depicts Dutch life and architecture. Amsterdam artist Rob Scholte is painting a major ceiling fresco in the reconstructed palace of Queen Beatrix.

Chinatown

Oriental oasis in oldest quarter

Amsterdam's Chinese community, numbering some 10,000, is experiencing a commercial and cultural renaissance. Their restaurants and shops, jammed cheek and jowl round the Binnen Bantammerstraat, expanded beyond de Waag on the Nieuwmarkt, spreading further on to the Geldersekade and Zeedijk. This new Chinatown, now centered on the Zeedijk, came about after the municipality cleared out the drug dealers who had dominated the street and restored many of the monuments into homes and commercial spaces. Hard-working emigrants, mostly from Hong Kong, eagerly took their place next to established Dutch cafés and shops, in the former notoriously dangerous area.

The metamorphosis of the historic Zeedijk area, which had been dyked against the raging IJ river in the late 13th century, resulted in a thriving Oriental oasis, where Chinese entrepreneurs provide their great diversity of specialized goods and services not only in the Netherlands, where there are over 80,000 Chinese residents, but also in Germany, France and Belgium. Besides the inevitable restaurants, whose specialities reflect the owners' regional origin, the myriad of shops range from a Chinese hairdresser and wedding service, to a women's tailor and health-restoring herb treatment clinics. The Chinese Medical Centre has opened on the Geldersekade.

Hifi audiovisual stores feature laser disks with universal favorites like *Beauty and the Beast* or *Snow White and the Seven Dwarves* in Cantonese version. The hottest Chinese pop stars are seen on oversized T.V. screens, while videos are rented, along with satellite disks for picking up a dozen Chinese T.V. channels. Amsterdam is home to the first Chinese channel in Europe, broadcasting news and other programs in Mandarin from TVB, the most popular Hong Kong T.V. station, as well as Chinese news gathered all over Europe.

The history of the Chinese in the Netherlands, who are among the country's oldest and largest minority groups, dates from 1911 when Dutch shipping companies sought cheap labor to replace striking sailors. After the strikes were settled, these Chinese employees kept their jobs and by 1927 some 3000 were working on Dutch ships. During shore leave, they stayed in houses around the Binnen Bantammerstraat, with restaurants, gambling houses and opium dens opening to serve them. Chinese community associations and secret organizations became

Chinese New Year's celebration with dancing dragons and fireworks on the New Market.

information and organizes excursions to bring the needy out of their isolation. The Tung Lok/Chen Hui and the Chun Pah senior citizens associations are actively concerned with providing institutional homes for the elderly.

In late 1995, Dutch and Chinese business leaders founded 'China Link' to provide special training for Dutch-born Chinese youth who are equally at home with both languages and cultures. Initiated by the Amsterdam restaurant entrepreneur Ho-Kai Yen, the program will prepare students for positions being developed by Dutch firms investing in China.

Regular manifestations reflect the rich Chinese culture. Chinese New Year's festivities, with dragon dances along the shops and homes, are accompanied by ear-splitting fireworks. The Chinese community is planning a Buddhist temple on the Zeedijk, to be built at a cost of 4.5 million guilders. Buddha Light International in Taiwan will finance most of the costs, while Chinese locals have subscribed for circa 1 million guilders. Sparkplug behind the project is Fu Wen Lo. The story goes that, as a young pilot, he had to flee the Japanese occupiers in China and found refuge in a temple underneath a Buddha statue. He swore that one day he would build a temple in gratitude. Now, some 50 years later, his promise will be fulfilled in Amsterdam's burgeoning ChinaTown.

very influential, with frequent fighting between the rival Bo'on and Sam Tin societies, each determined to protect their members against exploitation by shipping masters and boarding house owners. Following bloody conflicts between the two groups over the shippers' preferential treatment, over 200 were deported to China and the societies started to crumble. After coal was replaced by oil-fuelled furnaces, the Chinese had no work. They started selling peanut cookies on the streets with such success that Chinese from England and Germany came over to share in this lucrative trade. Amsterdam Chinese also went to the provinces, but by 1932 the peanut cookie trade had bottomed out and poverty surfaced. Amsterdam's Chinese population sunk to around 1000 in 1937. 'But we are back again, stronger than ever,' says K.M. Man, chairman of the Association of Chinese Entrepreneurs in Amsterdam and surroundings.

There is Wa Lai, an Amsterdam self-help organization working to help integrate Chinese into local life. In cooperation with the Amsterdam School for Adult Education and the Chinese School, Kai Wah, Dutch is taught to parents, while over 400 Dutch-born Chinese children take lessons in Chinese. Wa Lai helps students with homework courses, gives advice on schools, visits patients in hospitals and people requiring assistance at home, dispenses

Chinese shops, with everything from wedding dresses and beauty treatment to herb clinics and hi-fi specialists who sell popular Cantonese cds, have spread onto the Zeedijk in a major expansion of Chinatown.

Right: Tokos reach far afield with clients throughout the Netherlands and across the Continent.

Russian relations

Early traders, Czar Peter, royal links

Czar Peter the Great, with the Amsterdam Town Hall behind him, during his days as an apprentice shipbuilder.

The Amsterdam Chamber of Commerce won a competition based on twelve countries' bids for the most prestigious assignments in the European Union's vast program to implement the cis business infrastructure. The Chamber-led consortium of advisors was awarded the establishment of a Development Agency and Business Communications Center in Moscow and St. Petersburg. Market research, management, personnel training and other start-up activities are being realized in preparation for the operational activities.

St. Petersburg signed an official contract with Amsterdam — the first from the cis with a western relation — for an exchange of expertise on monument restoration. The Russians teach their Amsterdam colleagues special techniques in woodcutting, gilding and plaster moulding, while the Dutch instruct the latest technological advances, materials, management planning and subsidizing. Appropriately, this mutual sharing of craftmanship takes place in the Dutch capital, which served as the model for the 18th century plan of St. Petersburg. The classroom is the Amsterdam Monument Protection Association's storage space for old building elements in an abandoned synagogue on the Nieuwe Uilenburgerstraat.

Dutch relations, primarily in trade, existed long before Peter the Great came to Amsterdam in 1696. Coins minted around 1050 in the northern Dutch provinces of Friesland and Groningen were found alongside Russian rivers. Starting in the 13th century, Dutch captains bought wheat in the Baltic cities and Amsterdammers were eating Russian wheat well into the 16th century without knowing the country of origin. As early as 1547, Dutch bricklayers were working in Moscow. A Dutchman brought back the first furs from Russia in 1554 and 30 years later bilateral trade was flourishing. Dutch ships sailed to Russia with western goods and returned with grain and other bulk products. The first Dutch envoy went to Moscow in 1613, followed 50 years later by the first Dutch ambassador, who officially stated that: 'Since Holland renders Russia more services than all other European states, it hopes to receive far more advantages'. The ruling Czar complied with the request by immediately withdrawing the English exclusive rights to trade Russian tar. In the 17th century, a very special relationship with Holland as Russia's main trading partner existed.

Around 1631, Amsterdam merchant Andries Winius won the Russians' trust when he bought grain excess for fair prices. Their confidence opened up other trading channels and he moved to Moscow in 1634 with his wife and children. Winius became a very respected Russian businessman known as Andrej Denisovitsj Winius, who built Russia's first iron foundry at Tula, some 200 kilometers from Moscow. Another Amsterdam businessman, Hendrick Thesingh, personally accompanied annual

Zembla in 1596/1597 (see '... and the World'). An Amsterdam burgomaster, Nicolaas Witsen, with his broad knowledge of Russia, was instrumental in strengthening diplomatic and trade relations between the two countries in the 17th century. In 1665, at the age of 23, Witsen had gone to Moscow. Later, in Amsterdam, he built a political career, becoming mayor several times, and always showed Russian visitors around.

It was Witsen, Peter's confidante in Amsterdam, who personally supervised the building of a huge sailing ship and arranged its arrival in Archangel. After inspecting the galley, Peter, 22 years old, wrote in Dutch to Witsen, saying it was exactly as he wished, but, 'because Bacchus is always honored on these occasions and his wine leaves make the eyes so heavy,' a lengthy letter would have to follow. He proudly signed, 'Captain of the *Holy Spirit* ship'. Logically, Peter the Great turned to Witsen for support upon his arrival in Amsterdam in 1697.

In that year, aged 25, incognito as a petty officer called Peter Michailov, he came with a group of envoys. They visited Stadholder Willem III, who was at the same time King William of England, to request an alliance against the Turks, but this did not materialize. He also wanted to recruit crews, ships' carpenters and other skilled laborers and take back modern tools, instruments and techniques. Having just secured access to a seaport, he aimed to build Europe's strongest navy. Peter sought the Dutch as the world's most powerful seafaring traders. During his school years, he had been greatly influenced by the commander of his body guard, Colonel François Lefort, a Swiss officer of Scottish descent, who had spent many years in Holland's military service. Lefort spoke Dutch and had become a fervent sailor. Around 1684, Lefort asked a number of Zaandam boat builders to come to Russia to construct a small frigate for the young Peter, who learned Dutch and developed a love of sailing from them. As a child, Peter had been taught the use of an astrolabe from the Dutchman Franz Timmerman who, with compatriot Karsten Brack, also taught him basic navigation and assisted him in restoring an old English sailing yawl.

Peter was the first Russian Czar to travel outside his country. Soon after his arrival, he rented a modest laborer's house in Zaandam, a rural village not far from Amsterdam, and went to

shiploads of goods, starting in 1659, to the north Russian port of Archangel. He also had a profitable participation in the Moscovite Mast Contract, a monopoly leased out by the Czar for masts to be purchased in the north of Russia and exported to Holland via Archangel. Egbert Thesingh, who expanded the family business in textiles, masts and sawn timber after his father's death, secured a partnership share in a company

building and operating a water-powered sawmill near Archangel. His brother, Jan, received a monopoly in 1700 from Czar Peter the Great for printing land maps, sea charts, technical manuals and art books for shipment to Archangel and for sale throughout the Russian Empire. The Thesinghs also exported military equipment, raw materials and sent craftsmen, such as shipwrights, windmill builders and carpenters, to serve the Czar as workers or teachers. Egbert Thesingh, who himself worked on the mammoth project of moving a complete printing press with technicians to Russia, constructed the large Archangel warehouse at Leidsegracht 88 in 1702. A decade ago, it was converted into luxury apartments.

In 1694, a galley from Amsterdam arrived in Archangel. It was disassembled and put together again on a wharf in Preobrazjenskoje, near Moscow. Subsequently, 23 galleys were built following the Dutch model. Amsterdam's Rijksmuseum has an extensive collection of objects and curiosities related to contacts with Russia through the centuries, and early Dutch exploration in the Arctic Circle, such as Nova

Riga coat of arms, embedded as a gable stone in a house built around 1600 by the widow of Wessel Becker, commemorated the fortune her late husband had made trading on the Baltic Sea.

Mock sea battle on the IJ staged for Czar Peter.

work in a small shipyard. He was followed and harassed by the local populace who were intrigued by rumors of an important foreigner in their midst. It wasn't long before he was recognized by one of the shipwrights who had worked with him in Russia. He asked Witsen to secure a comparable position for him in Amsterdam. But even the influential mayor, a wealthy regent and director of the East India Company (VOC), was powerless to arrange for Peter to work as a ship's carpenter before the company's board voted in agreement.

During those days in late August 1697, when the official Russian delegation was being wined and dined by the city, Peter, the future Russian ruler, was naturally present at the festivities. On the night of the VOC meeting, Peter sat morosely, like a student awaiting final exam results, at the dinner in de Doelen until word reached him that he could work on the docks. Peter insisted on taking off immediately, despite the warning that at that late hour it was too dark and dangerous to travel. The sluices were opened to accommodate him on his journey by boat to Zaandam, where he arrived at one a.m. He fled early the next morning, after less than a week in Zaandam, to work in Amsterdam. With ten Russian volunteers, Peter began building the 100-foot

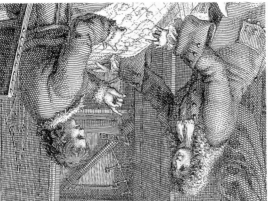

frigate, named *Peter and Paul*, specially commissioned for him on the Oostenburg island wharves. Witsen assured Peter privacy on the well-protected docks, as well as in the Rope Walks manager's mansion, where lodging was arranged.

The Amsterdam City Council's program organized for the official Russian delegation included a festive dinner in Hortus Botanicus, which Peter noted in his diary had 'strange trees and plants, even from India, which were protected in sheds from the winter cold'. There were visits to orphanages, a mental institution, a school, the Town Hall (now the Royal Palace) and the theatre. He was most excited by the mock sea battle on the IJ specially organized with dozens of big ships in his honor and he went on board to participate. Paintings of this spectacular happening are in the Maritime and Amsterdam Historical Museums.

In January 1698, after his five months' apprenticeship and the ship was completed and

Left: Peter the Great when he worked and resided in the Werkspoor; his portrait now hangs in those buildings, now a museum.

Above: Fire fighting equipment invented by Jan van de Heyden was demonstrated behind the Town Hall on the Dam. Czar Peter often visited the inventor's workshop on the Koestraat and took back water pumps and hoses to Russia.

launched, a certificate for Peter Michailov as a 'capable and very eminent shipwright', was presented by the company's master shipwright, G.C. Pool. Peter considered this piece of paper so important that he had it bound with key state documents which have survived to this day.

While on the wharf, the future Czar insisted on being called Pieter or Pieterbaas, becoming angry or ignoring anyone who addressed him otherwise. Though his Amsterdam domicile has since been demolished, the Rope Walk buildings of the East India Company and the Admiralty, virtually intact from that period, now serve as the Werkspoor Museum at Oostenburgerstraat 77. A bronze plaque in the Rope Walk walls commemorates Peter's work period. The modest Zaandam house has been preserved and is a revered site for Russian pilgrims.

The Czar founded St. Petersburg in 1703. With Dutch architects and craftsmen he had taken with him, Peter's new city was laid out like Amsterdam with canals and bridges. The Moika was designed to resemble the Herengracht, while the Fontanka simulated the Keizersgracht. His first residence was designed as a Dutch house and he had 2000 linden trees imported from Holland for the summer garden. Timber yards around the Admiralty were called 'Holland' and the Peter and Paul Cathedral spire was built by a Dutchman.

In 1716, Czar Peter again visited Amsterdam. Underlying this diplomatic mission was his desire to form an alliance with the Netherlands and France. He stayed for a time in the elegant residence at Keizersgracht 319 of Christoffel Brants, who had been given peerage for his contribution to Russian trade. A portrait of the Czar (dated 1733), is in the trustees' room of the Brants Rus Foundation at Nieuwe Keizersgracht 28-44.

In 1717, Peter was present at the death of his friend Witsen. With his entourage, he took over the mansion at Herengracht 527, occupied by the Russian ambassador/merchant Dimitri Solowjow — who was immediately sent packing. (Rumor has it that Peter contracted syphilis during one of his stays in the Netherlands.)

Extremely impressed by the effectiveness of fire-fighting equipment invented by Jan van der Heyden, he often visited his atelier on the Koestraat and took some early fire hoses back with him. He was morosely fascinated by the

anatomical collection — some 2000 preserved human and animal specimens collected by the internationally renowned professor Frederich Ruysch. Peter purchased the entire curiosity cabinet for exhibition in the Museum of Ethnography and Anthropology in St. Petersburg.

The Czar assembled a vast number of books, prints, drawings, artifacts and instruments during his Amsterdam visits, intending to help his people emerge from centuries of isolation by putting these on public exhibition. He himself learned to make engravings and took back a selection of Dutch graphics to instruct Russian artists. During his stay, he had commissioned a plan for the extension of St. Petersburg, which he realized upon his return.

At Peter the Great's request, Amsterdam rear admiral Cornelis Cruys led the Russian fleet in repelling Swedish attacks on St. Petersburg. Until today, much of Russia's maritime vocabulary is Dutch. The Netherlands was in dismay at the speed at which the Russians built up their fleet and world power — notably from the numerous Dutch naval officers, shipwrights, admirals and technical skill. The first Russian shipyard in Preobrazhenskoye and the first Russian ships in Voronezh were constructed under Dutch supervision. Cruys had been followed by many Dutch immigrants who made important contributions to Russia's industrial development.

Later, during Catherine II's reign, Amsterdam admiral Jan Hendrik van Kinsbergen assisted the Russian fleet in the Battle of the Black Sea. There is a warship, the Kapitan Kinsbergen in the Russian navy. He earned the nickname 'Hero of the Black Sea'. Another Amsterdammer, Robert Voûte, partner in the Mees & Hope bank, also supported Catherine the Great — but on the financial side. He spent an afternoon explaining how best to organize her monetary policies, while the ruler borrowed huge amounts of money for her military operations and art collection. Mees & Hope financed a considerable portion of the Russian national debt. A travel box used by the partners on their Russian trips is preserved at the bank's Amsterdam headquarters.

Czar Peter and Catherine II were desirous of equalling the grandeur of European royalty. They built magnificent palaces, established extensive imperial households and accumulated

Plaque memorializing Peter the Great's work period on the Rope Walk wall, now incorporated in the Werkspoor Museum.

Peter the Great's lodgings no longer exist but the West India Company shipbuilding wharves and the Admirality, scenes of his apprenticeship as a carpenter, have been preserved in the Werkspoor Museum. Early print shows the situation as the young Russian knew it.

works of art on a massive scale. Peter the Great commissioned a palace, which rivalled Versailles in size and magnificence, just outside St. Petersburg. He called it Mon Plaisir (My Pleasure). To decorate it, his agents scoured the European market buying up dozens of 17th century Dutch and Flemish paintings at a time. Rembrandt's *David and Jonathan* was purchased in 1716 for Peter at the Jan van Beuningen auction in Amsterdam. It was first hung in Mon Plaisir and later transferred to the Hermitage. In that same year, 280 more paintings, including work by Breughel, Rubens and Jan Steen, were secured for Peter in Holland and Belgium. This was the start of the Russian ruler's art collecting, spurred further on by Empress Catherine II, who engaged in a very extravagant living pattern financed in large part by the extensive loans from Amsterdam's Mees & Hope bank.

There had been very close relations between the Dutch and Russian royal families, the House of Orange and the Romanovs, in the 19th and early 20th century. King William II of Orange married the Romanov Princess Anna Pavlovna. Their son, later King Willem III, married Sophie van Würthenberg, whose mother was Anna Pavlovna's sister.

Therefore, it was not surprising that Russian bidders were in the forefront again in 1850 when King Willem II, in order to pay his debts, put his impressive collection on auction. The Dutch monarch was the brother-in-law of both Czar Alexander I and his successor, Nicholas I. A dozen or more magnificent Dutch paintings thus further enhanced the Russian state holdings. Complete collections, often several hundred at a time, were purchased. As a result, the Hermitage has one of the world's largest Rembrandt collections, as well as an overwhelming array of old Dutch masters — many bought in Amsterdam under the Rijksmuseum's impoverished nose!

Unfortunately, some major works by Dou, Potter, Metsu and Adrian van Ostade, bought by Catharine's agents at a 1771 Amsterdam auction, never reached Russia — the ship carrying them sunk in Finnish waters. A mediocre copy of a renowned triptych by Gerard Dou has been in the Rijksmuseum as a mild consolation since 1908.

Two original Rembrandts did return from Russia in 1933: the *Denial of St. Peter*, which had been bought for Catherine II in 1782, and *Titus in a Monk's Hood*, which was in a nationalized private collection. Both became available to the Rembrandt Society which provided the funds

Führer Museum planned for Linz, Austria. After the war, the Mannheimer collection, virtually intact, was brought back to the Netherlands as state property. The largest part was officially transferred to the Rijksmuseum, including the vase made for Czar Peter the Great. After a break precipitated by the bloody events in 1917, diplomatic and trade ties were resumed in recent decades. The privately-owned Stolichny Bank International N.V. chose to set up its first window in the West in Amsterdam at Herengracht 475, a stone's throw from the house Peter the Great usurped from the Russian ambassador.

and made the donations to the Rijksmuseum Through a circuitous route, an extraordinary Meissen porcelain vase commissioned by Augustus the Strong, Elector of Saxony and King of Poland, as a gift for Peter II on his ascension to the throne as Czar of Russia in May 1727, is now in the Rijksmuseum. This masterly example of ceramic art went into the Hermitage but in the 1930s was sold off with other works. It ended up in the celebrated collection of the Amsterdam banker Mannheimer. Shortly after he died in 1939, the banking house folded and his collection was appropriated by the occupying Germans. Money confiscated from Jews was used for the 'purchase' of such art works for the

Rembrandt's *Titus in a Monk's Hood*, as well as *The Denial of St. Peter*, both of which had been purchased by Catherine II's agents in Amsterdam in 1782, came back from Russia in 1933. The Rembrandt Society secured them for the Rijksmuseum.

Upper right: Contemporary Russian artists like Ilya Kabakov are greatly appreciated. His intriguing installation in the Amsterdam Stedelijk Museum, a labyrinth of offices for paper-pushing bureaucrats, drew large numbers of interested viewers.

The Arts

Cornucopia of cultural offerings

Traditionally, through the centuries, Amsterdam has always been the Netherlands' artistic center, with a magnetic pull attracting people in the arts. Against this backdrop, much of Holland's creative expression has been nurtured here.

The Leyden miller's son, Rembrandt van Rijn, came in 1624 to take painting lessons. Breitner, Witsen and Isaac Israels — the leading Amsterdam Impressionists — captured the turn-of-the century cityscape on canvas. Piet Mondriaan, son of a Calvinist school teacher in Amersfoort, enrolled in Amsterdam's State Academy in 1892 and stayed on for almost twenty years.

Karel Appel, the internationally-known COBRA painter, though he commutes between his New York and Monaco studios, still considers himself a real *Mokumer*. He had offered the city his entire private collection valued at well over 10 million guilders, but Amsterdam rejected the proposed one-man museum. Until 1973, when the Vincent van Gogh Museum was opened, there had never been a museum in Amsterdam dedicated to one artist.

Even Rembrandt is only one of many painters in the Rijksmuseum, though he is represented by 22 canvasses — four of which are city-owned. Rembrandt's beloved house was purchased by the city in 1906 on the 300th anniversary of his birth and a foundation was set up for restoration. With some etchings on permanent exhibition, this is the closest Rembrandt ever came to a one-man museum.

Rembrandt in Amsterdam

When the Rijksmuseum held a major tricentennial exhibition commemorating Rembrandt's death, artists staged an all night protest sit-in in front of the *Night Watch*. To dramatize their grievances against Dutch museum policies, they chose the most famous Dutch painting of all time as their backdrop. Rembrandt would have probably appreciated the artistic upheaval since he, in his time, was considered too avant-garde, had troubles with the bourgeois patricians who reigned during the country's Golden 17th century, and was plagued through his lifetime by his own nonconformist marital situations and money problems.

The only commission that Rembrandt ever got from the city of Amsterdam was by default. After building of the Town Hall was started in 1648 on the Dam Square, artists were asked to create allegorical paintings based on historical themes. The *Oath of the Batavians* (Claudius Civilis) was assigned to Govert Flinck for a high, curved niche in the large gallery. When he died suddenly, Rembrandt was called in to replace him. The work was painted in 1662 and hung in the building that summer until August when it was returned to Rembrandt for 'corrections and changes'. The proud artist revolted and he was never paid.

The individualistic, non-conforming artist was evidently perturbed by the interference. He probably cut down the 5.5 x 5.5 meter canvas to a more saleable size (2 x 3 m) and disposed of it. The work disappeared, as far as the records go, until 1734 when it was sold on auction for 60 guilders in its present smaller format to a Swedish family residing in the Netherlands. They took the painting with them to Sweden in 1766 and it was gifted in 1798 to the National Gallery in Stockholm, where it is called the *Night Watch of the North*.

Rembrandt is known for his impressive oeuvre (650 paintings, 300 etchings and 2000 drawings) and the inventory of his eclectic collection of *objets d'art*, recorded when he later became bankrupt and was forced to sell everything.

Rembrandt's *The Company of Captain Frans Banning Cocq*, popularly called *The Night Watch*, is the most famous Dutch painting of all times. When it was completed, the civil guardsmen complained and were reluctant to pay.

While the Dutch royal family did not retain any Rembrandt works, the wealthy patrician family of Jonkheer Jan Six van Hillegom, managed through nine generations to keep canvasses by this master painter within their ranks. Today's Jan Six is the 10th direct descendant of the man who became burgomaster after Rembrandt's death. The first Jan Six, who lived from 1618 until 1700, counted Rembrandt among his very close relations.

The paintings include the artist's most famous man's portrait, that of the then 36-year-old Jan Six, done in 1654.

Despite his friendship with men of means, and with extremely high earnings, in the period just before bankruptcy (his rates were 500 guilders for a full-length portrait, up to 1,000 guilders for

a biblical subject, plus good income from his students), Rembrandt continued to go deeper in debt as he fell out of favor with his powerful patrons.

Official rediscovery of the painter came only in the 19th century, after the French occupation ended and the newly-founded Kingdom of the Netherlands sought national heroes to glorify. The old Butter Market became the Rembrandt Square in 1852 with a dominant baroque statue of the great painter. (This is the oldest statue in town.) A few decades ago, a much more human representation of a kneeling Rembrandt was placed along the Amstel river where the artist often went to sketch. There is an old windmill behind him. Romantics idealized Rembrandt and made him into a demi-god. They clouded

and hid anything that was unpleasant in his bitter-sweet life, but the artist had lots of problems and these affected his work.

His marriage on June 22, 1634, to Saskia van Uylenburch, daughter of a Frisian burgomaster, started the happiest period in Rembrandt's life. She had a small dowry, became his favorite model, and her money enabled him to build up a priceless collection of paintings and *objets d'art*. In 1639, they settled on the Breestraat in what has been preserved as the Rembrandt House. It cost 13,000 guilders then and was never paid off before the artist was forced out by his debts in 1660. Saskia bore him four children, but three died as infants.

In 1642, Rembrandt painted *The Company of Captain Frans Banning Cocq*, now known popularly as *The Night Watch*. Though each of the sixteen guardsmen had agreed to pay around 100 guilders for inclusion in the mammoth group portrait, with the two officers paying higher fees for more prominent positioning, a number reneged, complaining that Rembrandt had taken too many liberties, not depicting them clearly enough in the accepted style of the day. After much haggling, Rembrandt received 1,600 guilders for this major civic guard piece.

Saskia died shortly after giving birth to their son, Titus. She left all her property to Titus, knowing what a poor manager of money the artist was, Rembrandt received the interest on the estate for life, providing he did not remarry.

Rembrandt had taken in a trumpeter's widow, Geertje Dircx, as dry nurse for Titus while Saskia was ill. She remained on for five years, though she was described as a 'shrew of a woman', and they quarrelled all the time. When she left, Rembrandt gave her an annuity but she dragged the artist into matrimonial court and accused him of improper relations and promise of marriage. She demanded that Rembrandt support her fully or marry her. Though Rembrandt denied everything, the court made him pay Geertje 200 guilders a year.

Undoubtedly she had become jealous when the painter brought in the 23-year-old Hendrickje Stoffels as a housekeeper in 1649 and fell in love with her. Though he never married Hendrickje, he considered her his 'second wife'.

The troubles went on. Hendrickje was reprimanded by the ecclesiastical court for illicit relations with Rembrandt and in 1654 was barred from taking Holy Communion. But they

Rembrandt's house in the old Jewish quarter, is now a museum with some 250 etchings on permanent exhibition.

Saskia with pearls in her hair depicts Rembrandt's young bride in 1634. She was responsible for the artist's happiest period. Financial and romantic problems plagued him after her early death. Etching is in the Rembrandt House.

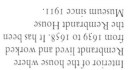

Interior of the house where Rembrandt lived and worked from 1639 to 1658. It has been the Rembrandt House Museum since 1911.

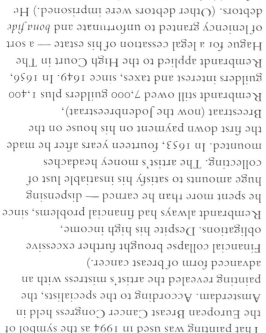

Self-portrait, open-mouthed, an etching from 1630 in the collection of the Rembrandt House.

stayed together and in October of that year they had a daughter, who was named Cornelia after Rembrandt's mother. (Earlier that year, Hendrickje had posed as Bathsheba bathing. That painting was used in 1994 as the symbol of the European Breast Cancer Congress held in Amsterdam. According to the specialists, the painting revealed the artist's mistress with an advanced form of breast cancer.)

Financial collapse brought further excessive obligations. Despite his high income, Rembrandt always had financial problems, since he spent more than he earned — dispensing huge amounts to satisfy his insatiable lust of collecting. The artist's money headaches mounted. In 1653, fourteen years after he made the first down payment on his house on the Breestraat (now the Jodenbreestraat), Rembrandt still owed 7,000 guilders plus 1,400 guilders interest and taxes since 1649. In 1656, Rembrandt applied to the High Court in The Hague for a legal cessation of his estate — a sort of leniency granted to unfortunate and *bona fide* debtors. (Other debtors were imprisoned.) He referred in his petition to 'losses at sea', indicating he probably also speculated in Dutch overseas trade.

Rembrandt drew up a twenty page inventory of his holdings, including 30 books of sketches, many finished and unfinished paintings, collected works by Dürer, Titian, Raphael, Rubens and Michelangelo, as well as costly *objets d'art*. The first auction in the Emperor's Crown Inn on the Kalverstraat yielded 3,094 guilders, while the second sale of etchings and drawings brought only 596 guilders. His house was sold in 1660 for 11,218 guilders. His son Titus was a major claimant, seeking 20,000 guilders owed to him, while Geertje Dirckx demanded her 200 guilder annual payments. Other attacked the painter for fraud. Rembrandt's marital situation and money dilemma led to abandonment by his high-placed patrons. Even his friend Jan Six demanded the immediate repayment of a 1,000 guilder debt after right Rembrandt had been forced to auction off his holdings.

They moved to a modest house at Rozengracht 184. Only Hendrickje remained loyal. She modelled for him, ran the house, cared for Titus and Cornelia, and founded a 'N.V.' (anonymous holding company) to protect Rembrandt against further debts. The year that *The Cloth Makers' Guild* was finished, Hendrickje Stoffels died,

leaving a nineteen-year-old son and an eight-year-old daughter. Rembrandt retreated further inwardly and painted some of his most searching, penetrating self-portraits. He wandered along the Amstel River a great deal in his period of despondency, sketching and searching for solitude.

In 1668, Titus was married but died a month later at the age of 28. One year after, heartbroken and declared 'insolvent', but not a pauper as the legends have it, Rembrandt died on October 4, 1669 — a forgotten man. He was buried in an unmarked grave in the Western Church with few mourners present. His final residence has been demolished. The present structure has a stone plaque high up on its façade for anyone really searching for Rembrandt's last address. Only a few decades ago, his beloved Saskia's grave was found in the Old Church and a plaque was placed to mark her tomb. Rembrandt's greatest memorial is the artistic legacy he left to the world. For those seeking physical links with the Amsterdam the artist knew: the view from his house to the Montelbaan Tower; the bend in the Amstel River where he kneeled to sketch the landscape and the now-gone Kostverloren *château*; the house he shared with his two great loves and an in-between 'shrew'. The clues he left behind, in etchings and on canvas, are the best guide to where Rembrandt roamed over three centuries ago.

However, Rembrandt is remembered not only for his masterpieces but by firms commercializing him as a brand name: a hotel, bar, restaurant, garage, diamond dealer, sightseeing boat, plane, train, movie theatre, postcard printer, glass cutter, office supplier and the town's tallest office tower. For many decades, the American maker of Dutch Masters cigars reproduced his *Staalmeesters* painting on its box, while Rembrandt low abrasion whitening toothpaste is now on the market!

Vincent van Gogh in Amsterdam

There were three Vincent van Goghs. The painter was conceived while his parents were still mourning the first Vincent Willem van Gogh who died at birth in 1852. A year later, to the very day, on March 30, another child, also named Vincent Willem, was born. The two Vincents, the stillborn and the healthy, were

registered under the same serial number, 29. The birth of the third Vincent Willem van Gogh, son of the art dealer Theo, and the painter's nephew, godson and namesake prompted him to write his brother Theo that 'he felt himself one mouth too many to feed' and 'that you were beginning to be alarmed at having to keep me. I often think of the little one. I think it is certainly better to bring up children than to give all your nervous energy to making pictures, but I am too old to go back on my steps'. The painter died by his own hand two months later at the age of 37 in the year 1890.

'The little one' was the late Vincent van Gogh, an engineer by profession, who inherited all of his uncle's unsold oeuvre. He greatly resembled the painter judging by his self-portraits, with

Rare Rembrandt full length portrait, a drawing with ink done in the period between 1655-1660. He was dressed in his painting smock and wore the same hat as in his etched self-portrait from 1648. It is in the Rijksmuseum.

Vincent van Gogh *Self-portrait with gray felt hat* shows the anguished artist in Paris in 1887. It is in Amsterdam's Vincent van Gogh Museum.

> *Vase with sunflowers*, Arles, January 1889. This oil on canvas is in the Vincent van Gogh Museum. A Japanese collector paid the record price of $40 million for one of the three versions of Van Gogh's *Still-life with fourteen sunflowers*.

'plucked-looking butcher's eyes', as the French poet Antonin Artaud called them. He had the same thin, tight lips, misty dark eyes and a sharply chiseled nose.

Vincent, later to become an artist, was 24 when he came to Amsterdam in May 1877 to prepare for the national examination before he could study theology at the university. He wanted to become a clergyman like his father and grandfather but since he had only completed several years of secondary school, he had to pass the entrance tests. His teachers were M.B. Mendes da Costa and his cousin, Teixeira de Mattos, both Sephardic Jews, who taught him classics at 1.50 guilders per lesson.

Vincent lived with his uncle, Jan van Gogh, rear

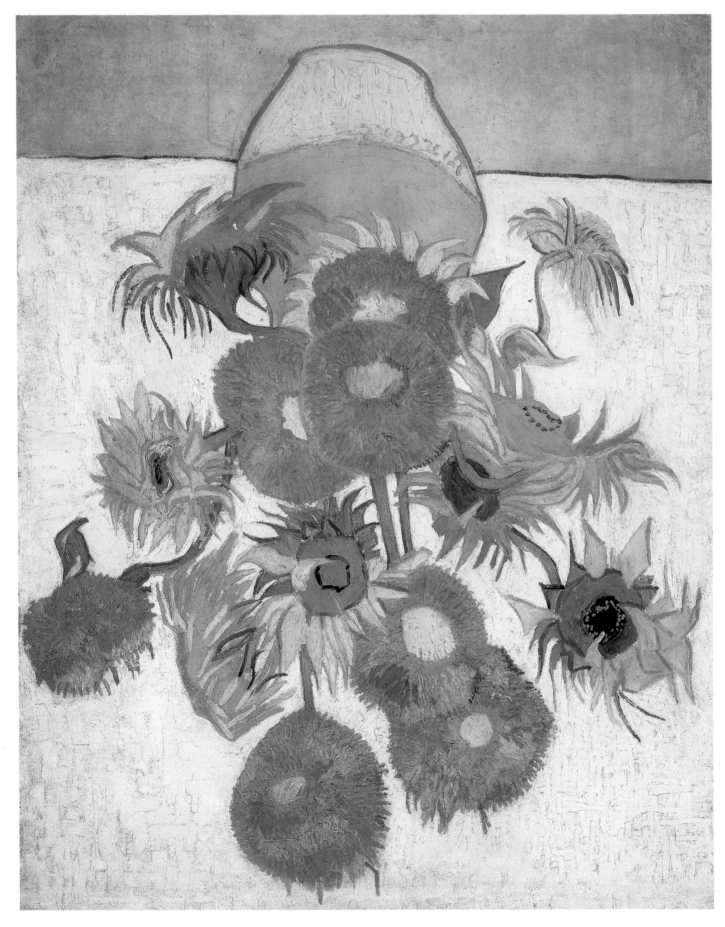

regularly went to reverend Stricker's home, where he encountered his cousin Kee. He already showed signs of being smitten by her. Vincent also visited Kee and her husband, Christoffel, in their home. In a letter to Theo, he wrote about his Amsterdam wanderings: 'I breakfasted on a piece of dry bread and a glass of beer — that is what Dickens advises for those who are on the point of committing suicide, as being a good way to keep them, at least for some time, from their purpose. And even if one is not in such mood, it is right to do it occasionally, while thinking, for instance, of Rembrandt's picture, *The Men of Emmaus*.'

But Vincent's inability to complete the preparatory studies, due to his problem of 'getting used to simple and regular work', was clearly evident. Mendes da Costa eventually felt obligated to advise the family to end the lessons. Vincent failed the examination. He had loved Amsterdam but was frustrated in his religious zeal to follow in the clerical footsteps of his father and grandfather. He left in July 1878 to work as an unordained preacher in a Belgian mining camp.

Three years later, the melancholic bachelor returned from Belgium for several days in order to talk to Kee. He came to the Stricker's home, where Kee lived after she was widowed. Earlier

admiral and director of the naval wharf on Kattenburg island, in a house that was part of the naval establishment. He had a number of other relatives in Amsterdam, including his uncle, Cor van Gogh, a prominent art dealer; his uncle, Johannes Stricker, a well-known preacher, whose daughter Kee was Vincent's secret love. Kee was married to Christoffel Vos, also a clergyman, who had retired due to ill health; and a distant cousin, Daniël Joost Vrijdag.

Though Vincent was a diligent student, he often had problems concentrating and left the wharf to seek diversion in churches, museums, art galleries and book shops. Not far from his tutors' house in the old Jewish quarter, he found the house where Rembrandt had lived. Though it was privately inhabited at the time, Vincent sought it out because of his great admiration for the old master, of whom he said: 'Rembrandt goes so deep into the mysterious that he says things for which no language has words.' In his letters to Theo, he described his visit to the Trippen House, the predecessor of the Rijksmuseum: '... this collection is beautiful and I have seen much that I had never come across before.' He was particularly impressed by Rembrandt's *Night Watch* and the *Syndics*. Vincent was often fascinated by his uncle Johannes' sermons in the Eastern Church. He

Vincent van Gogh, the artist's godson, nephew and namesake, was two months old when the painter took his own life in 1890. He had written to his brother Theo, an art dealer, that he felt himself 'one mouth too many to feed'.

View on the Singel with the Round Lutheran Church was only one of two Van Gogh Amsterdam canvasses. He painted from the provisional railroad station while waiting for a friend.

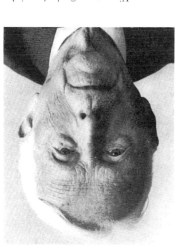

he had asked for her hand, only to be rebuffed with 'never, no, never'. His aunt and uncle received him but Kee stayed hidden. In a desperately dramatic move, he held his fingers in the lamp, while calling out, 'Let me see her if only for as long as I can hold my hand in the flames.'

In 1885, he was back in Amsterdam, only for a few days, for the last time. He visited the newly-opened Rijksmuseum and was mesmerized by Rembrandt's *Jewish Bride*. While Vincent sat in the provisional railroad station waiting for a friend, he painted *View on the Singel* and in the same period he completed *The Ruijter Quay with Tug Boats* — the only two known Amsterdam canvasses, though he had produced sombre drawings while he lived here.

After periods in Antwerp and Paris, Van Gogh moved to Provence in 1888, where he produced his most brilliant paintings. Two years later, the painter was dead.

On the subject of his uncle's difficult life and early death, the late namesake nephew cited from a letter that Vincent wrote to Theo just a few months before he committed suicide: 'We take death to reach a star.' It was engineer Van Gogh's dream that the new museum which he helped to shape would put the painter and his work in a new light because 'even after hundreds of exhibitions, Vincent remains, as he was in his lifetime, unloved and misunderstood.' The old engineer need not have worried. The Vincent van Gogh Museum became a living monument, which annually draws over half a million respectful visitors. Resourceful presentations have kept it from becoming a one-man mausoleum. This creative impact will benefit from expanded exhibition space on the Museum Square, thanks to a donation of 37.5 million guilders by the Yasuda Fire & Marine Insurance Company of Japan. The president of this company, Mr. Yasuo Goto, was in the international spotlight when he paid a record amount ($40 million) for one of the three versions of Van Gogh's *Still-life with Fourteen Sunflowers*.

Mondriaan in Amsterdam

Like Rembrandt three centuries earlier, Mondriaan, the strict Calvinist from provincial Amersfoort, would stroll along the Amstel river close to the popular Kalfje Inn. Many of the pastoral scenes, water and trees which had influenced Rembrandt, are recognizable in his early figurative style. This Amsterdam period, Mondriaan on the Amstel, resulted in 700 of the 850 paintings in his complete oeuvre. While Mondriaan lived here during those two decades, he had some ten addresses, mostly close to the watery, semi-rural areas he loved to paint on the city's southern fringes near the Amstel river, the 'Amsterdam Montparnasse' at the turn of the century. He had found his free expression here and by painting the same country landscapes over and over, he experimented with line, form and color, while continually reducing and simplifying, sowing the seeds for the style which later would bring him world recognition. During a traumatic and turbulent period which liberated him from his stern, Protestant

Mondriaan's *Mill by sunlight*, one of the 850 paintings completed during the artist's two decades spent around the Amstel River, in an area called the 'Amsterdam Montparnasse'. He experimented with free expression, repeatedly painting the same landscape in different styles.

background, he developed interest in theosophy, the mystical, Indian-inspired philosophy which would direct his artistic quest for absolute beauty.

After a short refuge from Amsterdam in 1904, offered by an artist friend in a north Brabant town, Mondriaan itched to return to the 'excitement and friction' of Amsterdam. He met artists whose work influenced him and like many of them, he sympathized with the anarchists

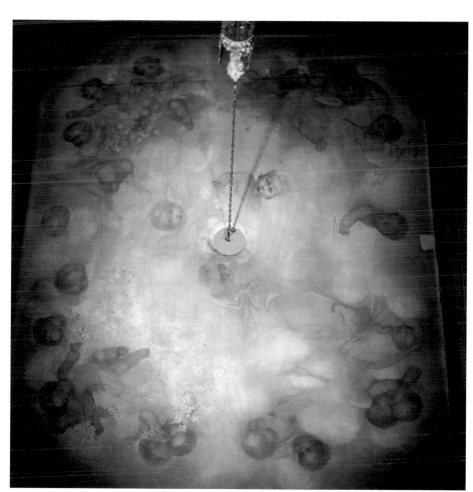

movement, clearly underscoring the break with his Calvinist background. When he showed works in 1909 at the Stedelijk Museum, visitors were shocked and abusive. Art critics found the canvasses 'raving, raving mad'.

Mondriaan left Amsterdam at the end of 1911 for Paris where he dropped an 'a' in his name. He had been an influential member of the De Stijl group of Dutch architects, painters and designers who were committed to new forms far from traditional art expression. The De Stijl artists limited their palettes to red, blue and yellow, with the neutral shades of black, grey and white,

while only using straight lines and right angles. Mondriaan was unquestionably the most renowned De Stijl artist.

He had already started on his tree studies by the time he left for Paris. This series clearly shows his development from figurative to abstract style. Early in his Amsterdam period, his trees had lost their color, had become an unmixed red and blue, and fauvism as an influence was clearly evident. But the countryside around Amsterdam, and the city and its artists, had already made its mark on the artist who would in the French capital, followed by New York, become one of the world's greatest abstract artists of the twentieth century.

Despite its relatively compact size, an absence of an extensive surrounding radius (such as Manhattan's 'bridge and tunnel public') and language limitations, Amsterdam offers a cornucopia of culture and art exceeding most comparable cities and rivalling other European capitals. Everything is here, from world prestigious orchestras, opera, dance, theatre and museums to concerts in the parks, musicians in the streets, marionettes on the Dam, itinerant performers on every corner and barrel organs churning away their tinny, romantic tunes on pedestrian routes.

Every month, around 2000 music and theatrical performances are staged in some 50 large and small theaters with a wide range from classical to experimental avant-garde. The Amsterdam attitude that culture is an integral part of daily life results in very casual dress. Tickets by international standards are relatively inexpensive, even for world premiere performances or concerts by renowned soloists. Films from all over the world are always shown in their original language in some 50 theaters ranging from the monumental Tuschinski, a glorious Art Deco movie palace, to miniscule art theaters.

The annual Holland Festival, started in 1948, unfolds every June as one of the most important events for music, theater and dance, with the focus on modern forms of expression. The Festival, through imaginative programming with Dutch and international performers, has become top ranking in the world of European culture. Amsterdam, with its 42 museums, supposedly has more museums per square meter than any city in the world, varying from the internationally

Mondriaan ceiling painting, commissioned by a family on the Keizersgracht to portray their children, was barely visible in 1995 until it was masterfully restored by Joop van Lürsenburg.

renowned 'big three' — Rijksmuseum, Stedelijk and Van Gogh Museum — to practically unknown ones devoted to every imaginable subject from bibles, piggy banks, cats, pianolas and trade unions to the role of sex in the history of mankind. The Rijksmuseum (National Gallery) is the country's largest museum, proudly called the 'Treasure House', with its collection of some 5,000 paintings, 30,000 pieces of sculpture and applied arts, including a large display of Delft blue, 3,000 Asiatic objects and close to one million drawings and prints. A section is devoted to the history of the Netherlands. The architect P.J.H. Cuypers built the museum in Neo-Renaissance style with brick towers and roofs, and Gothic elements like stained-glass windows. Dubbed a Gothic cathedral', the immense structure spreads over 30,000 square meters — the equivalent of three football fields.

In its 150 various sized halls, exhibitions include not only the work of 15th to 19th century Flemish and Dutch painters of international repute, but also collections of Italian, Spanish and French masters. While it would take four full days to view the Rijksmuseum's entire collection, most foreign visitors head straight to the Dutch 17th century painting section to zoom in on Rembrandt, notably his *Night Watch* and

Anatomy Lesson, as well as hasty glimpses of Frans Hals, Jan Steen, Paulus Potter, Van Ostade, De Hoogh, Hobbema, Avercamp and Van Goyen. When there are children in tow, a popular stop is in front of the two doll houses. Made as models, not toys, they contain 1,500 scaled-down objects, providing an authentic insight to domestic life in the late 17th century. The year 1676 is printed on a pin cushion in one of the houses.

The Vincent van Gogh Museum, based on designs by the architect Gerrit Rietveld, was

The Stedelijk Museum, which ranks among the Continent's most prestigious contemporary art institutions, is globally reputed for its collection and exhibitions. Director Rudi Fuchs redefined the museum's role in the changed art world of the nineties.

Mondriaan's Sarphatipark home and studio in 1908.

opened in 1973. It was constructed to house the works which Dr. Vincent W. van Gogh gave on permanent loan to the Dutch state. The artist left some 900 paintings and 1,200 drawings. The museum, with more than 200 paintings and almost 500 drawings, has the world's largest and most varied Van Gogh collection. There are also works by the artist's contemporaries, including Toulouse-Lautrec, Gauguin, Fantin-Latour and Monet, which Van Gogh had owned. The Vincent van Gogh Foundation is now responsible for the entire collection.

This open, light-filled museum welcomes visitors on the ground floor with a presentation of 19th century paintings. On the first floor, some 90 Van Gogh paintings provide a representative survey of the artist's genius, from his dark Dutch period via Paris to Arles, St. Rémy and finally to Auvers-sur-Oise, where he took his life. Many of the paintings are on permanent exhibition in chronological order, from the somber Brabant canvasses to the brightly-colored oeuvre from his late period. One can trace his artistic development while encountering some of his best known works, including *The Potato Eaters*, *Self-Portrait with Felt Hat*, *Still-Life with Sunflowers*, *A Pair of Boots*, *The Zouave* and *Wheatfield with Crows*. On the other floors one finds the print room, study collection, pastel cabinet and temporary exhibitions. In the library, Vincent's letters, mostly to his brother Theo, are on view.

The Stedelijk Museum (Municipal Museum), opened in 1895, was built in the Neo-Renaissance style like the Rijksmuseum. Over the years, the interiors were modernized and brightened in tune with contemporary norms and a new glass wing was added to provide more exhibition space. A major expansion on the Museum Square is planned. Willem Sandberg, who became director in 1945, started the Stedelijk on its route to becoming one of the world's most influential modern art showcases. Inspired by the Museum of Modern Art in New York, he envisioned a 'House of Museums', including fine art, photography, dance, theater, music and cinema. Pushing the old, mostly historical, collection into the background.

Breitner, a turn of the century painter, recorded Amsterdam with his palette and primitive camera. This view on the Oudezijds Achterburgwal backed by Zeedijk houses, is in the Municipal Archives collection.

The Rijksmuseum, National Treasure House, has more than 5,000 paintings, 30,000 sculptures and applied arts, 3,000 Asiatic objects and some one million drawings and prints reflecting the Netherlands' history. The largest Dutch museum's floor space would cover four football fields.

Sandberg staged avant-garde exhibitions and events which, despite the controversy they evoked, stimulated Dutch interest in modern art which has grown into today's large public. Over the decades, the Stedelijk has continued to be ranked among the Continent's most respected contemporary art institutions, with a global reputation for its collection and exhibitions, disproportionate to its relatively small budget and facilities. The wonderfully varied, all-encompassing presentation, further enriched by the successive directors, De Wilde and Beeren, includes painting, sculptures, drawings and graphics, video, photography, crafts, industrial design and posters. Among the 'modern classics' on permanent view are works by Monet, Van Gogh, Cézanne, Matisse, Picasso, Kirchner and Chagall. One of the world's most important collections of works by the Russian painter Malevich is owned by the Stedelijk and is used in a historical reference with paintings by Mondriaan and Kandinsky in exhibitions tracing the development of abstract art.

The lion's share of the collection consists of works from the second half of the 20th century, including Appel, De Kooning, Newman, Ryman, Judd, Warhol, Dibbets, Van Elk, Gilbert & George, Baselitz, Polke, Merz, Kounellis, Nauman and many others. The present director, Rudi Fuchs, undertook a redefinition of the museum's role in a much changed art world. In a series of 'Couplet' exhibitions, Fuchs created confrontations between the artists entrenched in the collection with works by contemporary artists. Simultaneously, he sought new art historical readings, highlighting works by lesser known Dutch and European artists within the framework of internationally recognized artists. Art is a part of Amsterdam life to be seen in the streets, on neighborhood murals and public

Karel Appel, world-famed COBRA artist, portrayed Stedelijk director Willem Sandberg in 1956. Sandberg first exhibited the controversial COBRA works in the late fifties by artists from Copenhagen (CO), Brussels (BR) and Amsterdam (A).

>Post Office, an imposing, turreted turn-of-the-century edifice behind the Royal Palace, became an upmarket shopping mall when the mailmen moved to modern quarters.

The Van Gogh Museum was opened in 1973 to house the works Dr. Vincent W. van Gogh gave to the state on permanent loan. The museum has the world's largest, most varied collection with over 200 paintings and almost 500 drawings.

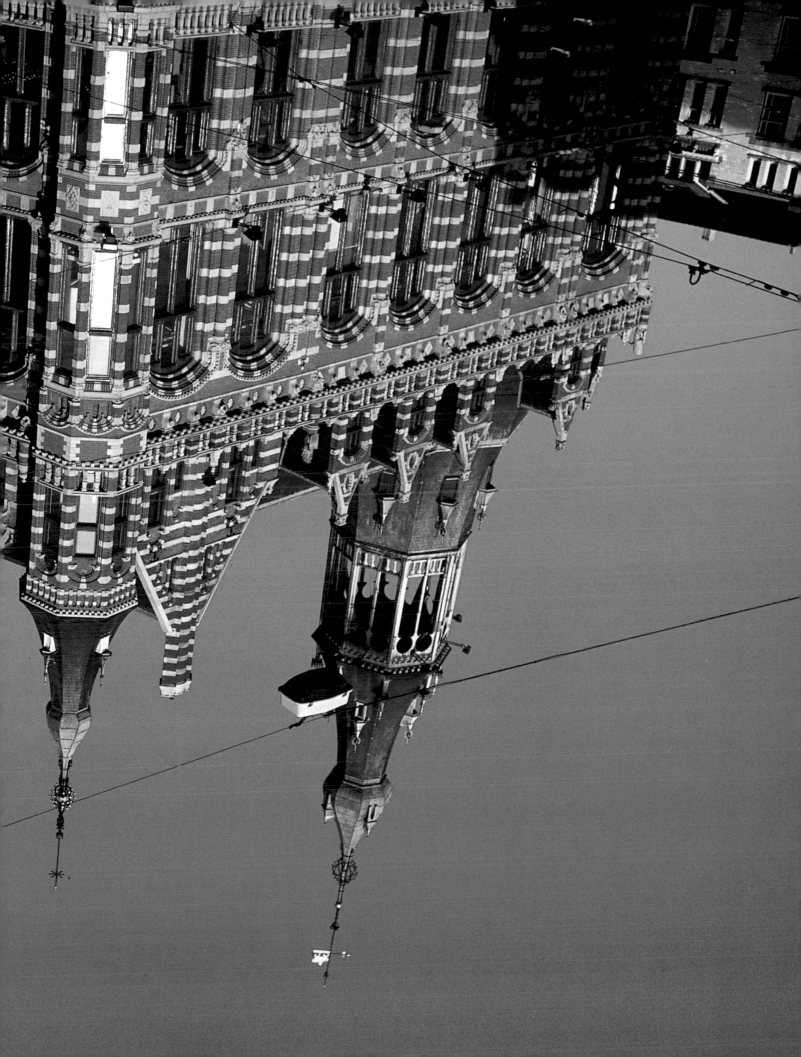

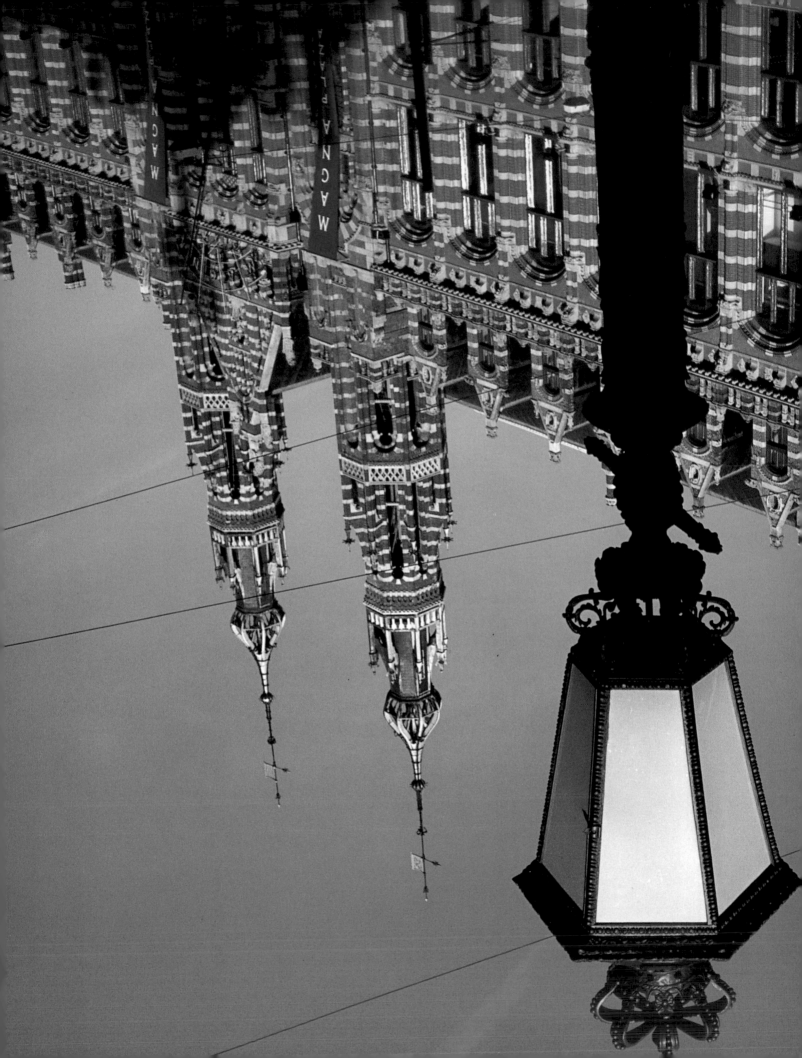

buildings, in the parks and squares, on the houseboats used as ateliers, in some 150 galleries, in cafés and in the auction houses. Major art schools, include the Rietveld Academy and the State Academy of Art. The prestigious Atelier '63 moved from Haarlem to Amsterdam inner city facilities, with a number of Holland's best-known artists evaluating the students' work. Many young hopefuls come to this art mecca from the provinces and foreign countries. The art scene is very prolific and hectic.

Beyond the 'big three', other museums of special significance include the Amsterdam Historical Museum, housed in a medieval convent and former orphanage, which traces the city's history in a very imaginative, visual manner. David and Goliath, figures with rolling eyes from a 17th century maze, guard over the restaurant. The Allard Pierson Museum houses Amsterdam University's vast archaeological collection of Greek, Roman, Egyptian, Etruscan, Cypriotic and West Asian antiquities. The Theater Museum, located in a magnificent canal house has opulent Louis XIV interiors. The National Shipping Museum, housed in the 1665 warehouse of the Admiralty of Amsterdam on the harbor, is devoted to Dutch seafaring history. Outside, an exact replica of the 17th century Dutch East India Company ship, Amsterdam, majestically dominates the port.

The Biblical Museum, situated in two stately canal houses, reconstructs life in biblical times, with Mesopotamian clay tablets, Palestinian pottery, Egyptian mummies, models of the Temple in Jerusalem and Jewish religious artifacts, along with a remarkable collection of antique bibles and biblical prints. The Dutch Film Museum, a 19th century pavillion on the edge of the Vondelpark, traces movie making. At the NINT Technology Museum, visitors of all ages can 'see' with their hands and follow developments in natural sciences. Under its auspices, there is the spectacular National Science and Technology Center, popularly called 'Impuls', which looks like a ship rising from waters of the eastern docks. The Tropical Museum shows its large collection of ancient and modern artifacts in a natural context, on a North African street, in a house on Java, an Indian village or in an African market, all reconstructed in true scale. There is also the TM Junior, which educates six to twelve-year-olds in these exotic cultures.

Egyptian tomb mask from the Allard Pierson Archeological Museum, which houses Amsterdam University's vast collection of Greek, Roman, Egyptian, Etruscan, Cyriotic and West Asian antiquities.

Wall painting on the Spuistraat reflects the young free spirit on the street scene.

Like the pace-setting museums, musically speaking, Amsterdam is a prime venue on the global network for concerts, solo performances and opera. When the Concert Hall opened in 1888, the festive inauguration attracted 422 carriages in a line-up that almost reached as far as

the distant Amstel River. For less privileged pedestrians, accessibility was more problematic until 1913 when horse-drawn trams stopped nearby. It was built on 186 wooden piles in the empty southern polder on the Museum Square. With its superb acoustics, it ranks among the world's finest three concert halls, along with Boston's Symphony Hall and Vienna's Grosser Musik Vereinsaal. While initially 60 concerts were scheduled annually, nowadays there are more than 500 concerts which attract over half a million people. An additional 150,000 come for the lunch concerts, radio broadcasts, meetings, receptions and private parties in the building. Besides the classical muse, other musical interests were served in the past often in a Jekyll and Hyde transformation with midnight jazz, rock and soul. Over the years, Louis Armstrong, Josephine Baker, Count Basie, Frank Zappa, Frank Sinatra, Diana Ross and many other great stars played the big hall. In the twenties to the forties, even boxing matches were held, something unthinkable today in this revered music temple. Prestigious programming keeps the Concertgebouw full all year round, primarily with the classics, but a jazz cycle has been initiated as a change of pace. A sign of the times in the mid-nineties, a new plague in the concert hall: cellular phones ringing during performances. And this started soon after the coughers had been quieted with free throat-soothing lozenges!

When the Concert Hall began to shake on its wooden piles, sink in the soggy ground and was in danger of collapse around 1983, director Martijn Sanders mobilized forces for a major renovation. Rotted wooden supports were replaced with 400 metal tubes which went deeper and were more solid in handling the building's 10,000 ton weight. The marketing-oriented executive capitalized on the emotional appeal of the impending catastrophe to get corporate sponsorship to meet all the urgent rehabilitation costs, as well as the addition of a desperately-needed extension. The old music temple is now more splendid than ever. Artists' and rehearsal facilities have been updated with modern amenities. The handsome all-glass annex hugs the building without intruding on its classical symmetry, while providing easier public flow and space for corporate, revenue-producing engendered events.

Sanders initiated sponsored summer concerts in a

period when the halls used to close their doors. He arranged the Great Soloists Series, which brought stellar performers like Jessye Norman, the Great Orchestra Series and many other programs which keep the Concertgebouw not only full but in the world limelight. He also organized the Mahler Festival in 1995 as an hommage to the great Austrian composer who, regularly directed his own pieces between 1903 and 1911 in the Concertgebouw and was last honored in 1920. A big music tent was pitched on the Museum Square to enable 2000 fanatic devotees to follow concerts by three of the world's greatest orchestras, conducted by foremost Mahler interpreters.

Amsterdam's Concertgebouw Orchestra is a national institution, a major tourist attraction, and one of the world's greatest symphony orchestras. Many great composers have conducted their works with the orchestra, among them Elgar, Glazounov, Schönberg, Ravel, Reger, Nielsen, Debussy, Richard Strauss and Mahler. In its first 100 years, the orchestra had only four permanent conductors, all of them Dutch, but the baton was passed more recently to the renowned Italian conductor, Ricardo Chailly, who has brought new vigor, ideas, challenges and interpretations to keep the orchestra at the forefront in the century to come. In one of the many favorable reviews during the 1995 international tournee, the *Boston Globe* headlined: 'A greatness born of profound balance.' A sub-headline read: 'The Royal Concertgebouw Orchestra Amsterdam has found a wonderful poise between clarity and

The Film Museum in the Vondel Park is housed in a 19th century pavillion. It traces movie making from earliest days and regularly screens film classics.

Right: The Concertgebouw-orkest (Concert Hall Orchestra) and chorus during intermission circa 1900.

The Golden Harp on the Concertgebouw (Concert Building) dominates the Museum Square.

The Amsterdam Concertgebouworkest in full glory in its own hall.

Above: The Concertgebouw, a late 19th century building, had a desperately-needed modern annex added without intruding on its classical symmetry. The great music temple is more versatile than ever since its major restoration.

Ricardo Chailly, conductor of the Concertgebouworkest, has brought new vigor and challenges to one of the world's greatest symphony orchestras.

warmth, power and subtlety, as it pursues an exceptionally adventurous repertory.

The range of music reaches far out of the Concert Building. There is baroque in the churches, modern music, jazz and improvised music, chamber and philharmonic orchestras. For several decades, Joseph Lam and the Bimhuis have been known for traditional jazz and jam sessions. Legendary American performers have played in these clubs. The Bimhuis is a laboratory for new developments in jazz and improvised music. The old Berlage Stock Exchange was renovated in the late eighties to provide two concert halls and exhibition space. The Dutch Philharmonic Orchestra is at home here. Classical orchestras and rock bands perform in the Vondel Park's open-air theater, a tradition started in the hippie days in the

seventies when bands like Slade played here. The 18th century Felix Meritis Theater has an elliptical concert hall, where St. Saëns and Grieg played.

The 1600-seat Music Theater became the pulse of Amsterdam's cultural life after it opened in 1986 with the resident Netherlands Opera, National Ballet, the Ballet Orchestra and additional programming. Of course, Amsterdam being Amsterdam, there was opposition to building the operahouse, which would be linked with the Stadhuis (City Hall). The battle cry, 'Stop the Opera', became 'Stopera', a name Amsterdammers still use for the complex.

The country had long needed a well-equipped, modern theater for opera and ballet. Amsterdam, as the cultural capital of the Netherlands, was the only city that could be considered as the venue. The Music Theater and Town Hall was designed by the architects Wilhelm Holzbauer and Cees Dam, and the complex rests on 3075 piles. The Music Theater, the largest building of its kind in the Netherlands, has a curved frontage behind which the auditorium and the 14-meter-high circular foyers are located. There are beautiful panoramic views over the Amstel River through the foyers' glass walls.

The Dutch artist Peter Struycken created a computer-directed star ceiling in the auditorium. In the main entrance, a metal sculpture of a violinist forcefully breaking through the marble floor appeared one night. All one can see is the head with a hat, a violin with a bow and a hand touching the strings. The anonymous artist of this *Music Rising* has never been identified. Surely, it's the same person who sculpted the faceless violinist, dressed in a trenchcoat, tipping his hat and carrying his violin case, which appeared one night in the Marnix Park.

There was no strong tradition nor real interest in the Netherlands Opera, founded in 1946 as a travelling company, until Pierre Audi came in 1988 from London to become its artistic director. Admittedly, he could utilize the well-equipped facilities of the Music Theater for large-scale productions, introducing his own direct, honest style, while building on the traditions started by his predecessors in renewing opera productions with daring producing teams and mainly young, fresh talent on the threshold of stardom. He works with the *stagione* system, meaning that for each production he hires a

The ice-breaker, just beyond the boat's bulk on the Amstel River, was an old inn used as a landing stage for barges towed with fresh water from the Vecht river. It took its name from the boats that kept navigation flowing. It's still a modern music center now.

separate artistic team and group of solo performers from Holland or abroad. The Netherlands Opera Chorus is a permanent part of the company, while the Netherlands Philharmonic Orchestra accompanies most of the performances. An average nine to ten productions each season with close to 100 performances, are staged in the Music Theater. Audi's daring and directness have resulted in constantly sold-out world premieres and new productions of everything from Monteverdi to Wagner, with rave reviews, wide international recognition and enthusiastic public demands for repeated curtain calls. Audi's highly acclaimed production of Monteverdi's *Il ritorno d'Ulisse in patria* went on to receive rare reviews at the Brooklyn Academy of Music. He premiered *Rosa: A Horse Drama* with music by the Dutch minimalist composer Louis Andriessen and

have taken up permanent residence in Amsterdam. The oldest and most important venues are the Municipal Theater, which celebrated its centenary in 1994, and the Royal Carré, built as a circus theater in 1839. Nowadays they both stage cabaret, musicals, ballet, opera and drama, frequently with foreign touring companies. The Elbow Children's Circus Theater and clubhouse was founded in 1948 as a social work project to give underprivileged children a recreational interest, keeping them from boredom and trouble in the entertaining framework of a pint-sized circus. New and unexpected venues are constantly being converted by the city for cultural purposes. Plans were being reviewed for a late-nineties, 20 million guilder transformation of a former gasworks in the western part of town. This will become a new cultural center with multi-functional spaces for modern media, music and theater. Even more ambitious is the city's blueprint for an expansive cultural center, budgeted between 100 and 200 million guilders, to rise on the banks of the IJ estuary. This will be on the Oostelijke Handelskade behind the Central Station, near the Passengers' Terminal under construction. There will be a center for new music; two concert halls, a 'black box' theater permitting experimental flexibility for staging and audience placement; housing for the Toneelgroep Amsterdam (the country's largest dramatic company), the Bimhuis jazz club and the IJsbreker (Ice-breaker), a modern music

Theater is an important part of the capital's cultural life. There are renowned local companies, but the Dutch language is a barrier for visitors. Several English language troupes have taken up permanent residence in

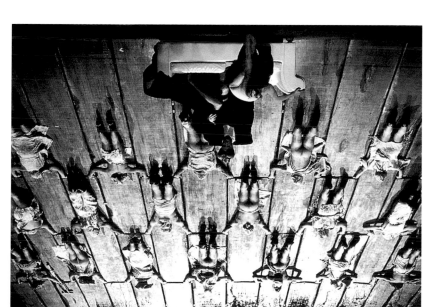

Rosa, A Horse Opera, also a world premiere, with minimalist music by the Dutch composer Louis Andriessen, had direction, visual conception and libretto by the British filmer Peter Greenaway.

libretto by the director Peter Greenaway, who brought cinematic technique to the stage, remarking: 'It's a film opera or an opera film.' Worldwide reviews promptly made it the most talked-about opera in Europe. This, and many other productions, have characterized Audi's imprint on the Netherlands Opera and its rise in international stature, as one of the world's most innovative companies.

Monteverdi's *L'Orfeo, Favola in Musica,* a Netherlands Opera premiere in 1995, stunned the public with its brilliant staging.

mecca. Also on the drawing board for inclusion in that center is a new central public library, after a move from cramped quarters on the Prinsengracht, and a shopping passage, a Dutch mall, which will extend into the Central Station.

Until such time, De IJsbreker will continue to stage some 200 concerts annually from its inadequate downtown housing. The broad focus is on music from the second half of this century. Renowned performers and emerging talents are among the Dutch and foreign soloists and ensembles. This institution's reputation has grown over the decades from the site of a 17th century inn with a landing stage for barges that were towed down the Amstel and Vecht rivers to bring clean, fresh water required by the Amsterdam brewers to make beer. To facilitate winter sailing, an ice-breaker was installed, which explains the café's name. After its destruction by fire, A.L. van Gendt was commissioned to rebuild the popular meeting place with an adjoining small concert hall. Van Gendt had already completed Amsterdam's impressive Concertgebouw (Concert Hall) in that same year.

More rehabilitation projects and new construction to showcase the arts are slated for realization around the turn of the century. Amsterdam continues to be a moving cultural feast.

Theater tram promotes music and theatrical productions in town.

Design for living

Amsterdam School to avant garde

serious housing problems.

The 20th century ushered in better building.
The outstanding architect Berlage — credited
with the Exchange, bridges and other landmarks
— completed rational plans around 1915 for the
new southern quarter as a unified mini-city with
housing, public transport, sports facilities and
parks. Berlage's concepts, influenced by his visits
to the United States and inspection of Frank
Lloyd Wright experiments, were adapted and
enlarged upon by innovative architects who
became known as the Amsterdam School. De
Klerk, Kramer and Van der Mei were among
the most important and their joint efforts on the
Netherlands Shipping House, built from 1912–
1916, ushered in a decade or so when the
Amsterdam School was in fullest bloom and
attracted architects and city planners from all
over the world.

The Amsterdam School reflected the socialist
utopianism of the City Council. The public
housing it commissioned would bring beauty
into the lives of Amsterdam's working class. The
buildings of this remarkable movement were
sculptures in brick. Function literally followed
form — the outer skin was designed before the
interior and allowed to dictate it. Form was
everything.

The Amsterdam School, proponent of
Expressionism in architecture, is roughly dated
from 1912 to De Klerk's death in 1923, but the
influence went on in new housing projects in the
western and other quarters of the city during the
years that followed. After De Klerk's death, a
woman wrote in a letter to a daily newspaper: 'Is
it not glorious to come home after a tiring day to
a house built for pure joy and domestic
happiness?'

Meanwhile, De Stijl School was more disposed
to theoretical formulations than the Amsterdam
School with its more varied tendencies. But

Architecture

While Amsterdam's old center remained an
intact architectural museum of stately building
styles, newer quarters sprang up during the 19th
and 20th centuries in former grazing fields and
swampland reclaimed to provide housing for the
expanding population. In a pattern of controlled
city planning, new Amsterdam spread in all
directions far beyond the limits of its 17th
century water web.

Areas that were once considered far out of town,
like the quarter bordering on the present
Museum Square and beyond the
Concertgebouw, came onto the map with
elegant town houses and spacious apartments
around the turn-of-the-century. In the 19th
century, large working class areas — De Pijp,
Staatsliedenbuurt, Dapperbuurt and the
Kinkerbuurt — were created with street after
street of crowded, low income housing. These
sections, lacking greenery and adequate living
space by current standards, became the core of

Queen Beatrix officially
opened the Netherlands
Design Institute. Smiling on is
the English director, John
Thackara, of this 'think-and-
do-tank'.

The Amsterdam School reflected socialist utopianism to bring beauty into the lives of Amsterdam's working class. These buildings were sculptures in brick with function literally following form. The movement peaked between 1912 and 1923.

there was a clear exchange between the two movements.

De Stijl's cooler, more linear building theories, realized chiefly between 1917-1925, resulted in a few Amsterdam showcase office buildings, shops and a public school.

The Nieuwe Zakelijkheid strived from around 1917 to uproot the other schools and implant functionalism as a way of building — a return to renewal of emphasis on sociological elements. In other words, that architecture must serve society, a theory already propounded by Berlage. Projects like Greiner's and Van Lochem's Betondorp (1924) — a reinforced concrete working class housing development in the Watergraafsmeer district — and the 'Open Air' School (1929-1932) on the Cliostraat, designed by Duiker, are outstanding inheritances of Amsterdam's functionalist architects.

During the post-war recovery period, when there was a dire housing shortage, the original expansion program of 1935 was continually updated and adapted to meet changing needs. Unfortunately, the architectural style did not reach the distinctive heights of this century's earlier decades.

Amsterdam's south-eastern extension started taking form in the late sixties.

The gigantic Bijlmermeer was developed as a satellite city with 2,250 acres of residential area, 625 acres of industrial sites, 500 acres for offices

The Amsterdam Medical Center, the world's largest, was realized in the newly developed Southeast area, which incorporates an expansive housing and business complex.

and socio-cultural facilities and 1,125 acres zoned for recreation. Like two-thirds of Amsterdam's post-war residential areas, the Bijlmermeer is subsidized as workers' housing with some 40,000 dwellings. There has been much social and aesthetic criticism levelled at the Bijlmermeer project — especially for its impersonal immensity.

But there were major problems. Adding fuel to

the flames were thousands of immigrants who had arrived in this period from Surinam and the Dutch Antilles, many of whom settled in the Amsterdam area, primarily in the subsidized Bijlmer. Accustomed to other living patterns, they had difficulty adjusting to the massive high-rise quarters and integrating into Dutch society. To ameliorate the violent problems, the city took action in the mid-nineties by demolishing a

Betondorp, a functionalist project by architect Van Lochem in 1924, was a reinforced concrete working class housing development in Amsterdam's Watergraafsmeer district.

W. Hartman

DIRECTOR MUNICIPAL DEPARTMENT
OF URBAN PLANNING, INNER CITY
DIVISION

Wim Hartman, reflected on architectural achievements: 'Around 50,000 rehabilitated or new living accommodations in twelve of the most dire working class areas were realized during the last 30 years. People had been crammed into miniscule apartments with tiny kitchens and toilets, no showers or any other comfort. To improve living space, two dwellings were often combined into one.

Subsidized rents enabled residents to stay in their neighborhood. Street patterns were retained, schools, parks and playgrounds were built. There have been many innovative architectural approaches to utilizing public spaces, often on difficult sites or by conversion of abandoned industrial buildings.

'The embattled Nieuwmarkt area, which had been devastated by subway excavations in the early seventies, was a hotbed of revolt as the locals fought to regain housing in their neighborhood. "Holes" were filled in, but the most spectacular solution for multi-housing was the "Pentagon" (Van Eyck/Bosch, 1984), a glass-fronted complex built on rubber blocks, which successfully eliminates vibrations from the subway running under the building.

'The Bickerseiland project, designed between 1975 and 1985 by architect Paul de Ley, was realized after a revolt against municipal plans.

'Other outstanding urban renewal projects were realized in dilapidated warehouses. On the islands of the KNSM shipping company in the old harbor area "Piraeus", a large residential block (Kollhoff/Rapp, 1994) was realized, next to other housing complexes (Albert, 1993, and Coenen, 1995).

'In the Entrepot West harbor area, 524 dwellings, with 50 different floor plans and parking facilities, were catapulted over the water (Atelier PRO, Van Beek, Nuis, 1993).

'An abattoir at Zeeburg in the eastern harbor was razed for distinctive housing (Lafour, 1989). More housing is planned on the Java and Borneo islands. The Alexander barracks were renovated for good, low cost dwellings.

'When a renowned American urban planner inspected the Frederik Hendrikplantsoen social housing project, she asked, to her great amazement, "But then where do the rich people live?"

'Leading architects have also approached social concerns with great sensitivity to the inhabitants' needs.

'Aldo van Eyck, who became world famous for the municipal orphanage complex of linked small dome units, designed the Moederhuis (1981), combining a 19th century building with new construction for single parents and their children. He kept everything in small scale and colorful for a very humane feeling. Incidentally, his "Tripolis" (1994), three office building units which turn their backs to the busy ring-road in their orientation to an inner plaza, have the former orphanage in the foreground.

'Pastel-tinted brick was used for a day nursery, with ten upper floor apartments, linked with a glass corridor to another building called the "Baby Temple" (Soeters, 1983).

'Some commercial buildings have made significant contributions to the cityscape, while others are less pleasing. The P.C. Hoofthuis deftly absorbed the Art Deco monument, the Witte Huis, with an university building for the language faculty which has clarity in its functional design (Bosch, 1984). Two concrete blockwork schools with the same basic shapes, outwardly looking like neighborhood houses, have classrooms grouped around central halls (Hertzberger, 1983).

'The light, functional halls added to the RAI exhibition complex in 1981 (Bodon), with solid and glazed horizontal bands, are aesthetically pleasing and efficient.

'The Music Theatre and City Hall, the Stopera, is a bit pompous on the outside, while the interior spaces, staircases and open views are better than the exterior. This was undoubtedly Amsterdam's most controversial building in ages (Holzbauer, Dam/Bijvoet, 1987). One gets used to Byzantium, with its combined dwellings, offices and shops after some time (Koolhaas/Christiaans, 1990). The Casino is 'pretty' architecture, trying to be urbane and pleasing, but I'm not fond of it (Ruyssenaars, 1990).

'The Wagon Lits and Ibis Hotel complex, straddling a narrow strip near the 19th century Central Station, introduce an unexpected futuristic design element in the center (Benthem/Crouwel, 1992). Its neighbor, the circular nerve center of the Netherlands Railroad, nicknamed the "flying saucer", adds to that modernistic corner. Naturally, many other interesting commercial buildings have been realized in recent years.

'One that remains unique in its approach is the ING office, which followed the anthroposophical belief that nature is the guiding line for architecture. This mammoth, S-shaped complex, with brick-clad, concrete towers linked into a pentagon shape, has few right angles and effectively saves energy (Alberts/van Huut, 1987).

'Noteworthy is the building of social housing planned in the Waterwijk as an environment-friendly and auto-free neighborhood where the city's water pipes and oldest pump station stood for over a century.'

number of the high-rise buildings, eliminating around 1000 dwellings, while planning construction of low-rise middle class housing, mostly for sale. Social housing with modest rents was maintained. This area, now called Amsterdam Zuidoost, incorporates far more than the troubled Bijlmermeer housing. An imposing financial and business center, shopping malls, office complexes, the Amsterdam Medical Center (the world's largest) have all been realized here. The ultra-modern Amsterdam Arena is under construction in this area.

Design

The Netherlands Design Institute (Vormgevingsinstituut), which became operational in the mid-nineties in the former

Amsterdam University's language faculty was harmoniously linked with the monumental 'White House', an Art Deco landmark on the Singel.

Upper right: Amsterdam's new Music Theater, combined with the Town Hall, rises majestically on the Amstel. Its conception and realization was widely protested but now the elegant facilities serve the opera and ballet to everyone's delight.

Rietveld's classic chairs, painted and zig zag, from the Stedelijk Museum collection.

Fodor Museum, is, according to its English director, John Thackara: 'a "think-and-do-tank" identifying new ways that design can contribute to the economic and cultural vitality of the community. It develops scenarios about the future and undertakes research projects to test them. The Institute's end product is ideas, knowledge and relationships to help companies, designers and researchers improve their capacity for innovation. This operation is probably unique among design institutes in that it is research-based. Our aim is indirect promotion of

ING Bank in Amsterdam Southeast is a splendid anthroposophical headquarters where there are no right corners.

B. Premsela

INTERIOR AND INDUSTRIAL DESIGNER

Benno Premsela is Amsterdam's design *éminence grise*, guru and doyen after 50 innovative years ruling the roost in artistic happenings.
As chairman of the Art, Architecture and Design Foundation, with stipendiary grants of circa 50 million guilders annually, he is a key player in the applied arts scene.
Premsela — a renowned interior and industrial designer with many credits for carpeting, lighting, home and office planning to his name — has influenced generations of developing designers. Premsela on contemporary Dutch design:
'Aldo van den Nieuwelaar designed a classic with a tall, narrow, free-standing storage unit which could also double as a space-divider. This simple box with a synthetic roll-down shutter was named "Amsterdammertje", after the ubiquitous dark red bollard that lines the city's canals and streets. Aldo was also the first to use fluorescent light for domestic lighting in lamps with white square backgrounds, with mobile or color variations in the minimal art tradition of Judd and Flavin, with an innovative Dutch twist. He has also designed carpeting and textiles.
'Geert Lap is unequalled in his ceramic vases. Rob Eckhardt does lamps and furniture in a new direction, like his amusing "tulip chair". Hans Appenzeller, one of the pioneers in jewellery, has been succesful with his chic boutique on Madison Avenue in New York.
'There are many more talented designers, such as Philip Sajet, who, in his non-conformity, mounts sharp, dangerous precious stones in rings, or embeds small street stones in bracelets.
'Dinie Besems, who is very conceptual, created a ring with a small saucer to catch a tear and a necklace of "ice cubes". It's interesting to analyze the intellectual processes behind these realizations.
'Though fashion is not our forte, there are some wonderful exceptions, like Alexander van Slobbe who took Paris by storm with his Orson & Bodil women's collection. The international press calls his simple architectural style "new modernism" and it sells from New York to Tokyo.
'Jan Jansen, an European trend-setting shoe designer since the sixties, developed new

Benno Premsela, Amsterdam's best known designer for close to half a century, was honored by H.R.H. Prince Bernhard with the coveted Silver Carnation award in recognition of his multitude of activities in support of the arts.

constructions and used unorthodox materials like bamboo, rubber and raw hide for women's footwear that was surprising, sometimes shocking, but never vulgar.
'Amsterdam, being so cosmopolitan in atmosphere and attitude, attracts creative foreigners who choose to settle here.
'Ulf Moritz, a German textile designer, has for many years found the right working climate for his exclusive home furnishings fabric collections.
'Czech-born Borek Sipek came to Amsterdam in the early eighties as an unknown designer. In the interim years, working from his Jordaan atelier, he has designed furniture, glass, ceramics and fabrics for Europe's most prestigious producers. He was even called back to Prague to serve as the official architect for President Vaclav Havel. But he always returns to Amsterdam.
'Industrial and public design is also important, such as the commission for glass ceilings given to the

artist Jeroen Vinken for the Post Office on the Singel, or the serene window conformity he planned for our Art Foundation (Fonds voor Beeldende Kunsten, Vormgeving en Bouwkunst) offices in an old Brouwersgracht warehouse.
'Friso Kramer, renowned for his classic "Revolt" chair and lantern poles lighting most of Amsterdam's streets, designed a never-executed project for door bells, mail slots and name plates for an entire social housing project to assure an aesthetic uniformity on the outside.
'Ruudt Peters, a jewellery designer, created a wonderfully welcoming iron fence for a residential development, while Narcisse Tordoir produced a lyrical screen as the entrance to the KNSM island housing. Of course, there is so much more to tell about design in Amsterdam, I should really write a book.'

Amsterdam's Rietveld Academy of Art annually graduates many creative designers in glass, ceramics, lighting, textiles, jewellery and furniture. Among the specialized Amsterdam showcases for established and upcoming talent include: Binnen, for furniture and textiles; Ra, for jewellery; Frozen Fountain features young Dutch furniture designers and Indoor has classic and contemporary glass. Leitmotiv presents edited classic designs, while Binnenhuis pioneers international design.

The architect Gerrit Rietveld is the grand-daddy of Dutch design. In the twenties, he created the landmark Metz & Co, and later planned the Vincent van Gogh Museum and the Amsterdam Academy Art which took his name. World recognition had already been achieved his red-blue chair, produced in 1918.

Decades of this intellectual baggage have helped Amsterdam designers of the nineties cross new frontiers in their innovative concepts.

design, not propaganda.' In view of this focused strategy, there are no public exhibitions but interested parties can arrange an appointment for a visit.

Sculptor Alexander Schabracq was commissioned by the city to create street furniture and lighting poles on the Damrak (seen near the Berlage Exchange) and on the Rokin.

KNSM Island was used for social housing. The Albert Complex, built by the Belgian architect Bruno Albert, used airy wrought iron entry gates for the successful housing project.

Leisure

Cosmopolitan forms of relaxation

Amsterdam has a myriad of man-made lakes, ponds and canals. Locals take to the water within the city for canoeing, sailing, rowing, motor boating, fishing, swimming and underwater diving. On rare occasions when the temperature drops low enough for a freeze, ice-skating is popular on the canals and lakes. Otherwise, people glide through the winter on artificial ice. Amsterdam has over 6,000 acres of recreational area including the 2,300-acre (with one third water) Amsterdam Woods, developed during the Depression years and finished by unemployed volunteers during the war.

There are some twenty parks — all colorful reflections of the city's imaginative planting department. When the first municipal park — the 125-acre Vondelpark (named after Joost van den Vondel, a famous poet) — was opened in 1865, a local newspaper proudly proclaimed that 'Amsterdam now has its own Bois de Boulogne'. It is a spot where, besides families, all kinds of people come to relax: Zen Buddhists, inline-skating grunge freaks, sweating joggers, loving couples, hash smoking neo-hippies, yuppies and dog walkers.

Amsterdam banker and philanthropist Pieter van Eeghen, who initiated the park plan in 1864, had to battle businessmen who were determined to erect a gasworks on that site, while the Dutch Railway Company wanted to build Amsterdam's

Skate boarding on the Museum Square. The city provided the room and facility for young people to work off their energy in shows of amazing athletic prowess. The Rijksmuseum serves as a backdrop.

>Ajax, winner of the Champions League 1995. When the Amsterdam *voetbal*-team returned home with the coveted trophy, the locals went wild. There was gleeful hysteria as the popular team sailed through the canals. Many an enthusiastic fan fell in the water.

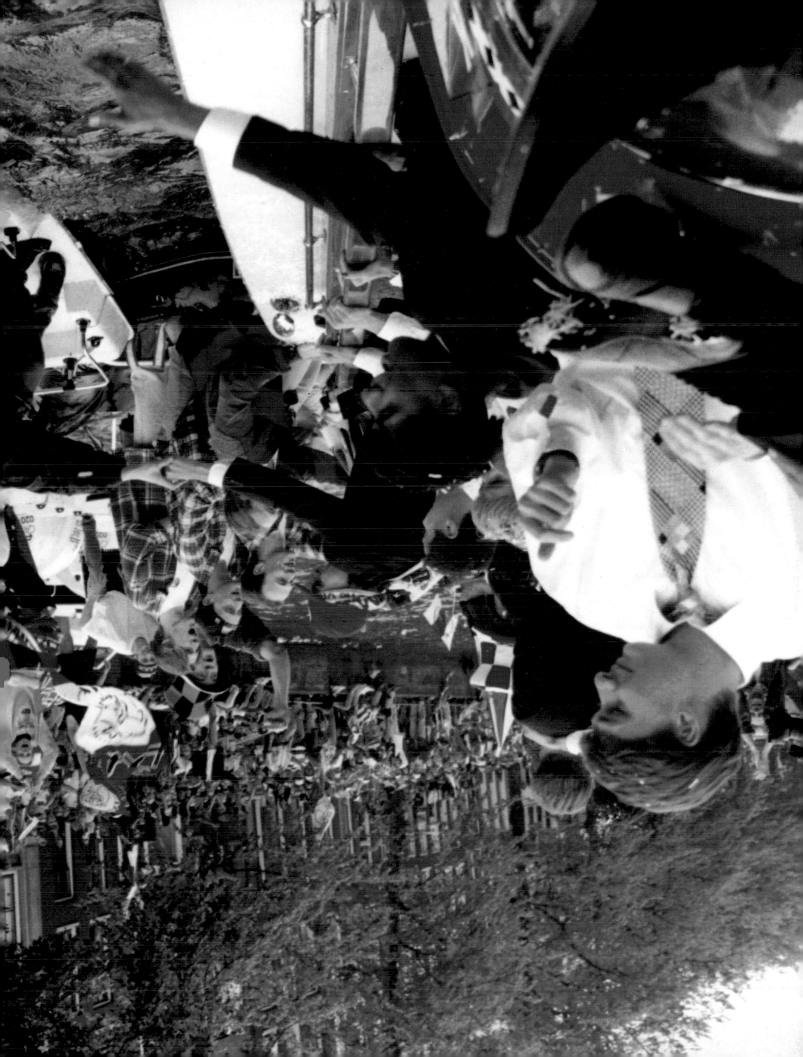

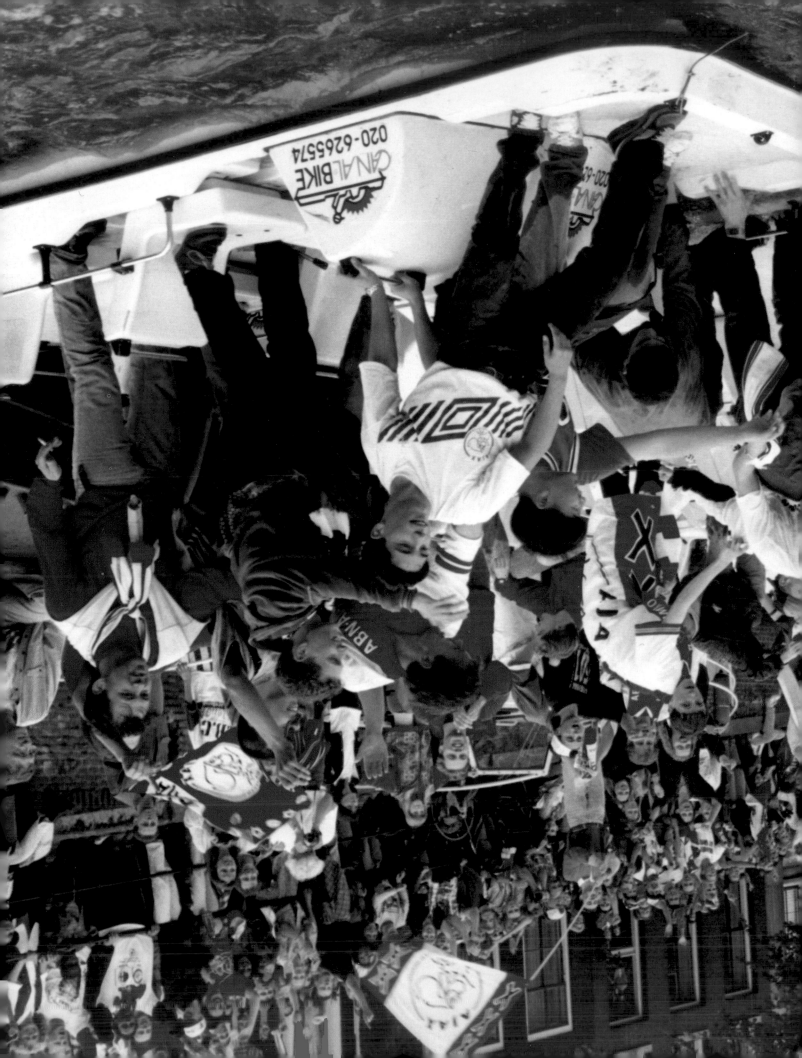

Central Station here. The visionary banker won out and had Jan Zocher, the landscape architect who also designed the Soestdijk Palace gardens, lay out the park.

A century later, when hordes of hippies in the sixties could no longer sleep on Dam Square, they were sent to the Vondel Park, which opened a luggage depot to store thousands of backpacks. This lasted until 1974, when sleeping in the park was also banned. The park's open air theater, where all kinds of performances are held, has always attracted record numbers of

Above: Rowers, individuals and in clubs, are regularly seen on the canals and Amstel River.

Ice skaters on frozen canals awakens memories of the beautiful 17th century winterscape paintings.

Amsterdammers. Architectural students come from all over to admire the blue tea house dating from the twenties. The Vondel Park Pavilion, built in 1878, houses a restaurant and the Dutch Film Museum, which regularly shows classic films.

The 128-acre Gaasperplas park, situated in Amsterdam South-East, was used for Floriade, a huge international flower exhibition organised once every decade. It has a campsite, barbecue and picnic facilities and lots of water for surfing, fishing and rowing among greenery.

The Amstel Park — a 38-acre inheritance from an immense garden event — has a maze, golf course, children's animal garden and pancake house. For over 6000 green-thumbed Amsterdammers who want to escape apartment life and public parks, there are 32 garden complexes, where one can rent, for a very nominal fee, a small plot of land.

Like all things Dutch sports facilities and participation programs are well-organized. No one need look far for a club or association of archery, badminton, basketball, billiards, bowling, bridge, boxing, chess or checkers, golf (a throwback to the 17th century Dutch *kolf* game of hitting a small wooden plug or ball), gymnastics, lawn tennis, handball, hockey, judo, flying, motor car racing, rugby, sharp shooting,

softball or baseball, soccer or football, table tennis, volley ball, ice hockey, weight lifting or greyhound racing. There is an indoor ski slope. Even sports that cannot be practiced in town, like hunting, have local clubs.

About 60 percent of the 750,000 Amster-dammers are active in some sport. Some 165,000 Amsterdammers are members of one of the 750 sports clubs. The ever-popular soccer clubs have over 45,000 members; tennis clubs, 17,000 (there are 270 outdoor and more than 50 indoor courts at twelve locations); and swimming and hockey clubs, each 4,500.

Rowing the canals, or (for non-athletes) gliding along them on little boats with outboard motors, is also one of Amsterdammers' favorite pastimes. Discovering the canal bike (pedal) boat is very

Kwakoe Festival. Dutch Surinamers who live in the Southeast region around the Gasper lake celebrate with the annual event which goes on for six weeks and attracts many Amsterdammers.

Sail Amsterdam, a mammoth water event staged every five years, draws the world's most impressive sailing ships to the city harbor for a splendid show of navigational beauty. Planning is already underway for Amsterdam Sail 2000.

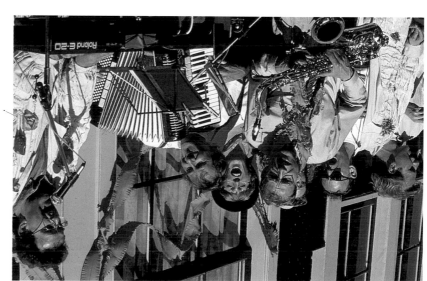

Queen's Day celebrants include children and adults who get made-up and dress wildly for the festivities. There's music in the air. Everyone seems to be playing or singing on this joyous holiday.

The Tuschinski Theatre, an Art Deco movie temple, must be one of the Continent's most extravagant relics from the twenties.

Right: Chess fanatics play on street corners and public squares.

popular among tourists.

Sports events like the annual canal marathon. The Dam to Dam Run (half a marathon) and the City Marathon attract athletes from all over the country and abroad.

The city has nineteen modern sports complexes and a covered ice hockey stadium that doubles as a concert hall. There are some 55 big, open areas with playing fields for a variety of sports, plus seven outdoor and eight indoor swimming pools (total water surface of 8,000 m²). The huge Sloterplas, a lake created when soil was hauled away for post-war housing developments, attracts Amsterdammers to its yacht harbor and beaches, and is popular for underwater diving and picnics. Kids can build sand castles, ride on swings, climb 'monkey bars', or wade in pools in over 650 playgrounds. There are several nearby golf courses, ranked among the best in Europe. And almost every Amsterdammer has a bike, by far the capital's most popular mode of transportation.

Spectator sports lure big crowds for important professional matches. The biggest playing field was the Olympic Stadium, built in 1928, when the Olympic Games were held in Amsterdam. It is being demolished to make room for housing. The Amsterdammers' Ajax mania and loyalty reaches hysterical proportions. When Ajax plays in town, or anywhere else in Europe, there are hordes of supporters in the stadium or glued to their TV sets. Conversation for days before and after every match is centered on the local soccer heroes. In coming years, Ajax will play in the multifunctional sports and events stadium — the Amsterdam Arena — being completed in the southeast section. When the name was announced, there were protests about associating this with the Romans' bloody gladiator spectacles. A Sleep-In, now called the Arena

M. van Praag

CHAIRMAN OF AJAX

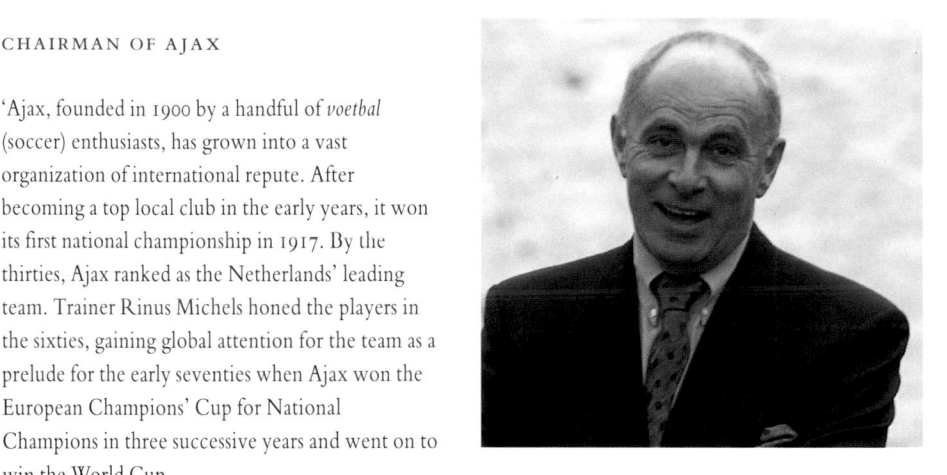

'Ajax, founded in 1900 by a handful of *voetbal* (soccer) enthusiasts, has grown into a vast organization of international repute. After becoming a top local club in the early years, it won its first national championship in 1917. By the thirties, Ajax ranked as the Netherlands' leading team. Trainer Rinus Michels honed the players in the sixties, gaining global attention for the team as a prelude for the early seventies when Ajax won the European Champions' Cup for National Champions in three successive years and went on to win the World Cup.

'Ajax's playing prowess was long established worldwide when in 1987 another laurel was added to its crown: the European Cup Winners' Cup in 1992. When the UEFA Cup was added to the trophy case, Ajax had won all of the three European competitions, an achievement equalled only by two other clubs, Juventus and Barcelona.

'In the 1994-1995 season, Ajax again successfully reached for the European crown. The team took its 25th National Championship before capturing the European Champions Cup for the fourth time. Ajax had emerged unbeaten in the elimination rounds of both the PTT Telecompetition and the Champions' League. The country went wild. The players were honored with ceremonies on Amsterdam's Museum Square where hordes of well-wishers proudly sang, *We are the Champions*. The hysteria around the European Cup swelled as the flotilla cruised along the canals to pressing crowds wanting to shout to their heroes and try to touch them. Many a fan fell into the water. All of Amsterdam was Ajax country — and even the uniformed police on control duty wore Ajax caps and scarves.

'As Ajax prepares for its centennial celebrations, the forecast is sunnier than ever. The club's popularity is soaring. Soon after the Ajax Supporters Association was founded more than 50 thousand members signed up — by far the largest number of any Dutch football club. When the club's first season (1996-1997) in the ultra-modern Amsterdam Arena was announced, ticket orders far exceeded the seat capacity.

'Sponsorship, with the ABN AMRO Bank in a lead role, has ensured the excitement of world class football but, equally important, the focus remains on finding and training talented youth as future stars. Through the years, the 'Ajax school' has groomed many juniors, including Johann Cruijff, Piet Keizer, Sjaak Swart, Marco van Basten, Frank Rijkaard, Dennis Bergkamp and Patrick Kluivert, all of whom won global recognition. Fans follow and identify with the young hopefuls as they emerge from their arduous training to take their place as players preparing for future Ajax victories.'

Youth Center, complained of the confusion this would evoke. There will be seating for 50,000 spectators who can flock into the stadium through 58 entrances. Built on a surface of 35,000 m², it will be one of Europe's most modern stadiums, with a unique, 38,000 m² transparent sliding roof, consisting of two 35 x 100 meters segments which can be opened or closed within fifteen minutes.

The stadium will have a two-tier underground parking garage for 2,000 cars. At walking distance from the stadium, there is parking for another 5,000 cars. Apart from soccer events, other sports like American football, motorcross or rugby can take place in this stadium. It's also a perfect venue for rock concerts and other gigantic events. The 200 million guilder project, scheduled for opening in August 1996, will also house an Ajax museum, television studio, various restaurants, meeting rooms and state-of-the-art facilities for the players.

Relaxation also takes the form of sunbathing — if the sun should shine — on café terraces, park benches, houseboat decks, chairs set up on canalsides, or on any inch of available space in the warm rays. Seeking the sun in this northern city is a fetish, while discussing the weather is a daily pastime. A night-time diversion is 'elbow-bending', lifting a beer or Dutch gin in a cosy pub filled with good conversation and an unmistakably Amsterdam ambiance. There are over 1,400 cafés in the city, always jammed with a faithful crowd seeking an unstrenuous form of night sport. Amsterdam is also home to more than 750 restaurants, catering for every taste.

An annual event, which attracts hordes of people from all over the Netherlands, is the Vrijmarkt, an unending market along all the canals and streets of the city center. Everyone is allowed to sell anything he wants without a permit on Queen's Day, a national holiday on 30 April (actually, celebrating the Queen Mother's birthday). People, young and old, stake out 'plots' on the pavements with ribbons or chalk and spend the night guarding their spot in anticipation of the next day's crowds.

Amsterdam is also home to an internationally famous zoo, Artis, annually drawing around one

for crew races and fishing. There are paths for horseback riding, cycling and walking, plus areas for picnics, ball games, kite flying, sleigh riding and a children's farm. A keep-fit course has obstacles to leap over, climb under and run around. One can surf, sail, canoe, play hockey, cricket or tennis, go camping or even bare one's soul in the specially designated, protected nudist areas. There is a wooded 'bird island' with botanical gardens. Marshy areas have remained

unchanged and are protected as natural reserves. A 24-acre animal enclosure is a home for European bisons and wild sheep, neighboured by the goat farm where cheese is made.

Large wooded areas have trees characteristic of Northwest European forests: oak, beech, maple and ash, as well as large stands of conifers, with the Norway spruce dominating. Fine specimens are marked with yellow spots when they are 40 to 50 years old and designated as 'future trees'. When the wood is thinned, they remain untouched.

Along the paths of the Amsterdam Woods are many varieties of very rare plants. One particular species — the Southern marsh orchid or *retorchis* — grows by the hundreds in the swampy areas near the lakes. They thrive on being trampled! The more they get stepped on, the more they blossom.

Circa 4 million people come to the Amsterdam Woods every year for the myriad of leisure possibilities it offers — from sports to stepping on rare orchids.

million visitors, with a collection of 6,000 animals. Unique attractions include an immense aquarium, a large 'nocturnal house' for animals from all over the world that would otherwise sleep all day, and a Planetarium.

The zoo, founded in 1838, had the first International Bell telephone in the Netherlands installed because the director wanted to 'try it'. Skeptics laughed, mockingly suggesting that he would use it to communicate with his animals.

The first known hippopotamus railway was built on the zoo grounds in 1856, for the hippos' transportation to bigger quarters.

The Artis collection includes several world rarities, such as a colony of blackfeet penguins, African wild dogs and Surinam Sea cows. There is also a lodging for the rare insect-eating claw monkeys.

The Zeiss Artis Planetarium, unique in the Netherlands, can project 8,900 twinkling stars on a 630 square meter surface. Multi-media techniques supplement the ultra modern Model-1 projector for dazzling sky tours which include visits to Mars, Jupiter and Saturnus. Changing shows continue to fascinate visitors of all ages, with themes like, 'Light on the Moon', dealing with the relationship of man and the moon, 'Walking space', and 'En route to the stars'.

Amsterdam also has a Hortus Botanicus, dating back to the 17th century, with over 6,000 plants. In early 1994, Queen Beatrix opened a new, 1,500 square meter hothouse, which contains three different warm-weather climate zones and their native flora: tropical, subtropical and desert. A rare specimen of the *Victoria Amazonica*, the world's largest water lily, opens only at night, two nights in a row, once or twice a year in the Hortus Botanicus. The subtropical flora collection is unique in Europe. A monumental palm greenhouse and herb garden was created, based on design and knowledge from 1638, the year that Hortus Medicus was founded.

Amsterdam's parks also have at least ten types of wild orchids and 70 protected plant species. For the wanderer, nature lover and sportsman, the Amsterdam Woods, 4 meters below sea level, is the most ideal and surprising get-away from urban stress. It has a hand-dug rowing channel

The Artis Zoo with sculpted falcons guarding its entrance. Tots are encouraged to touch the animals in the children's farm.

Right: Tropical trees and plants in the Hortus Botanicus triple climate hot houses can be examined from a five meter high bridge.

Protests

Centuries of locals in revolt

Amsterdammers have been tolerant of religious and political refugees from the earliest years. They have been benevolent and sympathetic to the underdog. They have meddled in other countries' politics and still do even today. The difficult Amsterdammers, because of their unusual international outlook, have made their city truly cosmopolitan in human terms, in the best sense of not being provincial.

Amsterdam has always known riots and protest strikes. Although some became violent and ended in deaths and severe injuries among protesters as well as police, none were aimed at injuring people, but rather at damaging property. Motivation behind protests and riots has changed over the centuries. From the 16th until the 18th century, religious reasons or taxation were behind many of the actions, whereas 19th and 20th century protests usually were sparked by political conflicts. Forms of protest have changed as well, from plundering opponents' houses to more orderly forms of protests like demonstrations, sit-downs and work strikes.

One common factor unites most riots: the time of year. Most took place in spring or summer. Only the 1969 riots were in the winter.

Nowadays, the Amsterdammer protests in peaceful picketing whenever he feels injustice is being done in any corner of the world. Then the Consulate of the erring nation becomes the target, or retail stores importing from countries where colonial oppression robs the natives of freedom, or tourist offices promoting destinations where dictators or military men deprive students and intellectuals of their voice. He pleads the cause of mothers of missing children in South America and other humanitarian causes. He has become violent in clashes with the police about vacation pay, traffic and pollution, housing, subway construction.

Combing the capital's history for protests and riots which characterized unrest through the centuries, a sampling follows: 'Streakers'

social problems and demands for changes in the political structure.

The Eel riot in the Jordaan (1886) ended with 23 dead and 140 wounded. Locals strung up eels across the canals. Standing in boats, they pulled them off, preferably by the heads.

In 1566, during the reign of statue breaking, a mob destroyed paintings in a church and two

appeared on the Dam in 1535 in the city's first major riot, the Anabaptist Rebellion. This religious sect, imagining they were in the Garden of Eden, ran naked across the great square, using violence in an attempt to gain control of the city. At least twenty policemen were killed, while the Anabaptists subsequently lost their heads on the gallows. This sorry fate did not, of course, befall three playful Amsterdam students who streaked across the Dam in 1974. Their heads and bare bottoms ended up on the front page of Dutch newspapers (see 'The Once-Holy Place')

There was even a 'children' riot in December 1663 when the ruling Calvinist regents banned *Sinterklaas* figures baked from spice cake since they deemed this tasty holiday treat to be sacrilegious and Papal nonsense.

During the Undertakers' Riot in 1696, mobs looted four houses, protesting new burial taxes. Scores of people were killed and hundreds wounded when the police opened fire. According to witnesses, the streets were filled with blood. When the riots ended after three days, twelve participants were condemned to death and hung. Many of the wounded fled from the hospital out of fear of being hanged.

Whereas Amsterdam regents enjoyed unprecedented prosperity through their world trade, the small people suffered untold economic deprivation. War with England added additional heavy taxes on the working classes and extra duties on funerals.

During the 1748 Tax Collector's riot, mobs pillaged the tax collectors' homes. When two protesters were executed at the Weigh House on the Dam, onlookers panicked. Soldiers on guard feared new riots and fired into the crowd, killing hundreds of people.

In 1848, while all of Europe was stirring with economic unrest, a Communist group formed under the banner of 'The Union for Moral Culture — All Men are Brothers'. It called for a meeting on the Dam. Police stepped in and seized all their pamphlets. People, warned to stay away, came to the Dam in droves. The speaker never showed up but youthful gangs and an angry mob caused a major riot. Militia volunteers and the police crushed the uprising and everyone went home.

A protest mounted when the old popular sport of eel-pulling was forbidden by law. The custom was to attach live eels, greased with green soap, to lines stretched across the Jordaan canals. From

monasteries. This riot was an offshoot of a religiously inspired Flemish movement, a forerunner of the Reformation, directed against church decoration.

A mob pillaged a house where Remonstrants were holding a religious gathering in 1626. This was called the Easter Riot.

When a few sailors were hanged in 1652, after protesting their low wages, soldiers feared that riots would break out and fired into the crowd of onlookers, killing an unknown number of people.

a wobbly row-boat, one tried to pull a wriggling eel from the line, or better yet, hold tight until the head was in his hands. To everyone's hilarity, many participants fell into the water. On a summer day in 1886, the police got word of preparations and charged in. The Eel riot ended with 23 people killed and 140 wounded.

The 1917 Potato riot resulted in ten people being killed and 113 wounded. On that occasion, mobs looted potato warehouses since no one could buy potatoes, though the warehouses were fully stacked with them — for export to England and Germany. Both of those countries, at war at the time, had a right to an equal amount of potatoes, but England refused to import its share, resulting in 5 million kilograms of potatoes rotting in the warehouses. In the same year, sympathizers with the Russian Revolution carried their political enthusiasm onto the city's main square in a show of solidarity with the Red cause, but their strike was quickly put down.

The 1934 Jordaan riot originated from complaints about decreased welfare support. Heavy fighting went on for three days, followed by turbulence. During the violent encounters, a protester was killed.

During the 1966 Telegraaf riot, construction workers marched on the national daily's building, then located in the center on the Nieuwezijds Voorburgwal, and burned a delivery truck. During their strike for increased vacation pay, a worker was killed. Since the newspaper attributed the death to natural causes, and not police brutality as originally presumed, the frenzied newspaper workers felt the newspaper had turned against them. They moved to the nearby Dam and to the Damrak, where further fighting with the police broke out. Heads were beaten, blood flowed, pavement stones were pulled up and thrown. It was several days before peace returned.

In the same year, the Provos (anti-Establishment provocateurs) picked the wedding of Crown Princess Beatrix and Prince Claus for their smoke bomb protests. Battles were fought in the Dam area. After the wedding incidents, there was an uneasy peace for a few months. Then the Provo riots started again in full force, and the police, who closed in hard, were accused of unnecessary brutality. All these events in 1966, with ensuing criticism of the City Hall and the police department, contributed to the resignation of both the burgomaster and the Police Commissioner. Youthful Dam sitters were the core of

Tax riot in 1835 when unpopular measures were enacted affecting house owners' tax obligations, rocked the city for months and resulted in the burgomaster's resignation.

controversy in 1967. A naval detachment arrived at Amsterdam's central railroad station, supposedly in a spontaneous act to rid the capital of its 'hippies' — a mixed bag of youthful travellers and students from all over the world. The young people had settled into the train station's halls and around the Dam memorial. The sailors, with hoses and buckets, went through their 'clean-up' with a vengeance. They charged through the station and then down the Damrak onto the main square, washing the international youth into dispersion. The next day there was mixed reaction in the newspapers. Amsterdammers doubted the merit of this deed. Everyone wondered who had really organized it. This city was characterized in the sixties and seventies by action groups of every sort, banded

Police arrived on the rooftops of houses occupied by squatters.

Under: Provos used the statue of 'Het Lieverdje' as an assembly point.

together to protest and seek reforms in causes that ranged from daycare for children of working mothers, feminism, sexual freedom, equal rights for homosexuals, concern over political situations all over the world, students fighting higher university fees, opposition to the subway construction, traffic problems, urban renewal plans which threatened a neighborhood's characteristic ambiance, squatters of unused buildings in the face of a severe housing shortage, to historical preservation societies, which combine private initiative and an unbounded drive for restoring the old monument buildings to their living function.

The Provos had also inspired student demonstrations on American college campuses and served as role models for the May '68 riots in Paris. Led by the bespectacled, bearded anarchist Roel van Duyn, they dressed in white jeans and rode white bicycles. Out with a vengeance, infused with humor, they sought to cleanse the city of its pollution from cars and industry, and bring more greenery and low income housing facilities into the center, while exerting pressure on money-motivated city decisions affecting the environment. With their white political platform, the Provos surprisingly captured one seat on the Municipal Council in the 1966 elections. Roel van Duyn and his closest lieutenants were officially in a ruling seat and they upset the decorum in the city chambers when they openly smoked hashish and impertinently sidetracked discussions to press for their own issues. (Van Duyn is still in office in the mid-nineties.)

A new activists' group calling themselves *kabouters*, meaning dwarves or little people, inherited the role of devil's advocate from the Provos in 1970. With support from all quarters, they got five men elected to the Municipal Council. Their actions, usually just bordering on lawlessness, were intended to embarrass city officials into reversing plans that might affect the living climate, primarily among the threatened working class. The party was successful in training neighborhood groups into speaking up loudly for their own causes, especially housing.

In the seventies, Amsterdam's women libbers, called Mad Minnies, successfully created day-care centers, evoked awareness of salary discrepancies and imaginatively asserted themselves in all kinds of contemporary social problems. They burst into a gynaecologists'

Feminists protested for abortion rights with BOSS over OWN BELLY signs.

convention with slogans painted on their middles — boss over our belly — seeking legalization of abortion. They got public toilets for women in the streets, a former masculine-only domain, after tying pink ribbons around street urinals. They marched in street protests for women political victims in other countries. Neighborhood action committees were formed to thwart the subway builders. The Safe Traffic Work Group protested with an exhibition exposing the cost to Amsterdam of its living climate by demolishing neighborhoods, besides the added strain on municipal funds. Residents of that working-class Nieuwmarkt neighborhood, the first victims of housing demolition, staged aggressive resistance, but to little avail.

In that same decade, the Amsterdam-based organization for Netherlands Sexual Reform, introduced more enlightened sexual information programs in schools and in their own clubhouses. There were contact evenings with naked partners feeling out problems of frustration. A condom called FUN was launched on the market. In contrast to 'men in white jackets' giving advice, they initiated café-like clubs where people with sexual problems, or desiring sexual information, could drop in for a

cup of coffee and talk freely.

The Netherlands Association for the Integration of Homosexuals also has its national headquarters in Amsterdam. Its COC clubhouse has long been a closed, protected gathering place for male and female homosexuals. The group associated itself with the Man-Woman Organization for joint

Violent protest actions against house demolition for the subway construction in the New Market area were common.

University student riots
centered on the Maagdenhuis
(Maidens' house) in the
sixties.

actions aimed at both homosexual and women's emancipation in society. The COC received a royal sanction and has a government subsidy for consultants working as advisors.

Action groups do not always take the form of protest. Some come to the municipality for help, or the city goes to them. Amsterdam takes the initiative to start or support groups with difficulty fitting into the normal pattern of society. It faces up to potential problems, such as drugs among the young or threatened violence by bands of disoriented Hell's Angels.

The city subsidizes cultural centers like Paradiso and the Melkweg, where soft drugs are permitted. Drug and alcohol patients are treated and efforts made to rehabilitate them. Several successful 'graduates', all ex-drug addicts, now run their own help service on a boat that sails the Amsterdam canals. They received a 25,000 guilder subsidy to purchase the boat and set up

'Drugs Anonymous'.

The squatter problem, which reached its zenith at the end of the seventies, has waned considerably since then. Squatters, anarchists and riot-mongers had disturbed Beatrix's inauguration in 1980 with very violent riots, forcing police to use teargas and water canons. The protestors shouted: 'Geen Woning, Geen Kroning' (No Housing, No Coronation). Relatively few houses are squatted in Amsterdam these days. Violent clashes between police and squatters during evictions have now become a relative rarity.

Today, as always, Amsterdam has more than its share of protest action groups for all kinds of causes. Some are disruptive, some constructive, some legal, some illegal — but they are all seen and heard by the decision-makers. Amsterdam remains a difficult city to govern since Amsterdammers are difficult

... and the World

Globe-spanning expeditions, exploration, trading

'It is just as rare for a Dutchman to reach 50, as for a Japanese to reach 100.' Not being blessed with longevity was ascribed to Dutch addiction to sexual excesses and drink.

'Their height is always wildly exaggerated, the prevailing opinion being that they are taller than other (or normal) people.'

'They have eyes like animals and no heels.' Their eyes resemble those of a dog and because the back part of their feet does not appear to touch the ground, they attach wooden soles to their shoes.'

'To urinate, they lift up one leg after the manner of a dog.'

And, it was widely believed in Japan that the Dutch possessed remarkable sexual powers which they heightened still further with potions and the like.

These marvellous misconceptions, firmly embedded in Japanese minds and scientifically explained in countless Japanese books, came from writer Hirate Atsutane (1777-1843), often called the theologian of Shintō, Japan's ethnocentric religion.

But the Dutch — who sailed for Japan in 1598 on a ship called *Charity* and were the only Western traders allowed to stay through the country's long period of seclusion — couldn't have cared less what the Japanese thought of them. While they entrenched themselves with a trading post, the Spanish, English and Portuguese were thrown out since they had been proselytizing. The Japanese government felt that Christians could not be good citizens. The Dutch Calvinists — who forced all of their seamen, including foreign recruits, to attend daily services on board ship — put away their bibles when business was at stake.

After they were confined in 1641 to the island of Deshima, they organized their love life in the licensed brothel quarter in nearby Nagasaki. The

HET GEZICHT VAN AANKOMST DER HOLLANSCHE SCHEPEN IN DE HAVEN VAN NANGAZAKIE

Dutch arriving in Nagasaki harbor.

Japanese saw the Dutch as 'red barbarians with webbed feet' and called their companions 'Keesjes' (Japanese prostitutes). Otherwise, they were content to stay among themselves, drinking gin, and concentrating on making money for their Dutch masters.

Once a year, the Dutch were allowed ashore to embark on their gift-bearing procession of homage to the Shogun's court in Edo (modern-day Tokyo). To stay in the Shogun's good graces, the Dutch painstakingly sought exquisite, costly offerings, many of which are still revered as national treasures. One such present, a splendid copper candelabra, almost cost the Dutchmen their heads. The Shogun's emblem had been engraved upside down in the Netherlands. A wrong gift or a wrong word could result in immediate death. Fortunately, the Shogun, so overwhelmed with the glistening work of art, missed the error.

There was a cult of *rangakusha* (Japanese scholars

inland waters and around Europe in search of new markets for trading. By the end of the 16th century, Amsterdam's entrepreneurs sought to take on an unknown world. During the Netherlands' maritime greatness, which extented through the 18th century, crews financed chiefly by Amsterdam merchants, bartered, colonized, conquered, explored, pillaged and set up trading posts and factories in all directions of the wind.

A small fleet, including a ship called *Amsterdam*, had gone through the Cape of Good Hope in 1595 to reach Java. One year later, two small ships tried to find the route north of Russia and Siberia to reach China and the Indies. One of those vessels got ice-bound and spent the winter of 1596-1597 on the island of Nova Zembla. The crew survived on polar bear meat in a large wooden shelter. (Their tools were found a century ago and given to Amsterdam's Rijksmuseum.)

On those voyages, the northerly region of Spitsbergen was also explored. The hardy seamen became whalers, dragging the whale carcasses to a nearby island, which they named Amsterdam, where they built sheds to live in and prepare the meat for transportation home. Whaling became a big business, especially after the Northern Company was organized in 1614 to regulate this trade. During the years 1610-1640, whaling was monopolized by those vested interests. The whaling trade reached even greater proportions after that time until well into the late 19th century when adventurous private enterprises hunted these mammals.

Besides whaling, the catching, curing and marketing of herring from the North Sea and cod from New Foundland had been one of the earliest sources of Amsterdam's prosperity. Before the 16th century closed, more ships had reached Bantam on Java's northern coast and the Moluccas. They returned with cargoes of exotic spices — pepper, cloves, nutmeg, cinnamon and mace — that brought the dazzled merchants tremendous profits. By 1602, there were so many Dutch ships — sailing from Zeeland as well as from Amsterdam — that prices soared in the Spice Islands as the seafarers bid against each other. As a result, the Dutch East India Company (VOC — Vereenigde Oostindische Compagnie) was formed as a unified front to deal with the natives, with a governing body of powerful regents, De Heren

of Dutch), which so admired the Hollanders' real or imagined virtues that their compatriots mockingly accused them of suffering from *rampeki* (Hollandomania). Of course the Dutch did leave their mark on Japan with their knowledge of navigation, geography, engineering, military science, horsemanship, chemistry, astronomy, culture, art, western learning and medicine. Many Dutch words came into daily use. Dutch was used as the official

Amsterdam, an authentic reproduction of the 17th century ship which sank on its maiden voyage, is moored at the National Maritime Museum on the harbor.

Japanese medium for communications with foreign powers, as well as for medical books, until the late 19th century. The Dutch had introduced technical instruments like binoculars, microscopes and varied medical equipment. Japan was only one of many distant places reached. For three centuries before that voyage, hardy Amsterdam settlers had been sailing from the marshy spot where the city began through

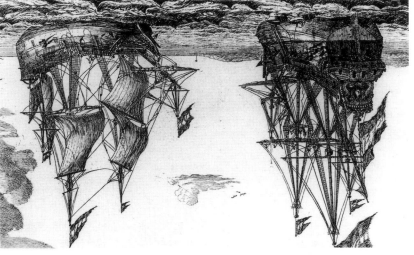

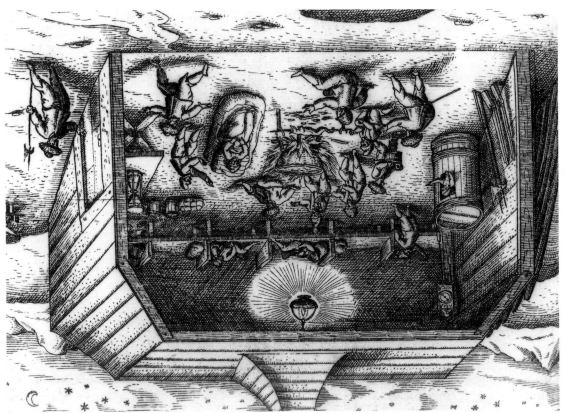

Under: The Cape of Good Hope with Dutch at anchor.

De Paerel, an East India Company ship, while *Den Dubbelen Arent* sailed for the West India Company.

On the island of Nova Zembla, the Dutch crew of an ice-bound vessel survived on polar meat throughout the winter of 1596–1597 in a large wooden house, as in this imaginary view. Their tools, found a century ago, were given to the Rijksmuseum.

XVII (Gentlemen 17). Another prime task set for the VOC crews was to combat British, Spanish and Portuguese traders and destroy their settlements.

The East India Company received sole trading rights in all lands east of the Cape of Good Hope and west of the Straits of Magellan. It had sovereign power, could make treaties, organize administration and defense systems, and wage war on the Spanish and Portuguese. The VOC lost no time in setting sail. No destination was too far nor any route too dangerous for an expedition to be dispatched by the money hungry merchant princes. On one of the first voyages in 1602, Ceylon, Malaya, Java and even Siam and China were visited. Two years later, the company's men successfully over-ran Molucca and set up factories on the Spice Islands.

There was a settlement from 1605 at Coromandel in India for cotton fabric trading. They established company headquarters for the entire eastern coast at Pulicat near Madras and later went into the interior of Bengal to barter spices for hemp and silk, and set up small dyeworks. Negapatnam was seized from the Portuguese in 1658 and later they took the Malabar coast from them. The Portuguese were

Above: Jan Pietersz. Coen was one of the Greatest Governor-Generals appointed by the VOC. He founded Batavia on the ruins of an old fort near Jacatra, from where the company later got control of all the East India trade throughout Asia.

Right: Dutch print from 1598 depicts the colonization of Batavia.

chased out of Cochin, which came under company rule in 1681. The Dutch were so powerful that around 1700 the English, who were competing with them in India, expressed fear of losing the territory to 'the most noteworthy company in the universe'. A trading station at Ayuthia, the old capital of Siam, was set up early in the game and functioned importantly in the trade between the Indies, Siam and Japan.

Willem Jansz., sailing with the *Little Dove* in 1606, explored New Guinea and recorded the earliest known sighting of the unknown continent of Australia. Dirk Hartogs landed on the western coast in 1616 and nailed an inscribed pewter plate to a post to establish his claim. (That plate, found in 1696, is now in the Rijksmuseum.) In 1641 the VOC was also granted a trade monopoly with Japan. Abel Tasman, on a voyage in 1642, discovered Van Diemensland, Tasmania and New Zealand. Two years later, he explored Australia's northern coast.

One of the greatest Governor-Generals appointed by the VOC was Jan Pietersz. Coen. He founded Batavia in 1619 on the ruins of old Jacatra, from where the company later got control of all the East India trade throughout Asia. Coen sent a ship in 1623 to the Persian harbor of Gamron to break the British silk trade monopoly. In 1638, the Dutch got a foothold in Portuguese-controlled Ceylon. Three years later, they took the town of Malacca, which had been considered an impregnable Portuguese stronghold — and with that victory the Dutch had supremacy in all the approaches to the Indonesian Archipelago. (The Dutch stayed in the East Indies until 1949 when that country became independent and changed its name to Indonesia. The capital Batavia became Jakarta.) To insure a fresh water supply for the VOC ships *en route* to the East Indies, the company established a settlement in 1652 at the Cape of Good Hope. Dutch farmers — fervent Calvinists who believed that colored people could never be converted — arrived three years later in South Africa. Their descendants still speak 'Afrikaans', a derivation from Dutch.

Trade was established with Arabia for coffee, gum, perfume and horses. Ceylon was conquered in 1661 and remained Dutch for almost 150 years until lost to the British during the Napoleonic wars. The Dutch bought silk, chinaware and tea in China, mostly in Canton. An artistic exchange developed between the Dutch porcelain industry in Delft and the Chinese producers. Delftware adapted many Chinese designs, while the Chinese used Dutch patterns on company-ordered chinaware that became known as *chine de commande*. The VOC, during its existence for almost 200 years, went to many other parts of the East on expeditions that gained land, power and riches, or lost territory, control and cargoes in constant encounters for supremacy with other colonizers.

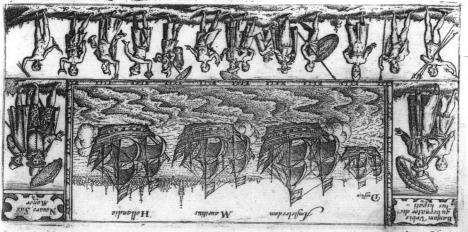

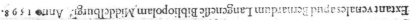

Extant venales apud Bernardum Langenesse Bibliopolam Middelburgi. Anno 1598.

But one expedition, back in the early years, ended in a 'wrong guess' — and the discovery of Manhattan island.

During the same era of its Nieuw Amsterdam settlement, the West India Company was active in other parts of the New World. It took Brazil from the Portuguese between 1630 and 1635. Vice-Admiral Piet Hein captured and burned Portuguese ships and added San Salvador, Rio de Janeiro and entire Brazilian provinces to Dutch holdings.

In 1634, the company captured the Caribbean islands of Aruba, Bonaire and Curaçao. (Bonaire and Curaçao are still Dutch territories today.) Three years later, after overpowering a Portuguese fortress on the African Gold Coast,

which gave them control of the area now called Ghana, slave trade became big business. The Dutch had replacing commodity dealing. The Dutch had some 60 men as agents on the West African coast specializing in the rounding up of Negroes for sale to the Spanish, who used them in back-breaking jobs on South American plantations. Cargo ships containing about 800 Africans — including many black prisoners of war sold by Africans to the Dutch agents — sailed regularly to Curaçao en route to South America. The Spanish government gave out official rights for these dealings which netted several thousand slaves a year. For a time, one wealthy Amsterdammer had the exclusivity of these rights.

Above: Vice-Admiral Piet Hein took Brazil from the Portuguese between 1630 and 1635 for the West India Company. He captured and burned Portuguese ships and added San Salvador, Rio de Janeiro and entire Brazilian provinces to Dutch holdings.

Under left: Dutch gin is distilled by West in the centuries-old manner in the heart of Amsterdam. This strong drink was the seamen's staple on the long global voyages of discovery and conquest. *Under*: Coffee and tea, among the earliest products brought back by the explorers' ships, is traditionally presented in the Keizer shop.

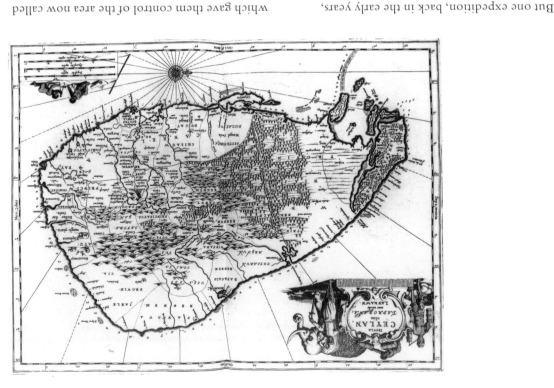

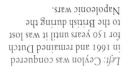

Left: Ceylon was conquered in 1661 and remained Dutch for 150 years until it was lost to the British during the Napoleonic wars.

The West India Company went on with the slave trade until the late 18th century, while combatting Spanish and Portuguese domination of the Western Hemisphere. But by that time, this company, as well as the VOC, had run its course and was disbanded.

While Amsterdam ships were circling the globe, merchants were also profiting from European trade around the Mediterranean, especially with Italy and France, and on the Baltic with industry and the staple market. The shipbuilding, wool and beer industries depended upon these imports. Since the local market was limited, products of grain, wood and wool had to be exported. Payments for the northern countries' goods was in household and luxury items which the traders had bought in southern Mediterranean lands, and later with exotic tropical products — like sugar, tea, coffee and spices — picked up in Amsterdam from the East

The castle and city of Batavia in this document printed in Amsterdam in 1652.

Germany and Scandinavia. A Dutch shortage of grain and wood meant seeking markets for raw materials needed for bread and shipbuilding. Bread was the lower classes' main food, eaten at all meals before the potato became known. As early as the 14th and 15th centuries, Amsterdam vessels picked up grain in Danzig, already a bustling export harbor at that time. But the big business was done in Scandinavia, not only for grain but also for wood, copper, zinc, iron and wool. This reached such proportions that it was called the 'mother' commerce of all Dutch trading — and became the basis for the important staple trade in which goods were carried to Holland for re-sale via export. So many flute-shaped ships plied the Scandinavian routes that a monopolistic system — like that arranged by the East and West India Companies in the territories they exploited — was unthinkable for these free traders. There was a thriving competitive situation to get the raw materials needed for domestic consumption, and West India Companies. From circa 1600, Amsterdam was the world's leading commodities market and the Dutch were Europe's biggest commercial carriers.

Sweden had become the most interesting market for the Amsterdammers. In the 17th century, Dutch merchant colonies settled in Finköping and Norköping and supported the Swedish King Gustaaf Adolf in his frequent wars against Russia, Poland and the German Kaiser. Trade in raw materials with the Netherlands flourished and many Amsterdammers used those Dutchmen in residence as contacts for expanding into new business ventures.

An outstanding example was Louys de Geer, an iron and copper goods dealer, who, around 1620, started shipping armaments to Sweden. The young king, extremely impressed with the Amsterdammer's clever dealings, appointed him quartermaster of his armies and made him the acting manager of the royal copper mines. He gave him Swedish citizenship. For his extensive

loans to the crown, plus investment in a Swedish/Dutch trading company he organized in West Africa. De Geer was made a Swedish nobleman and received all the land used by his mines and factories. Thus he became one of the richest landowners in Sweden. When the Dutch government reneged on an agreement to supply the Swedes with naval aid during a war with Denmark, De Geer recruited a naval force for them. Remaining an Amsterdam regent at heart, De Geer often came back to his mercantile palace, an orange brick house decorated with six Roman heads on the façade. It is still intact at Keizersgracht 123.

In Amsterdam this is known as the 'House with the Heads'. Legend: There were seven thieves breaking in. As each one entered, the maid decapitated him, up through the sixth. She married the seventh.

Other Amsterdammers, the brothers Louys and Hendrik Tripp were, like De Geer, deeply involved in Sweden in the early 17th century. Becoming incredibly wealthy from their dubious dealings in iron and weapons, they commissioned a virtual palace at Kloveniersburgwal 29 in classical French style with Ionic columns on the façade, pilasters and sculptures. The regal residence was so expansive that the brothers divided it into two dwellings with a separation line invisible from the canal. Wanting to immortalize the source of their poen (vulgar, vernacular Dutch for money) for all the world to see, the Tripps had canons carved on the roof chimneys and in the fireplaces. In 1812, the Royal Institute of Science, Letters and Arts occupied a part of the building, later sharing the space with the first Rijksmuseum (National Gallery). Today it houses the Royal Dutch Academy of Science.

Amsterdam harbor — home port for European and world trading — was still 'a forest of masts' in the early 18th century, just as a visiting German professor had described it back in 1550. But later in the century, maritime commerce had declined to almost a standstill, partly due to French occupation forces blockading Dutch ports to favor their own. Another important reason was that with the larger 19th century vessels and a competitive pressure for faster shipping, the harbor was not up to the times. There had always been a problem, since the earliest sailing days, for ships to reach the sea from Amsterdam's harbor, or come into port due to shallow waterways, ferocious winds and tides.

When the great North Holland Canal was dug in 1824, opening a direct route to the North Sea, Amsterdam's port took on renewed life. Industrialization of Amsterdam in the second half of the 19th century produced goods that could be shipped to the East, the Americas and northern European markets. To meet this need, the North Sea Canal was excavated in 1876 with a harbor mouth at IJmuiden. It has become, in the intervening century, the world's deepest and largest sea-shipping canal, bigger than either the Suez or Panama Canal. The 266-meter-wide North Sea Canal brought Amsterdam to within 10 nautical miles of the open sea. At IJmuiden two jetties extend 2 miles into the sea, an extraordinary hydraulic achievement, making one of the world's largest outer harbors, with a lock system creating a tide-free harbor for Amsterdam.

The Merwede Canal, completed in 1893, added further city links with main tributaries of the Rhine River. Over the years, all the waterways have been continually expanded for greater

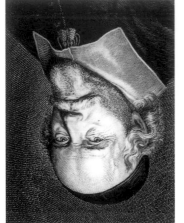

Under: Louys de Geer. His House of the Heads now serves as the Amsterdam Monument Protection office.

House of the Heads, built in the 17th century for Louys de Geer, an extremely wealthy arms dealer, is a flamboyant contrast to the more rigid neighboring house fronts. Legend is that a maid decapitated six thieves and married the seventh one.

The Amsterdam-Rhine Canal, opened in 1952, was a very important breakthrough, bringing the West German border to within 120 kilometers of the capital. This 65-kilometer-long 'back-door' route was deepened to some 5.5 meters by 1974. In the early eighties a widening project was completed. Annually, this canal handles over 100,000 vessels carrying some 42 million tons of cargo, making it one of the world's busiest manmade waterways. The Dutch inland waterway fleet is the world's largest and operates all over continental Europe's 4000 kilometers of rivers and canals.

carrying potential. Specialized harbors and storage facilities were added to the port complex.

Piet Hein, with dignitaries on board, cut the ribbon with its hull for the opening of the Amsterdam-Rhine Canal in 1952.

Automobile transport on the extensive waterways leading from the port of Amsterdam.

Port of Amsterdam continues
to expand as its gateway
function increases in
importance.

Three Mainports

Harbor, Schiphol, Teleport

G.C.G. *van der Heuvel*

EXECUTIVE DIRECTOR, PORT
MANAGEMENT OF AMSTERDAM

'The Amsterdam port region is a very significant and economic factor in the capital's balance sheet. Studies by the Netherlands Economic Institute revealed more being earned and achieved per ton per head here than in ports oriented purely to transport. With goods transshipment of 50 million tons per year, there is direct employment of 42,000 people and a turnover of circa 6.5 billion guilders. We are now ranked among the world's twenty largest port complexes.

'There are excellent opportunities for further economic growth and increased employment, particularly in port-oriented industries. By linking processing of goods to transport, transshipment and distribution, the Amsterdam port region's contribution to the economy will increase considerably. Likewise, we are seeking primary industries with environment-friendly activities.

'Economic growth depends upon long-term investment in infrastructure improvements, expansion of transport facilities, construction of business sites and the implementation of an umbrella management organization for the entire North Sea Canal region. Furthermore, national and local government authorities will have to develop more active policies to ensure our industrial growth.'

*A*msterdam is a three mainport gateway: Schiphol Airport, with KLM Royal Airlines as an integral partner in its global success, the Port of Amsterdam and Teleport — an extremely comprehensive air, sea and communications network. Together they provide transport and contact facilities unrivalled on the Continent. Located within a compact, highly accessible area of only 24 square kilometers, they jointly underscore Amsterdam's mainport function. Through its infrastructure facilities, Amsterdam plays a leading role in the European distribution industry: over three quarters of foreign companies with European headquarters in Amsterdam export goods from the Netherlands. The road, rail and inland waterway connections to the rest of Europe are excellent. Dutch truckers handle 30 percent of the European Community's cross-border road transport, while 60 percent of all inland water transportation is in the hands of Dutchmen.

Amsterdam lies at the center of the densely populated European Community Market, with 370 million inhabitants. By comparison, the United States of America has 250 million and Japan 125 million inhabitants.

The hectic daytime activity in the harbor is over, as evidenced by the cranes poised against the sunset.

The multi-functional port has
a smooth functioning
infrastructure and ultra
modern cargo handling
facilities. Raw materials such
as timber, might be stored or
handled for distribution to
another destination.

There are
scheduled shipping services to 150 ports in 90
countries. Amsterdam has ultra modern cargo-
handling facilities: roll-on/roll-off and
sideloading systems; oil, wine and liquid
chemical storage; container, grain, coal and ore
terminals; distribution areas and industrial plant
sites; and river, rail and highway links to
Europe's most important industrial centers.

Port of Amsterdam

Other highly-competitive ports stretching from
Hamburg to Le Havre handle 20 percent of the
world's seagoing goods traffic. In the nineties,
the Port of Amsterdam, Westpoort, located
within easy reach from the city, has emerged as a
bustling harbor. Amsterdam, and its neighboring
North Sea Canal ports of IJmuiden, Beverwijk
and Zaanstad, annually handle 50 million metric
tons of cargo, ranking the area as the fifteenth
largest seaport in the world and the fifth in
northwest Europe. The harbor has a clean
environment with no heavy, polluting
industries.

The North Sea Canal Ports generate circa 9
billion guilders annual business, while providing
employment for around 75,000 people. Towage
operations are among the essential services
required, with operations like Goedkoop
Havensleepdiensten, a firm specialized in the
vital tugboat assistance for large tankers and bulk
carriers for over 175 years.

Almost 9,000 ships annually berth in the
Amsterdam port region, with a joint
transshipment of 50 million tons. In the port area
there are over 2,000 stevedores employed, in the
total labor force of 42,000 people.

Amsterdam is the world's
largest cocoa harbor. Over
450,000 tons of cocoa are
received annually in
containers and sacks,
representing more than 20
percent of the world's annual
cocoa crop.

View of the western harbor area.

There is the smooth-functioning infrastructure: specialized terminals, modern distribution, transport centers and a large number of transport companies geared for fast and efficient distribution services covering all of Europe. As a multi-functional port, ideally located for European logistics, Amsterdam can fulfil all distribution requirements.

Amsterdam Westpoint, an international, multi-use storage and distribution center, is located in the Amerika Haven. This logistics center is within easy reach of ocean-going conventional and container vessels, feeders, inland waterway barges, rail and road cargo and, close by, air cargo. It is an ideal gateway to and from European markets. Cargo can be handled directly, either from vessel or warehouse on suitable transport for distribution, saving time and money. The logistics center offers a variety of warehouses (250,000 square meters) and 25,000 square meters of office facilities.

Westpoint has a 1000 meter sea quay, a special docking for inland navigation, with 300,000 meters of open storage room.

The municipality is developing a multi-million guilder face-lift of the old passenger terminal in order to meet Amsterdam's growing appeal as one of the most popular cruise harbors in Europe. The new International Passengers Terminal Amsterdam (IPTA) will consist of a gigantic, futuristic dome with a 50 meter span opening as a grand entrance hall, with tax free shopping, restaurants, tourist facilities, customs, and, possibly, check-in counters for Schiphol Airport. Next to it will be a multi-functional building, spread over 45,000 square meters, with a theater, conference rooms, offices, shops and a

tropical aquarium. There will also be parking space for the hundreds of touring buses which now clog the historic center.

Just as in past centuries, trading ships from all over the world are berthing at the Port of Amsterdam. It can accommodate vessels drawing up to 15 meters. Special deep-water port facilities outside the sealocks at IJmuiden handle dry bulk carriers with a draught of up to 19 meters. Large bulk carriers, mostly from North America, bring in cereals for transshipment throughout Europe.

Amsterdam serves as an outlet for Dutch exports centered on dairy products. After the United States, Holland is the world's second largest exporter of agricultural products. The city is also a gateway for foreign produce, including soy products, animal feed, grain and derivatives, as well as concentrated citrus juices.

Several port companies specialize in high value-added operations, ranging from upgrading oil products, coal and ore to the processing of minerals and assembling of electronic and other products. These companies process the incoming raw materials in the port itself, provide an added value to the Dutch economy of 9 billion guilders per year. It means that the Amsterdam port is one of the largest employers in the Netherlands.

Amsterdam is the world's largest cocoa harbor. Over 450,000 tons of cocoa are received annually in containers and sacks, representing more than 20 percent of the world's annual cocoa crop. The cocoa trade accounts for circa 10 percent of the jobs in the harbor, where a number of Amsterdam warehousing firms specialize in the storage and distribution of

H. Smits

PRESIDENT, AMSTERDAM SCHIPHOL
AIRPORT

'Our Corporate strategic goal is not to be the biggest, but Europe's best mainport. Though aviation will always be the foundation, the airport's non-aviation infrastructure is becoming increasingly important. First-class business centers, shopping malls like Schiphol Plaza, offices, hotels, conference rooms and adequate parking are essential for future growth.

'Mainport Schiphol's economic impact is felt far beyond our direct surroundings. The airport contributes, directly and indirectly, some 10 billion Dutch guilders to the economy, an equivalent of over 1.75 percent of Gross National Product. As we become a mainport in the European context, Schiphol-related earnings will contribute circa 30 billion Dutch guilders, some 2.8 percent of GNP.

'If you judge market place position by the number of EDCs (European Distribution Centers) set up by American or Japanese multinationals, we score well. Some 35 percent of all American distribution centers in Europe are located in the Netherlands. The Japanese have 40 percent of their EDCs here. Most importantly, we act as a magnet in attracting these clean industries, many close to Amsterdam Airport Schiphol.

'Increasing economic activity logically results in increased employment at the airport and its surroundings. Circa 37,000 people work at Schiphol. This will rise to 60,000 in the year 2015. Beyond the airport parameter, some 75,000 people depend directly or indirectly on aviation for their bread winning. An increase to at least 126,000 jobs is expected in 2015.'

---

cocoa. Holland has retained the dominant position since the 17th century in the global export of the three most important products from the cocoa bean. Through the years, there has been a very active Dutch cocoa association based in Amsterdam.

Amsterdam Schiphol Airport/KLM Royal Dutch Airlines

Amsterdam Schiphol Airport is located on land 4 meters below sea level, on the bottom of the Haarlem Lake, which was drained in 1852 and became a dry polder. On May 26, 1573, this was the dramatic setting for the bitter fight between the Spanish and Dutch fleets in the first large scale maritime action of the Eighty Years' War between the two countries. Hand-dug ring canals encircle the immense area where lake waters once roared and often flooded surrounding fields right up to Amsterdam's gates. A 1447 sea chart calls this area Schip Hol meaning Ship's Hole or Hell because of the many vessels lost here. Another explanation is that the name came into being when the words *scipua* (East Gothic for 'branch' or 'a cut piece of wood') and *hol* (a low-lying, marshy area) were joined together. Schiphol was thus the name of a low-lying wooded area. Other scholars in the field of nomenclature think that 'hol' refers to the depth of a ditch or river bed. That would indicate the passage of ships. 'Schiphol' might also be derived from *scheepshaal,* that is a slope over which vessels were dragged in earlier times. In the 19th century, a military fort was built on this site and took the name. An aviation center was built here, used the same name, and became one of Europe's safest havens for air ships. Two men were especially important in the early days of Dutch aviation: Anthony Fokker and Albert Plesman. Fokker was an imaginative aircraft designer and builder, while Plesman was the organizer and founder of KLM, the Royal Dutch Airlines. Right on Schiphol's grounds, a

First KLM flight to Brussels from Schiphol with a Fokker F3 in 1922. Pioneer Albert Plesman is in the middle of the group.

Fokker factory was established and still functions today. Between 1920 and 1934, almost the entire KLM fleet consisted of Fokker aircraft, which also made up two-thirds of the world's airline fleets. Schiphol Airport got its start in August 1916 as a military aerodrome during World War I. At the end of the war, there was a surplus of military aircraft. A number of businessmen wanted to use these machines for civil aviation. To interest the public in the possibilities of passenger air transport, two ex-Air Force officers, Plesman and Hofstee, organized an exhibition in Amsterdam in 1919. During this First Amsterdam Aero Exhibition, about 4000 visitors embarked on their first flight. Schiphol started commercial operations in May 1920, when KLM (founded in October 1919) began its first air service between London and Amsterdam, carrying two passengers and 15 kilos of cargo. The first aircraft was a De Havilland DH-16. KLM is the world's oldest existing airline.

By September 1920, besides its thrice-weekly London flights, KLM also had regular flights to Hamburg and Copenhagen. Civil aviation in the Netherlands was on its way. Airport authorities worked out of a small shed, formerly a military plane hangar. In that year, 440 passengers and some 50,000 pounds of mail and cargo were carried, but conditions were rather primitive. French pilots, fed up with sinking axle-deep into Dutch mud, dubbed it 'Schiphol-les-Bains'.

In 1926, the Municipality of Amsterdam, preparing for the 1928 Amsterdam Olympic Games, took over Schiphol administration from the government. Technical equipment was modernized, landing grounds improved and concrete aprons laid. A terminal building, large aircraft hangars and workshops, as well as wide approach roads, were built. It was Jan Dellaert, a former pilot, who became the first director. During his 40 years' management, until retirement in 1960, Schiphol developed into one of Europe's most modern airports.

The arrival of large numbers of the DC-2 and DC-3 in the early thirties was a watershed in aviation industry. They were the first light metal aircraft. KLM was one of the world's first airline companies — and first in Europe — to fly them. Almost 110,000 people travelled via Schiphol in 1938. In 1934, KLM had taken part in the London–Melbourne Air Races with a DC-2, winning first prize in the handicap section. In that same year, KLM covered the 10,488 kilometers separating Amsterdam from Surinam and Curaçao with a Fokker F. XVIII — and this became the start of the company's West Indies network.

A sister port relationship had already evolved between Amsterdam Schiphol Airport and Jakarta's National Airport. In 1929, KLM started a regular fortnightly service, which became a weekly service in 1931. Until the outbreak of

Arrival of the first KLM jet, a Douglas DC-8 at Schiphol Airport in 1960. The plane was named in honor of the KLM founder, Albert Plesman.

Aerial view (late 1995) of Schiphol Airport. While facilities are expanded, the 'one terminal' concept continues in this customer-friendly airport. Schiphol is regularly voted Europe's best airport.
Left: Schiphol Plaza shopping center successfully serves passengers but also attracts Dutchmen on weekends who make a day of shopping and observing the air traffic.
Right: New Schiphol terminals have been built in the continuing upgrading of client services. Rail and subway lines now come under the buildings for passengers' easy access.

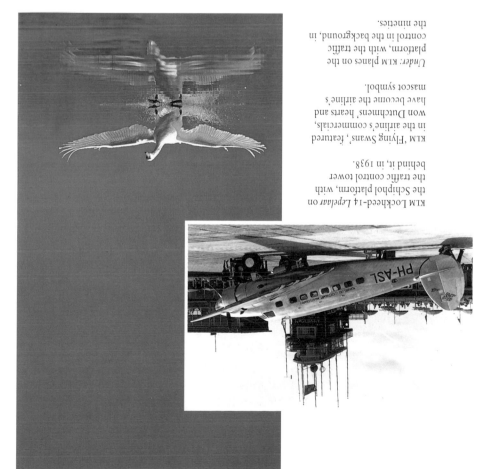

World War II, this was the world's longest air route.

On May 10, 1940, the bombs fell. The German Luftwaffe, after causing some damage, occupied the airfield. Then the Allies bombed Schiphol regularly in harassment of the enemy, until the end of 1944, when the Germans themselves blew up the airport. There was total ruin. Nothing remained.

Schiphol had to start all over. When the rubble was cleared within two months of the war's end, the first airliner could land. By November 1945, all runways were provisionally serviceable again and KLM could take off. In the same month, KLM's flights to Indonesia were resumed. In May 1946, KLM flew the first flight from Amsterdam to New York.

While KLM expanded its world routes, Schiphol resumed its importance as a port-of-call for many foreign airlines. It experienced a tremendous growth immediately after World War II. Plesman began rebuilding the airline. With the assistance of American President Harry Truman, he managed in 1945 to secure eighteen Douglas DC-4 'Skymasters' and some 30 DC-3 'Dakotas'. KLM was off again on its pioneering global air trails. Since then, new destinations have been added each year, building up today's

KLM Lockheed-14 Lodestar on the Schiphol platform, with the traffic control tower behind it, in 1938.

KLM 'Flying Swans', featured in the airline's commercials, won Dutchmens' hearts and have become the airline's mascot symbol.

Under: KLM planes on the platform, with the traffic control in the background, in the nineties.

P. Bouw

PRESIDENT, KLM ROYAL DUTCH
AIRLINES

'KLM and Mainport Schiphol must strengthen each other's capability to compete worldwide while safeguarding aviation's truly significant contribution to the Dutch economy. Look at the conglomeration of international firms focused around Schiphol.

'Our most substantial growth will be in mass tourism. This phenomenon only got underway in the seventies with the introduction of widebody aircraft. Though flying is becoming increasingly commonplace and undoubtedly cheaper, the majority of people are still far removed from being part of it. I foresee aircraft being developed to carry 800 to 900 passengers, twice the current maximum. The aircraft will be quieter too.

'I think KLM can play a major role in a world-embracing alliance, a Global Airline System. There's going to be a far greater distinction in passenger traffic between business and leisure travel. I expect a new fuel-efficient type of supersonic aircraft seating 200 to 300 passengers for the business market. The Concorde only carries 125 passengers.

'We will celebrate our first century as the world's first commercial airline in 2019. This is in the tradition of our 17th century United East India Company. We've always been a trading nation, great seafarers and road haulers, and now are great air transporters as well. KLM's strength and dynamism have been proven by the ability we have shown to meet the fundamental changes sweeping the industry head-on.'

route network to over 400,000 kilometers, linking 148 cities in 82 countries on six continents. More than 25,000 people are employed worldwide, including 5000 abroad. KLM has 350 offices in 250 cities in 94 countries. Its present fleet consists of nearly 100 aircraft, including those of the subsidiary KLM City Hopper. With an average age of 5.8 years, KLM's fleet is one of the youngest in the airline industry. KLM annually carries some 12 million passengers and circa 500,000 tons of cargo (turnover circa 9 billion guilders), thus ranking as one of the world's main passenger and freight transporters.

In a major strategic manoeuvre during the nineties, KLM joined forces with Northwest Airlines, forming the first truly global 'open skies' alliance. KLM and Northwest together have a worldwide network with synchronized schedules and a linked marketing program, offering over 350 destinations around the world in more than 80 countries on six continents. The two airlines' frequent flyer programs were combined to become the industry's best. The partnership also succesfully launched the World Business Class.

Though Schiphol had continually expanded and improved facilities in its old location on the eastern side of the dried-up lake, necessity meant starting anew in the sixties on another site in that polder land to keep pace with KLM and international airline traffic needs. Determined to remain a customer-friendly airport, Schiphol insisted that everything from architectural design to directional signing should underscore a welcoming, efficient attitude. The formula worked, as evidenced by the annual independent surveys among business and holiday travellers. In 1994, for the eleventh consecutive year, Schiphol was voted Europe's best airport. The 'one terminal' concept scores highly with transit passengers who don't have to shuttle to other areas.

Now, the 2000 hectare Schiphol terminal area is larger than New York's Kennedy Airport. The four runways, each about 3,300 meters in length, can carry aircraft weighing more than 400 tons. The terminal building, with separate levels for departures and arrivals, offers passengers all the luxuries of modern travel, from baby baths, Europe's best stocked, lowest priced tax-free shops to the world's first casino in a major airport, a joint venture with Holland Casinos, providing roulette, blackjack, slot machines and the Chinese dice game, Sic Bo.

Schiphol has a 'Junior Jet Lounge' for children traveling by themselves. Passengers can also tee-off on Schiphol's indoor golf simulator, with professionals on hand to give tips. The golf center is located behind the customs area in the

Teleport management

L.J. van Gelder, PROJECT MANAGER, CITY OF AMSTERDAM
T.B. Haeser, DIRECTOR, TELEPORT DEVELOPMENT
P.C. van Bladeren, PTT TELECOM

Confident that the Amsterdam Teleport will be Europe's most formidable telecommunications complex upon completion in the year 2010, the management team commented: 'This area has been realized in a unique cooperation between public and private sectors. Besides the many high quality buildings, Amsterdam Teleport continues to attract international, communication-sensitive businesses.

'By pioneering we've succeeded in creating a business center to meet the demands and requirements of the approaching era. The total telecommunication facilities offered in our call center have been recognized as unequalled, which attracted international firms to set up their European headquarters here. Concentrated activities within the Teleport area enhance Amsterdam's good business climate.'

west wing and is specifically aimed at transfer passengers. There is also a tax-free golf shop. The Schiphol Plaza shopping center, with its broad assortment, links the railway station to the terminal building, further increasing travellers' comfort. Schiphol Plaza has a remarkable, environment-friendly feature: an organic roof. Approximately 7000 square meters of grass lawn were planted on the slightly curved canopy covering the main hall. The turf is 25 millimeters thick, with 50 percent of it moss to facilitate drainage. The lawn is not only aesthetic but is also an effective energy-saving insulator.

Schiphol has excellent rail and road connections: a twenty-minute train ride to downtown Amsterdam's international railway terminal. There is easy accessibility to the national Amsterdam–The Hague–Rotterdam highway, with a cut-off close to the terminal building complex. Before the turn of the century, Schiphol will be linked to the TGV and ICE nets, the high speed French and German trains.

In the area surrounding the airport, there are 400 companies, including numerous non-EC companies, that benefit from Schiphol's very efficient 30,000 square meter bonded warehousing system which provides duty-free storage areas for transit shipments. There is also more than 50,000 square meters of shed space used by over 100 freight forwarders. With the world's largest flower auction in neighboring Aalsmeer, Schiphol handles an overwhelming number of flower and plant shipments every day. International trucking combinations offer road–air transport possibilities as part of the airport's

very successful distribution center function. Schiphol co-owns several business parks close to the airport, for operations which generate air traffic such as freight forwarders, European distribution centers and corporate headquarters. There are excellent hotel, meeting and telecommunication facilities in the area. A World Trade Center will open at Schiphol Airport in 1996. After Vienna, Schiphol will be the second international western airport with such a facility. The 27,000 square meter World Trade Center, to be connected directly to the airport's single terminal building, will function in cooperation with the Amsterdam WTC. As an international meeting point, accessible by plane, high speed train, bus and car, the center will have a five-story parking garage, four eight-story and four six-story office towers. Five-star Sheraton and Hilton hotels, office space and meeting facilities will be included in the 100,000 square meter Schiphol Business City complex. Schiphol developed as a leading European gateway, while KLM expanded its global network to become one of the world's main carriers, number five in air cargo and number eight in passenger transport. An amazing success story for the airline and the airport, both disproportionately large for the small country they represent.

Teleport

Amsterdam's Teleport development is based on the combination of real estate, urban planning and state-of-the-art telecom and facility management services. Located in the Sloterdijk area, its partners are Dutch PTT Telecom (telecommunications and facility management services), the municipality of Amsterdam (actual physical development of the site) and Teleport Development (real estate development and overall coordination). There is a comprehensive full-service office environment, combining the advantages of shared telecommunications with good real estate and centralized facility management services. When fully completed around the year 2010, some 25,000 people will work in an area spread over 100 hectares, with office space utilizing 600,000 square meters. Teleport is easily accessible by train, bus, tram or car. The train ride from Amsterdam Central station to Sloterdijk station takes five minutes and from Airport Schiphol thirteen minutes.

Amsterdam Teleport combines state-of-the-art telecom and facility management services. It has proven to be a prime location for European call centers and for communication-led companies.

Teleport has direct highway access, while the Amsterdam docks are nearby.

For reducing costs and improving customer satisfaction, Amsterdam Teleport has proven to be a prime location for European call centers and for communications-led companies. In order to compete in the single European market companies need expansion potential. Amsterdam Teleport offers extensive opportunities and one-stop shopping. In one meeting subjects can be discussed from ground lease to incentives, from available office space to telecommunication requirements. In cooperation with the City of Amsterdam and the buildings' owners,

Amsterdam Teleport offers all required support in research and/or facility planning free of charge.

Amsterdam Teleport's telecommunications infrastructure, capable of handling all forms of data transmission from voice to video to text, is among the most sophisticated available. This was a decisive factor for the Société Internationale de Télécommunication Aeronautique (SITA), which operates the world airline industry's computerized reservation system, in establishing its European headquarters at Amsterdam Teleport.

>Teleport, with Schiphol Airport and Amsterdam Port, is a key in the city's effective Three Mainports access. Communications-led companies, such as the Dutch PTT Telecom, are based here.

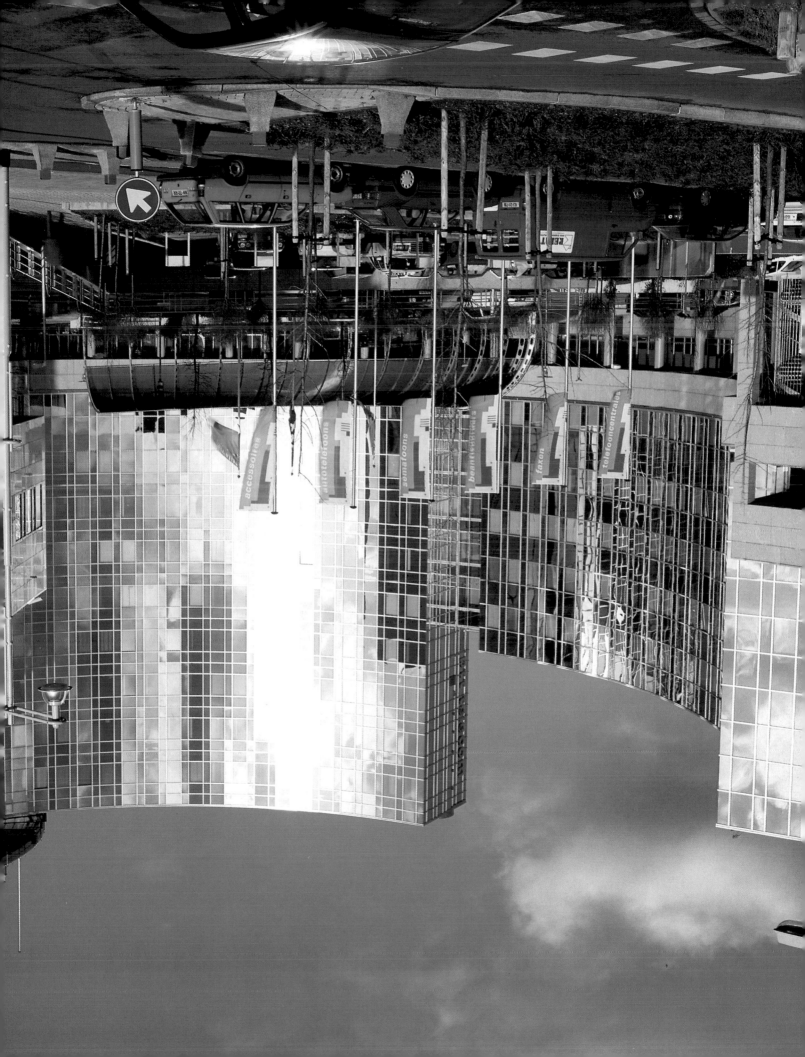

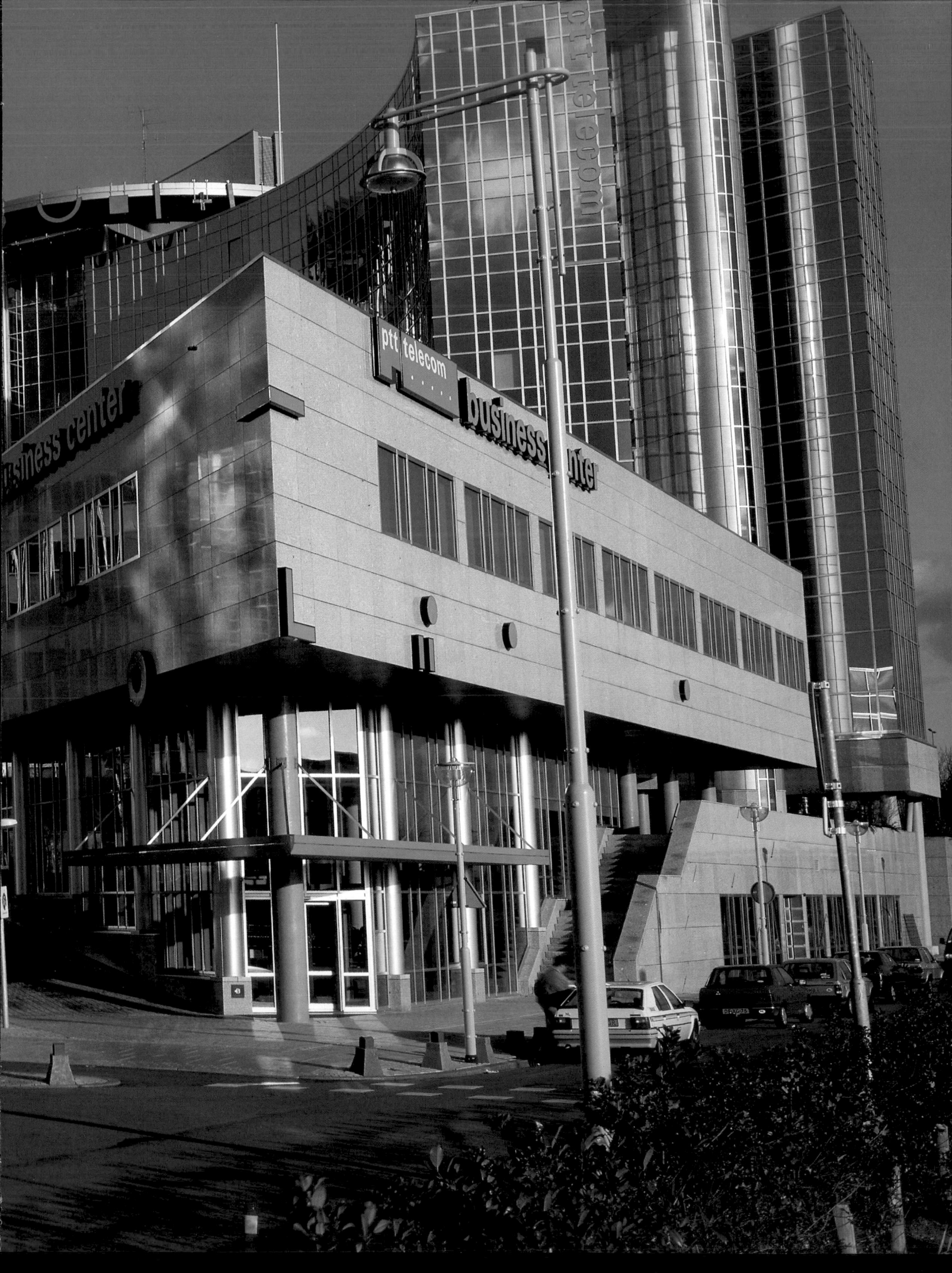

Business scene

International financial service center

*M*oney has been a driving motivation for Amsterdam's merchant princes right from the city founding over seven centuries ago — and that pattern has persisted until today. Amsterdam, with a work force of 650,000, has developed its long-standing international orientation with a focus on financial and commercial services, trade and tourism as the city's main economic activities. Trade, transportation and services together account for well over 50 percent of Dutch GNP, much of this generated by Amsterdam enterprises.

Amsterdam, a unique commercial center with unrivalled Euro access, ranks among the five best cities in Europe for a company location. The mercantile spirit is evident from the earliest records of enterprising seamen and the active commerce that prompted the granting of toll privileges in 1275. In a letter dated 1514, Amsterdam's burgomasters stated that the city's main occupation was trading and explorations to the East and West. Cornelis Anthoniszoon embellished the first ground plan in 1544 with the words: 'the renowned merchant city of Amsterdam.'

During the city's Golden era, its citizenry was reputed for hard bargaining and glossing over the niceties of business. Foreigners' uncomplimentary feelings were summed up by a 19th century British diplomat: 'In matters of commerce, the fault of the Dutch is offering too little and asking too much.'

When the East India Company was founded in 1602, Amsterdam's citizens could sign the company's stock registers and get a share in the daring enterprise. This was the first company in the world with a legal status similar to the present limited liability company. Its shares were the first ever to be traded on a public exchange.

Investors were then paid off in dividends (until 1796 the average annual dividend on the VOC shares was not less than 18 percent) of pepper and other spices brought back from the East by the company. These commodities were sold on the local market. Though these shares were made out in the individual buyer's name, a lively trade developed and marked the start of modern share trading, giving Amsterdam a claim as the world's oldest Stock Exchange. The Amsterdam Stock Exchange served as a model for many other stock exchanges.

At that time, trading took place in the primitive setting of shop porches, on the bridge over the Damrak and, in rainy weather, in the St. Olof's Chapel or the Old Church. The City Council saw the need for a proper building benefiting the growing commerce and commissioned Hendrik de Keyser to design an imposing Exchange. This was completed in 1611 on the Rokin as a tight link with the moneyed law-makers of the Town Hall, who were making Amsterdam into a rich, powerful city/state with worldly possessions. (The Exchange building was demolished in 1835 after it started to shake on its pilings and sink into the sandy base.) The arched passage in the area still retains the name Exchange Gateway.

In 1609, the Amsterdam Exchange Bank was founded by the municipal authorities to put an end to the chaotic monetary affairs that arose from the traders' far-flung dealings all over the world. Since a great deal of foreign money was in circulation, many money-changers and bankers withheld sound currency in order to force up the exchange rate. The Exchange Bank put an end to this and other manipulations, while encouraging merchants to pay by transfer. The bank soon developed into Europe's largest clearing house. From that time, Amsterdam became known as the place where acceptance

The Mint Tower on the Singel was used to coin money when a war in 1672 cut off the central supply. The crafty ruling regents had already conceived a double bookkeeping system in 1664 to maintain financial stability.

credit was applied on a large scale. The origin of modern international payment transfers can be traced to the city's initiative. In addition, Amsterdam developed into a high finance center after numerous prominent bankers began specializing in the emission of foreign loans, a field in which they acquired international reputations.

In an ode to the city's monetary genius, Adam Smith wrote in his classic *Wealth of Nations:* 'At Amsterdam ... no point of faith is better established than that for every guilder circulated as bank money, there is a correspondent guilder in gold or silver to be found in treasure of the bank ... each new set of burgomasters visits the treasure, compares it with the books, receives it upon oath and delivers it over, with the same awful solemnity, to the set which succeeds ...' Speculation was in the Amsterdam air. The same shares changed hands as many as five times a day. Lotteries were popular with all classes obsessed by winning money. Merchants filled their warehouses with goods that they bought cheaply when supplies were plentiful and held until a seller's market meant big profits. Amsterdam became known as the city in Europe where money could buy anything. When Genovese marble was desired for the building of Versailles, the French came to Amsterdam for the purchase. Amsterdammers were monopolizing markets and carrying goods with a calculated risk on re-

The Old Church was one of the sites where business was done before the first Exchange was built by Hendrick de Keyser on the Rokin in 1611.

OUDE-ZYDS CAPEL

sale when the time was opportune! (Precursor of the European Options Exchange.)

Perhaps even Calvinism fostered the money cult by preaching that man had a moral obligation to work as hard as possible — and bankruptcy was a prime sin.

When the war cut off the central money supply in 1672, Amsterdam minted its own in a rampart fortification that is still known as the Mint Tower. The crafty city fathers even devised a double bookkeeping system in 1664 (and kept it going until 1811) as a technical aid to staying financially stable.

The 17th century Amsterdam philosopher Baruch Spinoza summed up the situation with: 'In this flourishing republic, this city second to none, men of every nation and every sect live together in the utmost harmony; and all they bother to find out, before trusting their goods to anyone, is whether he is rich or poor and whether he is honest or a fraud.'

Anybody's money was welcome in Amsterdam. While the British fleet was battling the Dutch, their vessels were insured by Amsterdam brokers. That's the reason there wasn't always rejoicing after the Dutch won a sea battle. Dealing with the enemy was an established tradition. Amsterdammers were known for doing business on both sides whenever the Dutch Republic was involved in a conflict. Prosperity from world trade and financial dealings continued up to the last decade of the 18th century, when the French occupation began. Harbor activities then came to a standstill, commerce and industry were immobilized, unemployment reached gigantic proportions and thousands of people lived in squalor. The city lost its important foreign connections, its role as the staple market center and the carrying trade was taken over by others. By the time the French left in 1813, the Netherlands was in economic shambles — and the hardest hit was the newly-proclaimed capital city of Amsterdam.

After the liberation, Willem, Prince of Orange, became the sovereign. King Willem I earned a reputation as the 'merchant king' for his efforts to restore Amsterdam's economic life, beginning in 1814 with the establishment of the Netherlands Bank. He initiated many other efforts to revive the city's commercial life. A

number of institutions had run their course and ceased operations. The Exchange Bank, after functioning for more than 200 years, closed its doors in 1819. The East and West India Company division, the Tea Warehouse Masters, managed to continue its trade with China. In 1824, the Netherlands Trading Company was launched to regain the Dutch share of world trade and the great North Holland Canal was opened to give Amsterdam ships a direct and safer passage to the North Sea. In 1825, the Amsterdam Steamship Company was established on the former East India Company wharf on Kattenburg island, along with a company that developed into the Werkspoor Engineering Works. New road and waterway connections with the city were built and, in 1839, the Amsterdam-Haarlem railroad line started operating.

However, it took Amsterdam almost 50 years to really recover from the economic setback. (In retrospect this was a blessing, since Amsterdam's greatest architectural heritage was saved from demolition and monstrous modernization.) It was only during the second half of the 19th century that the city began to recoup its financial stability. More shipping companies were started with an eye to trading around the Mediterranean and Baltic Seas, as well as providing regular service to the United States and the Far East. Amsterdam regained its importance as a staple market. Companies were founded to operate plantations in the Netherlands' overseas colonies.

Recovery around the turn of the century laid the groundwork for Amsterdam's revival as a center for finance, stock trading, insurance, industry, ready-to-wear fashion, diamonds, commerce and freight handling. During the first decades of this century, Amsterdammers engaged in a feverish flurry of activity in all money-making spheres. Not since the Golden era, three centuries before, were so many people busy working for the city's economic resurgence — and their own financial gain.

The Amsterdam Stock Exchange

The Amsterdam Stock Exchange was a prime mover in the city's financial revival. Just as the 17th century had spawned powerful worldwide companies, the 20th century produced Philips, Royal Dutch, Unilever, AKZO and KLM — and

the Amsterdam Exchange assisted these firms in their global expansion. As the shares of these and other Dutch companies were introduced on more and more exchanges abroad, foreign investors showed interest in Dutch shares. As a result, the Amsterdam Stock Exchange evolved into an important international arbitrage center. A century earlier, the Amsterdam Stock Exchange played a key role in the reconstruction of the Dutch economy and, after 1850, redeveloped its foreign business, including financing large parts of American and Canadian railroad construction. By the first part of the 20th century, the Amsterdam Stock Exchange also developed into the leading market for American securities outside of the United States, when numerous certificates of American shares were introduced here.

The second Exchange, a neo-Greek classic mercantile temple, was built by the architect Zocher on the site of the old fish market on the Dam. Opened in 1845, it was demolished 60 years later when the structure, like its predecessor, started to sink in its sandy base. The site was sold for 825,000 guilders for a modern department store patterned on those in Paris and London. The Dam merchants panicked at the prospect of this competition and attempted to block the sale. An agitated Amsterdam group raised 825,000 guilders in three days and presented the money to the Town Hall. They wanted the land used for a Colonial Institute and Museum that was being moved from Haarlem to the city that had most profited from colonial trade. This was to be a monumental structure in the heart of Amsterdam. The city fathers did not budge in their decision to bring new business to the Dam and used the collected money for the

The Amsterdam Stock Exchange, bustling more than ever with modernized techniques and systems, under the watchful eye of Mercurius.

Baron B.F. van Ittersum

CHAIRMAN, AMSTERDAM STOCK
EXCHANGE

'After a major restructuring program designed to
strengthen our position as the international market
for Dutch securities, we introduced Trading System
Amsterdam (TSA) in October 1994. The strategic
thinking behind TSA immediately paid off as two
dealing systems, separating and simultaneously
interlinking the wholesale and retail markets, took
effect. Likewise, the jobbers' role with the retail
markets provided an American style stock specialist
service, while computerized, screen-based dealing
for the wholesale markets was introduced.
'Those changes, which expanded the Exchange's
capacity, efficiency and accessibility, followed the
previous year's introduction of the Amsterdam
Treasury Bond Market (ATM). This unequivocally
demonstrated cheaper, faster and easier dealing in
Dutch government bonds.

'The Bourse has never been healthier or more
optimistic as turnover record levels are regularly
surpassed and the 1 trillion guilder barrier was
broken. It has become extremely attractive for
companies to seek a Dutch listing, as well as for
overseas investors to seek access to companies
quoted on the Amsterdam Exchange.

'Our new system will give us a competitive edge
and position of strength to meet foreign
competitive challenges when the scheduled
harmonization of European securities markets
becomes operative'.

De Bijenkorf, the first Dutch
department store, was built on
the Dam site, though
opponents wanted this
location for the Colonial
Institute and Museum when it
moves from Haarlem.

Institute of the Tropics which was built in the
town's eastern quarter. Thus the country's first
grand department store, de Bijenkorf (the Bee
Hive), was built on the Dam.
In 1896, the municipality of Amsterdam
commissioned the architect Berlage to build a
new (third) Exchange on the Damrak. The
securities business took place in this building.
But in 1913, the Association of the Amsterdam
Stock Exchange (ASE) opened its own Exchange,
the Effectenbeurs, designed by architect
Cuypers, where it still operates. The old
Exchange now serves as a cultural and exhibition
center.
Annually, circa 1,600 different stocks and bonds
are traded, among which some 400 foreign
bonds and shares. More than 100 American
companies are listed on the ASE. The ASE has a
strongly international profile with around 45
percent of total market value owned by non-
Dutch institutions and individuals. The
European Community countries, other
European nations, North and South America,
Australia and Asia are strongly represented in this
trading. Since many large Dutch companies
listed on the Stock Exchange make the bulk of
their turnover abroad, investments made on the
Amsterdam Stock Exchange have a very
international character.

In its pre-eminent European position as one of
the leading international capital markets,
Amsterdam attracts a never-ending flow of
foreign companies wanting to be listed, with
Japanese, American and British firms among the
largest number, as well as a few French

companies. Dozens of foreign security companies set up operations in Amsterdam in view of the city's strength as an international financial center. Characterizing this was the decision by Yamaichi in the seventies to operate here soon after the Japanese Finance Ministry gave approval for security companies to do commercial banking business abroad. Their Amsterdam office was opened as the first fully-owned company within the worldwide Yamaichi Group to go into this business. The Japanese, as so many other foreigners, were encouraged by the liberal Netherlands Central Bank regulations, which offer clients a complete range of financial services. Three of Japan's four biggest stockbrokers are located in Amsterdam in order to serve over 150 Japanese firms established in the Netherlands. Only a few are listed on the ASE or participate in syndicated loans. Some 30 Japanese companies are listed on the Amsterdam Stock Exchange, most with their original shares.

Amsterdam is fifth in terms of turnover among Europe's stock exchanges, after London, Paris, Frankfurt and Zurich, and, worldwide, in ninth place. A small comparison: while German GNP is five times that of the Netherlands, the German Stock Exchange is only twice the size of the Amsterdam Stock Exchange. Amsterdam's average investment profit during the last decade was only surpassed by the Hong Kong Stock Exchange.

European Options Exchange

The European Options Exchange (EOE), based in an ultra-modern building close to Dam Square, was Europe's first when it was founded in April 1978. The Amsterdam EOE, Europe's fifth biggest options exchange, ranks twelfth in the world, ensuring liquidity and price competitiveness. The demand for a regulated market in options listed on an exchange has increased tremendously: average daily turnover has risen from less than 1000 contracts in 1978 to 53,000 in the mid-nineties.

Options are traded on Dutch stocks, Dutch stock indices, Dutch state loans, currencies, precious metals and a pan-European Index. Annual EOE options turnover averages some 700 million guilders on a total of around 11 million options contracts.

J.Ch.L. Kuiper

GENERAL DIRECTOR, EUROPEAN OPTIONS EXCHANGE (EOE)

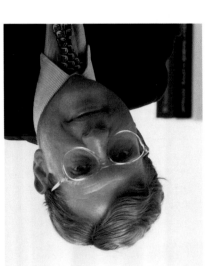
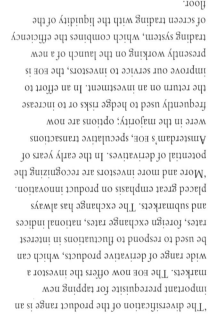

'The diversification of the product range is an important prerequisite for tapping new markets. The EOE now offers the investor a wide range of derivative products, which can be used to respond to fluctuations in interest rates, foreign exchange rates, national indices and submarkets. The exchange has always placed great emphasis on product innovation.

'More and more investors are recognizing the potential of derivatives. In the early years of Amsterdam's EOE, speculative transactions were in the majority; options are now frequently used to hedge risks or to increase the return on an investment. In an effort to improve our service to investors, the EOE is presently working on the launch of a new trading system, which combines the efficiency of screen trading with the liquidity of the floor.

'The EOE will continue to be the place where the supply and demand for derivatives meet in a well-regulated, transparent market. On the exchange, an investor can monitor changes in the value of his positions on a day-to-day, minute-by-minute basis. Risk can be adequately calculated at any given moment.'

Amsterdam's top two financial institutions — the Stock and Option Exchanges — now present a united front, boosting the Dutch capital's role in the competitive world of international finance. The first important step was the launch of a joint equity index on the first day of trading in January 1994.

This Amsterdam EOE-Index (abbreviated to 'AEX'), is used by both the Amsterdam Stock Exchange and the EOE. It is a reliable measure representing all important sectors of the Dutch economy: transportation, food, electronics, energy, banking, insurance, chemicals and publishing.

The AEX gives a weighted average of the 25 major and most actively traded Dutch stocks, selected annually on the basis of effective turnover during the past three calendar years on the Amsterdam Stock Exchange. These 25 stocks represent 80 percent of total market capitalization of the Dutch stocks quoted on the Amsterdam Stock Exchange, according to its chairman, Baron Boudewijn van Ittersum, who commented: 'The two markets are increasingly seen by investors as being complementary. This

is something which the two exchanges and their members must take advantage of.

Options and futures have been successfully traded on the EOE-Index since the late eighties. The Index likewise measures and compares the performance of Dutch share portfolio performances, making risks controllable and manageable.

Insurance

Amsterdam has been a major international insurance center since 1585 when the first premiums were noted in the open air exchange. Present day high tech dealing takes place in the Amsterdam Insurance Exchange, built in 1989 across from the World Trade Center. In this Exchange — the first such building in over four centuries — some 30 underwriters and insurance companies, as well as the Dutch Insurance Exchange Association (VNAB), are actively involved with co-insurance. The traditional form of co-insurance has existed since the Golden Age when cargoes of coffee and spices on the East India Company ships were covered, whereas today the risk factors are container transport or super tankers, drilling islands and chemical installations, environment responsibility and high tech companies. The common denominator is either the enormity or the special character of the risk requiring a number of insurers to become involved for underwriting in its entirety at the Exchange. The VNAB handles the entire administrative information flow for the Dutch co-insurance market. Besides local companies, there are many foreign firms among the risk-takers with an equity in the Dutch insurance operations.

The European Options Exchange, opened as the first of its kind on the Continent in 1978, has retained an influential position. Close cooperation with the Amsterdam Stock Exchange strengthens their joint trading position.

'three mainports' and prestige positioning are important factors, a prime motivation, unquestionably, is the low corporate taxation rate.

In this internationally-oriented city, educational facilities keep pace with the incoming foreign executives' requirements. The International School of Amsterdam (ISA), with some 550 pupils from 38 countries, has programs based on the Anglo-Saxon model, with English and Dutch as compulsory subjects. Graduates complete their education with an international baccalaureate, recognized for university admission in most countries.
A new 30 million guilder complex, with 5 million guilder municipal underwriting, accommodates 700 students, when it opens in late 1995.
There are also British, French and Japanese schools in Amsterdam, plus the Korean Saturday school in neigboring Amstelveen.

Left: The Insurance Exchange, opened in 1989, near the Amsterdam World Trade Center, is the first collective building despite more than four centuries' trading. In house: over 30 insurance companies.

Foreign companies

Foreign companies have also found Amsterdam an ideal operational base, especially after the Common Market was established. Holland offers favorable fiscal regulations and has more foreign tax treaties than any European country. Close to 600 foreign firms have set up operations around the capital, among which 150 Japanese, 270 American and 30 Asian companies. They have manufacturing, marketing and distribution facilities, centered close to Schiphol, the port, plus several other prime locations throughout the city.

Amsterdam has become European headquarters for circa 160 international corporations. While comparatively low rents, geographical advantages, local workforce's linguistic facility,

H. Grosveld

DIRECTOR OF ECONOMIC
DEVELOPMENT, MUNICIPALITY
OF AMSTERDAM

'As far as Continental competition is concerned, Amsterdam's economic structure is dependent for some 50 percent on large-scale, internationally operating manufacturers and activities in the trade and transportation sector. The percentage is far higher if you incorporate spin-off effects in the commercial service sectors as a result of international trading activity.
'In the last five years, some 60 to 70 Asian companies, primarily Japanese, have entered the European market via Amsterdam. This can produce a chain effect throughout Asia. A Korean Business Center is operational. In the year 2000, I expect the Taiwanese to be even more visibly present in Amsterdam and, possibly, there will be companies from Thailand, Malaysia and China.
'Positioning of European company head offices presents both opportunities and threats for Amsterdam. A country choice has a lot to do with economic and political stability, facile continental and intercontinental travel and the fiscal climate. In this respect, Amsterdam is interesting for the establishment of European support centers, headquarters and holding companies, ranking among Europe's five most preferred cities today. Amsterdam's Euro Access is a key pluspoint for doing business on the Continent.'

Industrial versatility

Few of the world's major cities can match Amsterdam's operational versatility — over 3,500 industries employing more than 30,000 people — with the metal industry as the nucleus. The footwear and ready-to-wear industries, employing some 14,000 people, have always been important. Chemical and pharmaceutical industries abound.

The printing trade, with some 4,500 employees, has been a traditional Amsterdam craft through the centuries. There are liquor and Dutch gin factories and distilleries, cocoa and chocolate producing plants, leather and rubber processors and manufacturers, furniture makers, electrical engineering works, the building trade, as well as the revitalized diamond industry.

Other products manufactured in Amsterdam include airplanes, computers, diesel engines, energy-saving devices, food, generators, hydraulic pumps, chewing gum, stained-glass windows, tobacco products, sunflower seed oil and offshore equipment. Amsterdam's industry is also characterized by many small workshops located all over town. The capital's many-sided industrial enterprises led to numerous technical training schools, unequalled elsewhere in the Netherlands. Industrial research is also carried out on a major scale.

Amsterdam Science Park, located on a 49-acre site in the Watergraafsmeer, will bring the business world and the scientific community closer together, eventually employing up to 10,000 people. Scientists and technicians can commercially exploit the research and spin-off. In the first development phase, the Matrix

The Netherlands Central Bank has its national headquarters in the heart of Amsterdam. Initiated by King Willem I in the early 19th century, the Bank gradually became the banker to the Dutch banks. The Bank's interest rate influence Dutch interest rate levels.

Dr. W.F. Duisenberg

PRESIDENT, THE NETHERLANDS BANK

'Like the other countries of Continental Europe, the Netherlands is recovering from the recession and is groping its way towards renewed sustainable economic growth. Recent research, covering more than 100 countries, suggests that, in the long run, economic growth is dampened by inflation and stands to benefit most from sound fiscal policies in the sense of lower public deficits and from a stable monetary environment. It is essential that policy makers should consistently set their sights on the creation of sound conditions for economic and monetary development, meaning sound public finance, moderate wage movements, appropriate and stable exchange rates and a monetary expansion geared to the real growth trend of production at no or very low inflation. Steady perseverance in the pursuit of such a firm and consistent policy should lessen uncertainty and thus contribute to economic recovery.'

Banking

With the head offices of more than 30 Dutch banking institutions and some 50 branches and twenty representative offices of foreign banks, Amsterdam is one of Europe's leading financial centers. The Netherlands Central Bank has its headquarters here. Over 60,000 people work in the capital's banking industry, with its a centuries-old international tradition.

After the French occupation came to an end, the country was brimming with worthless French paper money, assignats. Trade, the very pivot of the economy, came to a virtual standstill while the existing credit system did not boost economic activity. After King Willem I had initiated the Netherlands Bank, enterprises and private individuals could take up credit through the purchase (discount) of bills of exchange or against collateral of securities and goods. The Bank was not permitted to grant unsecured credit. It was also charged with stimulating the circulation of money through the issue of banknotes. Consequently, the Bank's credits were mostly paid out in banknotes, which could be exchanged for gold and silver coins. However, bitter memories of the assignats made the general public distrustful of paper money. Public confidence was gradually won since the Bank started backing the banknotes with precious metals.

The Bank also began trading in coins and bullion and managing the government's receipts and payments, becoming cashier to the government. In the second half of the 19th century, new and dynamic commercial banks emerged, gradually taking over the Bank's lending to industry and the general public. The use of book entry money was then still in its infancy. Credit was usually taken up in the form of banknotes. In order to obtain these banknotes, the budding banks themselves were compelled to obtain credit from the Netherlands Bank, which gradually became the banker to the banks. Through the interest rate which the Bank charges for its loans, it can exercise an influence on interest rate levels in the Netherlands.

Gold reserve at the Netherlands Bank.

In the seventies, there was a widespread internationalization of Dutch banking. Moreover, many Western banks, viewing Amsterdam as a 'bridge' for reaching across the Continent and entry into the Common Market, opened offices. With all the major Dutch banks here, the city, rediscovered' as a major international financial center, also attracted far-flung institutions.

The BCA Bank Europe NV (Bank Central Asia), part of the Salimgroep, incorporating some 500 companies employing over 200,000 people, opened an office in Amsterdam. The BCA Bank, building has 21 companies which are involved in science, technology, biology, physics and computer research.

P.J. Kalff

CHAIRMAN OF THE NETHERLANDS
BANKERS ASSOCIATION AND
CHAIRMAN OF THE BOARD OF
MANAGING DIRECTORS OF ABN
AMRO BANK

'The Dutch banking system has a good international reputation.

'Following the Dutch banking system's internationalization in the seventies, the eighties was a decade of mergers. Some banks affiliated with insurance companies, resulting in the creation of insuring banks, with the Netherlands in the European forefront. The Dutch regulatory system for combined banks and insurance companies was taken as a model for European legislation in this field.

'The Dutch banking system has always been very internationally oriented. The Nederlandsche Handel-Maatschappij, for instance, one of the banks from which ABN AMRO Bank developed, had a branch in Jakarta in Indonesia as early as 1825. In 1859 it was the first foreign company to open a branch on the island of Deshima. Today almost half of the bank's staff, for example, works abroad.

'Another aspect of Amsterdam's international nature as the "financial gateway to Europe" is with a strong home base in Indonesia, has a major international network.

'The Amsterdam office of the Russian Stolichny Bank is the first of its kind in Western Europe. It serves companies as well as private individuals. Stolichny Bank has 30 Moscow branches.

'Amsterdam is also home to five Taiwanese banks: the Chang Hwa, the Bank of Taiwan (Europe), Chiao Tung Bank Europe, the International Commercial Bank of China and the Medium Business Bank of Taiwan. These banks all concentrate not only on trade finance but also on developing their loan businesses — largely Taiwanese subsidiaries and Chinese restaurants. They are also involved in exchange dealing, inter-bank business and trade in international markets.

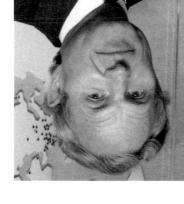

the fact that a lot of foreign banks have branches or offices in the Netherlands. Being the financial capital of the Netherlands, Amsterdam is an attractive location for foreign banks. The Amsterdam Institute of Finance also functions as an international training center for potential top banking officials from all over the world.

'Whereas many other countries have separate organizations for different types of financial institutions, in the Netherlands virtually all the commercial banks, cooperative banks, mortgage companies, savings banks and investment credit institutions are united in a single organization. This is in the interest of the entire banking industry.'

Services

Naturally, Amsterdam has all the commercial, legal, financial and administrative services required to support its bustling financial hub. Amsterdam's commercial services include: accountancy and auditing firms (circa 1,000), economic consultants (950), engineering companies (700), computer services (600), real estate agencies/brokerages (500), law firms (300), press/communication services (175) and advertising agencies (75).

Most operations also serve customers outside the Amsterdam region and internationally. The trend for international cooperation has made the business services sector of great importance for the Amsterdam region's economic development. Many service operations are situated in the southeast, Sloterdijk and new south, close to the World Trade Center.

The 35-floor, 135-meter-high Rembrandt Tower, near the Amstel station, is the city's tallest commercial building with 30,000 square meters of office space.

Business leaders dine and confer at the exclusive, members-only De Industrieele Groote Club in the curious Industria building dating from 1913 in the inner city heart at Dam 27. The prestigious Amstel Club, with an extensive network of national business leaders, has a very diversified program, organized from its handsome club rooms in the Amstel Hotel.

RAI Exhibition and Congress Center

Situated at European crossroads, Amsterdam has through the centuries attracted buyers and sellers. Nowadays the capital city annually draws some 2.5 million visitors to its RAI Exhibition and Congress Center. This state-of-the-art complex has under one roof 87,000 square meters exhibition space in eleven multifunctional, air conditioned halls, as well as 22 fully equipped conference areas that can accommodate over 10,000 delegates. With circa 1100 congresses, symposia and performances organized annually, along with 75 exhibitions and trade fairs, the RAI regularly fills Amsterdam's 29,000 hotel beds.

Some 400 people are employed directly and another 800 indirectly, while visitors' spin-off spending on taxis, hotels, restaurants, bars,

florists, theaters and nightclubs is estimated at 600 million guilders.

Additionally there are revenues from conference fees, exhibition space, services, facilities, entry tickets, parking, food and beverage collected directly by the RAI.

The authoritative Union of International Associations ranks Amsterdam among the world's top ten international conference venues. Generally some 40 percent of the most prestigious conferences are medically oriented. The RAI's high tech facilities include a satellite-linked video system, which can transmit live broadcasts of surgical operations held in Amsterdam's Academic Medical Center. Also there is a chipcard voting system for rapid assessment of audience response.

The RAI is in the city's southern area, close to the Beatrix Park, within walking distance of hotels and the World Trade Center. From Airport Schiphol to the RAI station is an eight-minute train ride. Trams, busses, subways and taxis are nearby. Space for 2650 cars is provided below the complex in the country's largest underground garage. The RAI is just off the Amsterdam ring road linked with the European motorway network into Germany, Belgium and France.

A.A.L. Minken

MANAGING DIRECTOR, RAI EXHIBITION AND CONGRESS CENTER

'Though ranked in a relatively modest position among middle-sized Dutch companies in terms of turnover and staffing, the Amsterdam RAI's reputation and image surprisingly soar afield in this country and abroad. This is truly remarkable since our facilities and congress center are not the world's largest, nor even the biggest in the Netherlands. Nevertheless, the RAI's authority and influence in international commerce, industry and science has global impact.
'In the Netherlands, the RAI has been synonymous for over 100 years with exhibitions and trade shows. The first RAI exhibition was held in Amsterdam in 1895. Therefore, in the public mind, the Amsterdam RAI is often identified with the extraordinary developments in science, industry and technology which occurred in the ensuing century.

'Exhibitions and trade shows have had a demonstrable and undeniable influence on the purchasing preferences of private consumers and industry, as well as commerce at large. They drive the proliferation of new products and services in many fields. And, in this sense, act as an economic stimulus which, inevitably, has a wider social impact.'

The RAI complex, with eleven multifunctional exhibition halls and a congress center, annually draws some 2.5 million visitors.
The RAI Congress Center, hosts many medically oriented congresses. A satellite-linked video system is capable of transmitting live broadcasts of surgical operations in Amsterdam's Academic Medical Center.

World Trade Center

Amsterdam's World Trade Center (WTC) was opened in 1985. It has over 53,000 square meters of fully equipped office space (from 60 square meters upwards), meeting rooms, exhibition space, banks, a post office, café, coffee shop and restaurants, Trade Information Center, shopping arcade, World Trade Center Club and parking facilities for 1200 cars. Secretarial, translator and interpreter services are available. Excellent communication facilities link the WTC in ten minutes with Airport Schiphol by rail or highway and the city center is equally accessible. In the late 1990s, three new office towers, with a 100,000 square meter surface, will be added to the present four gleaming steel blue WTC towers. The WTC houses 350 companies with a total of 2500 employees of 30 nationalities. Every day 3500 to 6500 people visit the complex. Rolf Draak, the dynamic director of the Amsterdam World Trade Center from soon after its inception, has been responsible for the successful developments as well as the planned expansion at the end of this decade. Draak is also the driving force of the second World Trade

World Fashion Center

Four towering buildings, spread over 3 hectares, form the gigantic World Fashion Center (WFC), located on the ring road encircling Amsterdam's city center like a necklace.

The World Fashion Center was established in 1968 to provide Dutch garment manufacturers and wholesale traders with the infrastructure and facilities necessary to design, show and sell their products under one roof. Fifty percent of the 1400 Dutch fashion businesses are headquartered here. Approximately 550 wholesalers and importers, collectively representing over 1200 brand names from some 40 countries, have their showrooms/offices in the WFC complex. Annually more than one million buyers visit the center.

Retailers from the United Kingdom, Germany, Benelux and Scandinavia buy on a cash-and-carry basis, one of the WFC's main attractions. Many of the businessmen in the WFC have foreign origins, with 10 percent of the tenants

Center to be opened at Schiphol Airport in 1996.

The Amsterdam World Trade Center, open since 1985, has four office towers housing some 350 companies from 30 countries with more than 2,500 employees. The success of this World Trade Center will be mirrored in the new Schiphol WTC to be opened in 1996.

from Turkey, Morocco and Asia.

Amsterdam's WFC is the oldest and largest of eighteen fashion centers in western Europe. There is no comparable fashion complex on a single site anywhere else in the world. Apart from clothing, merchandise offerings also include shoes, belts, sports clothing, sunglasses, leatherware and accessories. The WFC is a comprehensive lifestyle center, where anything that can be worn is sold.

Immigrant entrepreneurs

Amsterdam business has opened its doors for immigrant entrepreneurs. The hotel and restaurant trade has the largest number, with some 1300 out of a total work force of 4300. The number of other branches in which they are heavily represented is growing. Activities in trade are no longer limited to the retail sector (close to 1000). Nowadays more foreign-born residents operate businesses in the wholesale sector (circa 1000). In the industrial sector, there are roughly 300, in the business service sector 100, in other service sectors 375, and an additional 300 foreign entrepreneurs.

Industrial companies (most of them in the ready-to-wear sector) are run by Turkish entrepreneurs. Construction companies have Italian management, as do most ice cream parlors. Pharmacies are run by Vietnamese. Money exchange offices are to a large extent in the hands of Indians and Egyptians. Indians and Pakistanis are very well represented in the textile trade. Egyptians are active in the snackbar industry, Moroccans in the coffee shops. A large number of Ghanese work in the trade sector, while Chinese entrepreneurs run restaurants, as do a large number of Italians. Many Surinamers work in the insurance industry, real estate and service sectors.

About 1000 of these Amsterdam residents stem from Surinam and the Netherlands Antilles, an equal number from Turkey, 900 from the north African countries, 450 from southern Europe and about 1750 from various other countries.

Tourism

Money-making is done on all levels in Amsterdam, from ten picturesque daily and four weekly street markets to hundreds of off-beat

Tourism, one of Amsterdam's primary sources of income, accounts for some two billion guilders annual revenue, with employment provided for some 20,000 people. A modernistic passengers' terminal for cruise ships is being realized.

J.E. Moreu

DIRECTOR, VVV AMSTERDAM
TOURIST OFFICE

'There are many positive developments which will foster increased tourism. Expansion of Amsterdam Schiphol Airport to become one of Europe's leading "mainports", with the TGV link-up to Paris, London and Frankfurt, will be an invaluable stimulant. European city tourism will flourish with faster rail connections.

'In the historic inner city, many underground garages will be built, making parked cars on the street something of the past. This will enhance the exceptional architectural inheritance of the concentric web of our 17th century canals.

'By the turn of the century, while everyone will still first flock to the center, the Museumplein will become even more appealing. After expansion of the Rijksmuseum, Van Gogh Museum and Stedelijk Museum of Modern Art, and completion of underground parking facilities, this cultural square will be face-lifted into a pedestrian-only green enclave with gardens, paths and recreational areas.

'Also around the year 2000, Tourport Amsterdam is planned. This will welcome passengers arriving on cruise ships, sightseeing boats and excursion buses. This terminal, to be situated on the IJ harbor just behind the Central Station, will have a handling capacity of 3 million passengers annually. This impressive addition to our tourism infrastructure will, in itself, also become a fascinating attraction.'

Early Heineken posters, using a traditional Dutch image, contributed to the company's successful positioning as the most popular imported beer in the United States.

fashion boutiques, art galleries and antique shops that have mushroomed all over town. Major pedestrian shopping streets, business centers and bustling department stores make this city the Netherlands' shopping mecca. Buying fever infects foreign visitors who love the city's myriad offerings. Unprecedented numbers come to shop and sightsee in the monumental center. Since the advent of the jet age, tourism has become big business. Today Amsterdam ranks as the seventh most popular European destination.

The tourist industry is one of Amsterdam's main sources of income and employment, annually generating circa 2 billion guilders and providing employment for 20,000 people in hotels and restaurants, shops, the service sector and museums. Incoming tourism to the Dutch capital underscores Amsterdam's international image. Day tourism is a growing trend accounting for about 10 million visitors annually and generating approximately 1 billion guilders in revenue.

The cruise industry contributes importantly to tourism income: annually over 100,000 cruise tourists come to Amsterdam, 60,000 from overseas and the rest on Rhine cruises.

Tourists can select lodgings in all price and comfort categories from camping, youth hostels to the luxury five-star hotels. Among the 900 dining possibilities, having dinner can be as simple as a snack from a street automat set in the wall or at a herring stall on the canal to the most elegant Michelin-star restaurants.

Amsterdam, world famed as a city of diamonds, has some 1000 persons employed in this industry, which accounts for an annual turnover of around half a billion guilders. The Amsterdam Diamond Exchange has circa 200 members. One million visitors tour the diamond works every year. Promoting the country's most popular attraction, the VVV Amsterdam Tourist Office works on a tight budget with a dedicated staff. Though the Dutch capital's unique charm has been a magnet for centuries, new destinations and shifting vacation patterns have wrought increased competition. To assure its continuing, significant support to the Amsterdam economy, the VVV Amsterdam Tourist Office, in cooperation with KLM and the Netherlands Board of Tourism, regularly creates cultural theme events which resound in global success.

Beer

Before coffee and tea were introduced in the 18th century, Amsterdammers' favorite drink was beer. Researchers believe that from 1300 to 1650 the average annual beer consumption per capita in the Low Countries was between 400

R.S.L.M. de Vilder

PRESIDENT OF THE AMSTERDAM CHAMBER OF COMMERCE AND INDUSTRY

'On a national level, we play a special role. When you think of Holland, you think automatically of Amsterdam. We are the showroom of the Netherlands. Chambers must lobby to promote an improved business environment. We lobby the city governments on behalf of the business community for better roads, airports, services. Simultaneously, we lobby the national government for improvements to the total infrastructure.

'Of prime importance is strengthening our position as a leading distribution center, with Schiphol Airport, the expanding port activities and road/rail transportation facilities. Tourism, emerging as a leading motor of the economy, must be supported with civic improvements, while we project a positive image to make Amsterdam even more attractive. This is true, of course, also in gaining foreign companies' confidence in investing here.'

The Amsterdam Chamber of Commerce and Industry

The Amsterdam Chamber is the vital link to all of the Dutch capital's business sectors, including finance, tourism, trade, services, communication and transportation. Over 70,000 companies, 12,000 foundations and 6,000 associations, representing 12 percent of the country's business, are logged in the regional Trade Register, making Amsterdam the largest of the Netherlands' 32 chambers of commerce. Likewise, the Amsterdam Chamber, with its 240 employees, is the leading model for the 'Enterprise House' concept in which the chamber hosts and coordinates numerous services to industry and trade, particularly small businesses, under one roof.

The Amsterdam Chamber's trade information and promotion departments maintain a worldwide network with sister chambers. Beyond the European Community, they set up trade clubs and associations in Central and Eastern Europe, Japan, the People's Republic of China, Indonesia and Suriname, with trade missions to most of these destinations. Several thousand enquiries received annually from all over the world are handled via computerized trade searches to match them with potential Dutch importers.

As an untiring mercantile director, Rob de Vilder, chamber president, is virtually 'Mr. Amsterdam'. He was also elected president of Eurochambres by delegates of 1,300 chambers representing 12 million businesses in 29 European countries.

Amsterdam Promotion Foundation

The Amsterdam Promotion Foundation (AMPRO), with some 50 members from municipal organizations and private enterprise, works to project the Dutch capital's strength as a financial center, while underscoring Amsterdam's positive image. Goals include attracting foreign companies' investments and settling here, organization of international congresses and trade fairs and development of extended incoming tourism.

An AMPRO European promotional offensive, based on a five-year business plan utilizing marketing communications and sales promotion tools to 'sell' the city, has been entrusted to Fred Minken, RAI director. Success of the dynamic strategy will be evaluated early in the year 2000.

and 450 liters. The first Amsterdam brewery was founded in 1442. In the 16th century, ten breweries operated in the city, increasing to twenty in the 17th century.

Gerard Adriaan Heineken, who became the world's second biggest brewer, was 22 when he bought the Haystack brewery on the Nieuwezijds Voorburgwal in 1864. At that time, it was the Dutch capital's largest brewery, founded in 1592. Heineken was a very shrewd businessman. The company had outgrown its premises by 1867 and started building on the Stadhouderskade. That new facility had the world's first brewing laboratory for quality control of the basic ingredients and finished product. While this brewery is no longer operational, a large section of the historic building serves as the Heineken Visitors Center. Freddy Heineken, the founder's grandson, retired as CEO after positioning his product as the world's most popular export beer. In 1968 Heineken also took over the Amstel Brouwerij N.V., founded in 1873 on the Mauritskade.

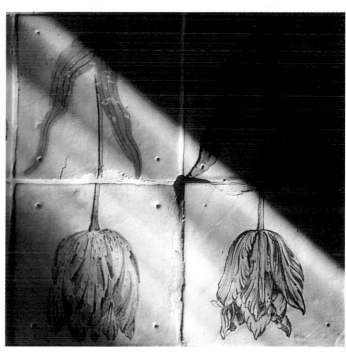

Right: These wavering, streaked flowers were proudly recorded on tiles and paintings, such as this still life by Hans Bollogier, in the 17th century.

Tulipmania during Amsterdam's Golden Age had incredibly wealthy burghers competing for bulbs producing streaked or speckled flowers. Houses, ships, cattle plus thousands of guilders were traded. Unknowingly they bought bulbs with a virus.

Tulipmania

Though the first tulips arrived over 400 years ago from Turkey, it was a century later, during Amsterdam's Golden Age, that a strange madness overtook the otherwise staid, conservative burghers as they competed for tulip bulbs which produced flowers with irregular, wavering streaks. Little did they know that these speckled and jagged petals were 'sick' — victims of a virus.

An Amsterdam merchant, rich from trade with the East, would exchange a ship, house, cattle, farmland, sometimes with thousands of guilders thrown in, to acquire this status symbol. In the 1630s, a clever dealer bought up bulbs in the winter, selling before he actually had the stock, for future delivery. Deals were noted on negotiable pieces of paper — and the world's first futures market had been initiated. Prices were soaring. An *Admiral de Maan* tulip, which sold for 15 guilders in 1634, fetched 175 guilders three years later. Between 1634 and 1637, all hell

broke loose. A single bulb was traded for two carts of wheat, two carts of rye, four fat oxen, eight fat pigs, twelve fat sheep, 5000 liters of wine, 1500 kilograms of butter, 500 kilograms of cheese, a bed, a silver cup and a suit. The popular scarlet and white *Semper Augustus* sold for 3000 guilders in 1633. But in 1637 three *Semper Augustus* bulbs went for 30,000 guilders. This at a time when the grandest canal house with garden and coach house cost 10,000 guilders. The average annual wage was 150 guilders. Cafés had separate rooms where bulbs were traded and children used as spies. Painters like Rembrandt, Vermeer and other Dutch masters recorded the virus on canvas. Artists and artisans used the exotically veined flowers as themes on tiles embedded in the walls of wealthy burghers' homes. This was the time of the 'Tulipmania'. The frenzy reached such a feverish pitch that the influential Calvinist church protested against the outrageous behavior. Ministers denounced the flowers from the pulpits as frivolous vanity. When this

unorthodox commerce endangered the Dutch economy, the government stepped in and issued controls. But the big crash did come.

It was only a few decades ago that a wily phytopathologist at the Laboratory for Flower Research discovered that bulbs, like people, can get a virus. He proved that the exotic streakings were tell-tale signs of sick bulbs. This resulted in flowers with spots, broken colors or flame patterns. Nowadays, only two growers are permitted to deliberately produce these 'sick' bulbs — but are strictly forbidden to grow them in the vicinity of healthy ones. Today, everything is done to protect this backbone of the burgeoning tourist business and worldwide export. And, naturally, to prevent a recurrence of the Tulipmania crash that shook Amsterdam over 300 years ago.

Centerpoint, Amsterdam Southeast. This new business and financial center has eye-blinding modernistic architecture commissioned by Dutch banks and concerns which have concentrated their international activities here.

The Former planetarium in Amsterdam Southeast, on the Gaasperplas (lake), now houses a congress center and an architect's office.

Illustration Credits

The publisher has made every effort to ensure that all illustration material has been properly credited and compensated according to legal regulations. Despite this endeavor for total accuracy, any unintentional omission can be brought to the publisher's attention.

Cover (front) Photo's: Christian Sarramon
Cover (back) Photo: Jan van der Weerd
2, 3 Photo: B&U International Picture Service
6 Photo: Christian Sarramon
7 Photo: Gemeente Amsterdam
8 Source: Gemeentearchief Amsterdam
9 (u.l.) Photo: Haags Gemeentemuseum
10 Photo's: ANP foto
11 (a.) Photo: Piet Schreuders
(sec.fr.a.) Photo: Gemeentearchief Amsterdam
(3rd.fr.a.) Photo: Piet Schreuders
(sec.fr.u.) Photo: Gemeentearchief Amsterdam
(u.) Photo: Anefo
12 (a.r.) Photo: Amsterdams Historisch Museum
13 (a.) Photo: ANP foto
(u.) Source: The Grand Amsterdam
14 (l.) Photo: B&U International Picture Service
(r.) Photo: Paul C. Pet
15 (a.r.) Photo: Gemeentearchief Amsterdam
(u.l.) Photo: Willem Middelkoop
(u.r.) Photo: Christian Sarramon
16 (a.) Photo: W. Krook, Afdeling Archeologie/Stedelijk Beheer Amsterdam
(insert) Photo: ANP foto
(u.l.) Photo: W. Krook, Afdeling Archeologie/Stedelijk Beheer Amsterdam
(sec.fr.l.) Photo: W. Krook, Afdeling Archeologie/Stedelijk Beheer Amsterdam
(u.,m.) Photo: W. Krook, Afdeling Archeologie/Stedelijk Beheer Amsterdam
(sec.fr.r.) Photo: W. Krook, Afdeling Archeologie/Stedelijk Beheer

Amsterdam
(u.r.) Photo: W. Krook, Afdeling Archeologie/Stedelijk Beheer Amsterdam
17 (a.l.) Photo: Christian Sarramon
(a.r.) Photo: B&U International Picture Service
(u.r.) Source: Gemeentearchief Amsterdam
18 (a.l.) Photo: VVV Amsterdam Tourist Office
(a.r.) Photo: VVV Amsterdam Tourist Office
(u.l.) Photo: Gemeentevervoersbedrijf Amsterdam
(u.r.) Photo: Christian Sarramon
19 (a.) Source: Canal Bike B.V.
20 Photo: A.A.M. van der Heyden
21 Photo: Paul C. Pet
22 (a.) Source: Stichting Atlas van Stolk, Rotterdam
(u.l.) Photo: Christian Sarramon
(u.r.) Photo: B&U International Picture Service
23 Photo: Christian Sarramon
24/25 Photo: Paul C. Pet
26 (a.) Photo: Christian Sarramon
(u.) Photo: Christian Sarramon
27 (a.) Photo: VVV Amsterdam Tourist Office
(m.) Photo: Gemeentearchief Amsterdam
(u.) Photo: Gemeentearchief Amsterdam
28 (a.l.) Photo: ANP Foto
(a.r.) Photo: B&U International Picture Service
(m.) Source: Rijksmuseum, Amsterdam
(u.) Photo: Siegfried Wijnschenk
29 (a.l.) Photo: Ronald Hoeben
(a.r.) Photo: VVV Amsterdam Tourist Office
(u.) Photo: B&U International Picture Service
30 (a.) Photo: Paul C. Pet
(u.) Source: Amsterdam Ports Association
31 Photo: Martin Kers
32 Source: Gemeentearchief Amsterdam
33 (a.l.) Source: Gemeentearchief Amsterdam

(a.r.) Source: Gemeentearchief Amsterdam
34 (u.) Photo: A.A.M. van der Heyden
(a.) Source: Gemeentearchief Amsterdam
35 (u.) Source: Gemeentearchief Amsterdam
36 Source: Gemeentearchief Amsterdam
37 (a.) Source: Gemeentearchief Amsterdam
(u.) Photo: Paul C. Pet
(a.l.) Photo: Willem Middelkoop
(a.r.) Source: Amsterdams Historisch museum
(u.) Photo: Hollandse Hoogte
38 Source: Gemeentearchief Amsterdam
39 Source: Stichting Atlas van Stolk, Rotterdam
40 (a.) Photo: Benelux Press
(u.) Photo: Benelux Press
41 (a.) Photo: Gemeentearchief Amsterdam
(u.) Photo: Copyright © RVD, Photo: Thuring B.V.
42 (l.) Photo: C. Veldkamp
(r.) Photo: Serge Ligtenberg
43 Photo: J. Dalhuijsen
44 (l.) Photo: Paul C. Pet
(r.) Photo: Paul C. Pet
45 Photo: Christian Sarramon
46 (a.l.) Photo: Christian Sarramon
(a.r.) Photo: A.A.M. van der Heyden
(l.m.) Photo: Christian Sarramon
(m.) Photo: A.A.M. van der Heyden
(r.m.) Photo: Christian Sarramon
(u.l.) Photo: Christian Sarramon
(u.r.) Photo: A.A.M. van der Heyden
47 (a.) Photo: Hollandse Hoogte
(u.) Photo: Christian Sarramon
48 (l.) Photo: Christian Sarramon
(r.) Photo: Christian Sarramon
49 (a.) Photo: Christian Sarramon
(u.) Source: Museum van Loon
50 (a.l.) Photo: Maarten Brinkgreve
(a.r.) Photo: Christian Sarramon
(u.) Photo: Christian Sarramon
51 Source: Stedelijk Museum, Amsterdam
52 (l.) Photo: Spaarnestad Fotoarchief
(r.) Photo: Ronald Hoeben
53 (u.l.) Source: Gemeentearchief Amsterdam
(u.r.) Photo: B&U International Picture

Service

54 Source: Firma Blommers

55 (l.) Photo: Ben van Meerendonk

(r.) Photo: Ben van Meerendonk

56/57 Photo: Christian Sarramon

58 (l.) Photo: Hollandse Hoogte

(r.) Photo: Christian Sarramon

59 Source: Rijksmuseum, Amsterdam

60 (a.l.) Source: Joods Historisch Museum, Amsterdam

(a.r.) Source: Joods Historisch Museum, Amsterdam

(u.l.) Source: Joods Historisch Museum, Amsterdam

(u.r.) Photo: Han Singels

61 (l.) Source: Joods Historisch Museum, Amsterdam

(r.) Source: Joods Historisch Museum, Amsterdam

62 (a.l.) Source: Joods Historisch Museum, Amsterdam

(a.r.) Source: Joods Historisch Museum, Amsterdam

(u.) Source: Rijksmuseum, Amsterdam

63 (a.) Source: Joods Historisch Museum, Amsterdam

(u.) Source: Joods Historisch Museum, Amsterdam

64 Source: Joods Historisch Museum, Amsterdam

65 (a.) Photo: Han Singels

(u.l.) Photo: Han Singels

(u.r.) Source: Joods Historisch Museum, Amsterdam

66 (l.) Source: Joods Historisch Museum, Amsterdam

(r.) Source: Gemeentearchief Amsterdam

67 (a.) Source: Gemeentearchief Amsterdam

(u.l.) Source: Rijksinstituut voor Oorlogsdocumentatie, Amsterdam

(u.r.) Source: Museum het Rembrandthuis, Amsterdam

68 (a.r.) Photo: Jeroen Nooter

(u.l.) Photos: AFFS/AFS, Amsterdam, the Netherlands

69 (a.) Source: Gemeentearchief Amsterdam

(u.) Photo: ANP Foto

70 (a.) Source: Gemeentearchief Amsterdam

(u.) Source: Het Parool

71 (l.) Photo: Christian Sarramon

(r.) Source: Gemeentearchief Amsterdam

72 (a.l.) Source: Golden Tulip Barbizon Palace

(a.r.) Source: Golden Tulip Barbizon Palace

(u.l.) Photo: B&U International Picture Service

(u.r.) Source: Gemeentearchief Amsterdam

73 (a.l.) Photo: Jan van der Weerd

(a.r.) Photo: Jan van der Weerd

(u.) Photo: Christian Sarramon

74 (a.l.) Photo: B&U International Picture Service

(a.r.) Photo: B&U International Picture Service

(u.) Photo: Hollandse Hoogte

75 (a.) Photo: W. Krook, Afdeling Archeologie/Stedelijk Beheer Amsterdam

(u.l.) Photo: Hollandse Hoogte

(u.r.) Photo: Hollandse Hoogte

76 (a.) Photo: B&U International Picture Service

(u.) Photo: Anton Veldkamp

77 Source: Joods Historisch Museum, Amsterdam

78 (a.l.) Photo: Jaap Pieper

(a.r.) Source: Gemeentearchief Amsterdam

(u.) Source: Gemeentearchief Amsterdam

79 (a.) Source: Amsterdams Historisch Museum, Amsterdam

(u.) Source: Amsterdams Historisch Museum, Amsterdam

80 (a.) Source: Gemeentearchief Amsterdam

(u.) Source: Gemeentearchief Amsterdam

81 Source: Gemeentearchief Amsterdam

82 Source: Maison Descartes, Amsterdam

83 (a.) Source: VVV Amsterdam Tourist Office

(u.) Source: Maison Descartes, Amsterdam

84 Source: Algemeen Rijksarchief Den Haag

85 (a.) Photo: Maarten Brinkgreve

(insert) Source: Gemeentearchief Amsterdam

(u.) Source: John Adams Institute, Amsterdam

86 (l.) Source: Gemeentearchief Den Haag

(m.) Source: John Adams Papers, Collectie Massachusetts Historical Society, Boston

(u.) Source: Gemeentearchief Amsterdam

87 (a.) Photo: Christian Sarramon

(u.l.) Photo: B&U International Picture Service

(u.r.) Photo: Christian Sarramon

88/89 Photo: Christian Sarramon

90 Photo: American Chamber of Commerce in the Netherlands

(u.) Source: Hotel Pulitzer Amsterdam

91 Photo's: Stanley Gontha

92 (l.) Source: Rijksmuseum voor Volkenkunde, Leiden

(r.) Source: Rijksmuseum voor Volkenkunde, Leiden

93 (l.) Photo: Ronald Hoeben

(r.) Photo: Taeke Henstra

94 Photo's: Jan Derwig

95 (a.) Source: Nissan Europe N.V.

(u.) Photo: Taeke Henstra

96 Source: ABN AMRO Bank N.V.

97 (a.l.) Source: Okura Hotel

(a.r.) Photo: Taeke Henstra

(m.) Source: Dai-Ichi Kangio Bank Nederland N.V.

(u.) Photo: Nederlands Bureau voor Toerisme

98 Photo: Rob Scholte B.V.

99 Photo: Albertina da Rosa

100 Photo's: Aatjan Renders

101 Source: Werkspoormuseum

102 Source: Amsterdams Historisch Museum

(insert) Photo: Vereniging Vrienden van Amsterdamse Gevelstenen

103 (l.) Source: Werkspoormuseum

(r.) Source: Universiteitsbibliotheek van Amsterdam

104 Source: Werkspoormuseum

105 Source: Werkspoormuseum

106 (l.) Photo: B&U International Picture Service

108 Photo: B&U International Picture Service

109 (a.) Source: Museum 'Het Rembrandthuis'

(u.) Source: Museum 'Het Rembrandthuis'

110 (a.) Source: Museum 'Het Rembrandthuis'

(u.) Source: Museum 'Het Rembrandthuis'

111 Source: Museum 'Het Rembrandthuis'

112 Source: Van Gogh Museum, Amsterdam

113 Source: Van Gogh Museum, Amsterdam

114 (l.) Photo: A. Petersen

(r.) Source: Stichting P. en N. de Boer

115 Photo: B&U International Picture Service

116 Photo: Paul de Jong

117 (a.) Photo: R. Drektraan, prive collectie
(u.) Photo: B&U International Picture Service

118 (a.) Photo: B&U International Picture Service
(u.) Source: Gemeentearchief Amsterdam

119 (a.) Photo: B&U International Picture Service
(u.) Source: Collectie Mr. Power, Londen

120/121 Photo: Christian Sarramon

122 (a.) Source: Allard Pierson Museum
(u.) Source: VVV Amsterdam Tourist Office

123 Photo: B&U International Picture Service

124 (a.l.) Photo: Thijs Wolzak Fotografie
(insert) Photo: Hans Samson
(a.r.) Photo: Sybolt Voeten
(u.r.) Photo: Clive Barda
(u.l.) Source: Gemeentearchief Amsterdam

125 (a.) Source: De IJsbreker
(u.) Photo: Kors van Bennekom

126 (a.) Source: Het Muziektheater, Amsterdam
(u.) Source: Het Muziektheater, Amsterdam

127 Source: Gemeentevervoersbedrijf, Amsterdam

128 Photo: ANP Foto

129 (a.) Photo: Christian Sarramon
(u.) Photo: Christian Sarramon

130 (a.) Photo: B&U International Picture Service
(u.) Source: Academisch Medisch Centrum

132 (a.l.) Photo: B&U International Picture Service
(a.r.) Photo: A.A.M. van der Heyden
(m.) Photo: Christian Sarramon
(u.) Source: ING Bank

133 Photo: ANP Foto

134 (a.) Photo: ANP Foto
(u.) Source: Alexander Schabracq

135 Photo: B&U International Picture Service

136/137 Photo: Persbureau Louis van de Vuurst

138 (a.) Photo: B&U International Picture Service

139 (u.) Photo: F. Middelkoop
(a.) Source: Amsterdam Ports Association
(u.) Photo: ANP Foto

140 (a.l.) Source: VVV Amsterdam Tourist Office
(a.r.) Source: VVV Amsterdam Tourist Office
(u.l.) Photo: Christian Sarramon
Photo: Diana Molina

141 Photo: Persbureau Louis van de Vuurst

142 (l.) Photo: Artis, Amsterdam
(r.) Photo: ANP Foto

143 Source: Gemeentearchief Amsterdam

144 Source: Gemeentearchief Amsterdam

145 Source: Gemeentearchief Amsterdam

146 (a.) Photo: Ronald Hoeben
(u.) Photo: Het Vrije Volk

147 (a.) Photo: ANP Foto
(u.) Photo: ANP Foto

148 Photo: ANP Foto

149 Source: Rijksmuseum voor Volkenkunde, Leiden

150 Source: Amsterdam Ports Association

151 (a.) Source: Vereeniging Nederlandsch Historisch Scheepvaart Museum
(m.) Source: Vereeniging Nederlandsch Historisch Scheepvaart Museum
(u.) Source: Vereeniging Nederlandsch Historisch Scheepvaart Museum

152 (l.) Source: Vereeniging Nederlandsch Historisch Scheepvaart Museum
(r.) Source: Vereeniging Nederlandsch Historisch Scheepvaart Museum

153 (a.l.) Source: Vereeniging Nederlandsch Historisch Scheepvaart Museum
(a.r.) Source: Vereeniging Nederlandsch Historisch Scheepvaart Museum
(u.l.) Photo: Christian Sarramon
(u.r.) Photo: Christian Sarramon

154 Source: Vereeniging Nederlandsch Historisch Scheepvaart Museum

155 (a.) Photo: A.A.M. van der Heyden
(u.) Source: Vereeniging Nederlandsch Historisch Scheepvaart Museum

156 (a.) Source: Amsterdam Ports Association
(u.) Source: Nationaal Foto Persbureau B.V.

157 Photo: Bob Fleumer

158 (a.) Source: Gemeentelijk Havenbedrijf, Amsterdam
(u.) Source: Hollandse Hoogte

159 (a.) Photo: Willem Middelkoop
(u.) Source: Amsterdam Ports Association

160 Photo: Hollandse Hoogte

161 (a.) Source: N.V. Luchthaven Schiphol
(u.) Source: KLM

162 Source: KLM

163 (a.) Source: KLM aerocarto luchtfotografie
(u.l.) Source: N.V. Luchthaven Schiphol
(u.r.) Source: N.V. Luchthaven Schiphol

164 (insert) Source: KLM
(a.) Source: KLM
(u.) Source: N.V. Luchthaven Schiphol

165 Source: KLM

167 Source: Teleport Amsterdam

168/169 Source: Teleport Amsterdam

171 (a.) Source: Gemeentearchief Amsterdam
(u.) Photo: Christian Sarramon

173 Source: Effectenbeurs, Amsterdam

174 (a.) Source: Capital Press
(u.) Photo: B&U International Picture Service

175 Photo: Frits Gerritsen

176 Source: EOE Optiebeurs

177 (l.) Source: Hollandse Hoogte
(u.) Source: Gemeente Amsterdam

178 Source: De Nederlandsche Bank N.V.

179 (a.) Source: De Nederlandsche Bank N.V.
(u.) Source: De Nederlandsche Bank N.V.

180 Source: ABN AMRO Bank N.V.

181 (a.) Source: Rai, Amsterdam
(u.) Source: Rai, Amsterdam
(insert) Source: Rai, Amsterdam

182 Photo: Fotoburo Jaap Meijer

183 Photo: B&U International Picture Service

184 (a.) Source: VVV Amsterdam Tourist Office
(u.) Source: Heineken

185 Photo: Rob List Fotografie B.V.

186 (l.) Source: Rijksmuseum, Amsterdam
(r.) Photo: Christian Sarramon

187 (a.) Photo: Martin Kers
(u.) Source: Van den Oever, Zaaijer, Roodbeen & Partners

SO-AJN-739

CHABOT COLLEGE-HAYWARD

2 555 000 061764 +

100001   PS
                                          3513
Gorey   0614
                                          A8
Amphigorey

Date Due

JA 28'74	JAN 24 '80	APR 18 1991	
AP 17'74	JUL 16 '80	FEB 01 1994	
MAR 5 '75	MAY 25 '83		
APR 17 '75	FEB 05 '87		
DEC 15 '75	JUN 18 '87		
MAR 24 '76			
OCT 2 '76	MAR 21 '88		
APR 20 '77	OCT 12 1988		
MAR 0 2 '78	NOV 14 1988		
FEB 13 '78	NOV 30 1988		
JUN 6 '79	FEB 07 1989		
	APR 27 '89		

CHABOT
COLLEGE
LIBRARY

25555 Hesperian Boulevard
Hayward, CA 94545

AMPHIGOREY

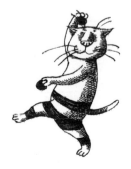

Fifteen books

by Edward Gorey

G.P. Putnam's Sons   New York

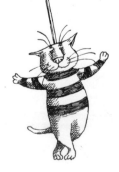

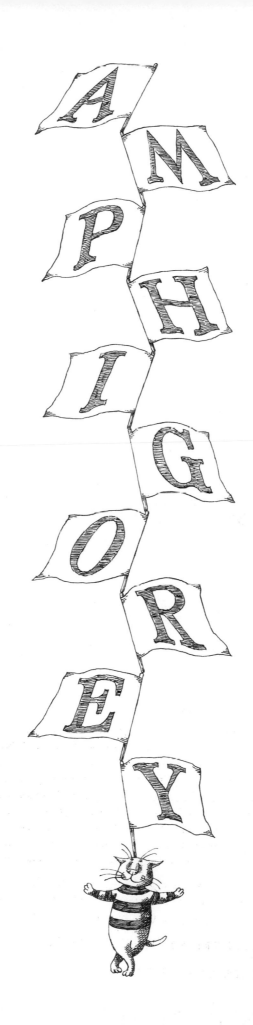

PS
3513
O614
—
A8

Copyright © 1972 by Edward Gorey

The works in the present volume were first published as indicated:
The Unstrung Harp, 1953 , *The Listing Attic*, 1954, Duell, Sloan and Pearce–Little Brown;
The Doubtful Guest, 1957, *The Object-Lesson*, 1958, Doubleday & Company, Inc.;
The Bug Book, 1960, Epstein & Carroll ; *The Fatal Lozenge*, 1960, *The Hapless Child*, 1961,
The Curious Sofa, 1961, *The Sinking Spell*, 1964, Ivan Obolensky, Inc.; *The Willowdale
Handcar*, 1962, The Bobbs-Merrill Company, Inc.; *The Wuggly Ump*, 1963, J.B. Lippincott
Company ; *The Gashlycrumb Tinies*, 1963, *The Insect God*, 1963, *The West Wing*, 1963,
The Remembered Visit, 1965, Simon and Schuster. The author and publisher
acknowledge with special thanks all courtesies of the foregoing publishers.

All rights reserved. This book, or parts thereof, must not be
reproduced in any form without permission. Published on the same
day in Canada by Longmans Canada Limited, Toronto.

Library of Congress Catalog Card Number: 72-80859
SBN 399-11003-8
Printed in the United States of America

For my mother

100001

Amphigorey is made up of books first
published between 1953 and 1965. They are
now difficult and often expensive to come
by: hence this compilation. Its title is
taken from amphigory, or amphigouri,
meaning a nonsense verse or composition.

E.G.

THE FIFTEEN BOOKS

The Unstrung Harp

The Listing Attic

The Doubtful Guest

The Object-Lesson

The Bug Book

The Fatal Lozenge

The Hapless Child

The Curious Sofa

The Willowdale Handcar

The Gashlycrumb Tinies

The Insect God

The West Wing

The Wuggly Ump

The Sinking Spell

The Remembered Visit

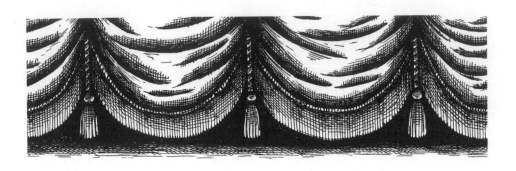

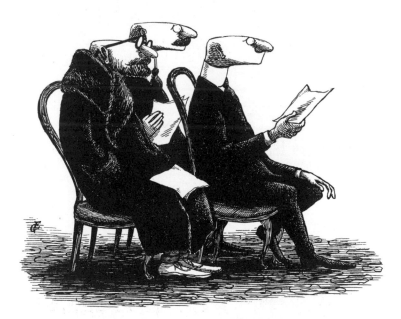

Mr Gorey, Mr Earbrass, and a Knowledgeable Friend.

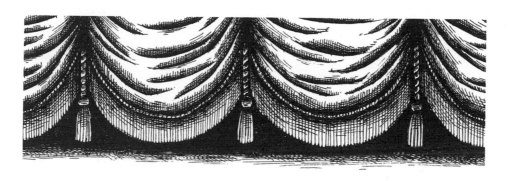

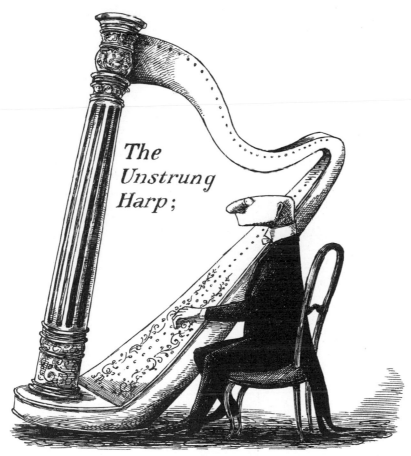

The Unstrung Harp;

or, Mr Earbrass Writes a Novel.

Mr C(lavius) F(rederick) Earbrass is, of course, the well-known novelist. Of his books, *A Moral Dustbin, More Chains Than Clank, Was It Likely?*, and the Hipdeep trilogy are, perhaps, the most admired. Mr Earbrass is seen on the croquet lawn of his home, Hobbies Odd, near Collapsed Pudding in Mortshire. He is studying a game left unfinished at the end of summer.

On November 18th of alternate years Mr Earbrass begins writing 'his new novel'. Weeks ago he chose its title at random from a list of them he keeps in a little green note-book. It being tea-time of the 17th, he is alarmed not to have thought of a plot to which *The Unstrung Harp* might apply, but his mind will keep reverting to the last biscuit on the plate.

Snow was falling when Mr Earbrass woke, which suggested he open *TUH* with the first flakes of what could be developed into a prolonged and powerfully purple blizzard. On paper, if not outdoors, they have kept coming down all afternoon, over and over again, in all possible ways; and only now, at nightfall, have done so satisfactorily. For writing Mr Earbrass affects an athletic sweater of forgotten origin and unknown significance; it is always worn hind-side-to.

Several weeks later, the loofah trickling on his knees, Mr Earbrass mulls over an awkward retrospective bit that ought to go in Chapter II. But where? Even the voice of the omniscient author can hardly afford to interject a seemingly pointless anecdote concerning Ladderback in Tibet when the other characters are feverishly engaged in wondering whether to have the pond at Disshiver Cottage dragged or not.

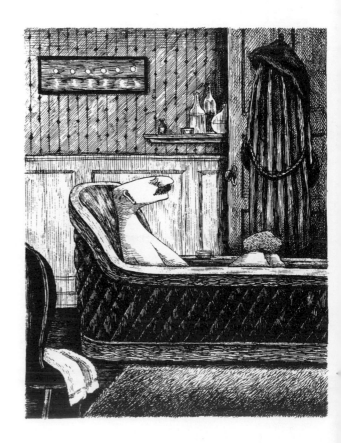

Mr Earbrass belongs to the straying, rather than to the sedentary, type of author. He is never to be found at his desk unless actually writing down a sentence. Before this happens he broods over it indefinitely while picking up and putting down again small, loose objects; walking diagonally across rooms; staring out windows; and so forth. He frequently hums, more in his mind than anywhere else, themes from the Poddington *Te Deum*.

It was one of Mr Earbrass's better days; he wrote for so long and with such intensity that when he stopped he felt quite sick. Having leaned out a window into a strong wind for several minutes, he is now restoring himself in the kitchen and rereading *TUH* as far as he has gotten. He cannot help but feel that Lirp's return and almost immediate impalement on the bottle-tree was one of his better ideas. The jelly in his sandwich is about to get all over his fingers.

Mr Earbrass has finished Chapter VII, and it is obvious that before plunging ahead himself he has got to decide where the plot is to go and what will happen to it on arrival. He is engaged in making diagrams of possible routes and destinations, and wishing he had not dealt so summarily with Lirp, who would have been useful for taking retributive measures at the end of Part Three. At the moment there is no other character capable of them.

Out for a short drive before a supper of oysters and trifle, Mr Earbrass stops near the abandoned fireworks factory outside Something Awful. There is a drowned sort of yellow light in the west, and the impression of desolation and melancholy is remarkable. Mr Earbrass jots down a few visual notes he suspects may be useful when he reaches the point where the action of *TUH* shifts to Hangdog Hall.

Mr Earbrass was virtually asleep when several lines of verse passed through his mind and left it hopelessly awake. Here was the perfect epigraph for *TUH*:

A horrid ?monster has been [something]
    delay'd
By your/their indiff'rence in the dank
    brown shade
Below the garden…

His mind's eye sees them quoted on the bottom third of a right-hand page in a (possibly) olive-bound book he read at least five years ago. When he does find them, it will be a great nuisance if no clue is given to their authorship.

Mr Earbrass has driven over to Nether Millstone in search of forced greengages, but has been distracted by a bookseller's. Rummaging among mostly religious tracts and privately printed reminiscences, he has come across *The Meaning of the House*, his second novel. In making sure it has not got there by mistake (as he would hardly care to pay more for it), he discovers it is a presentation copy. *For Angus—will you ever forget the bloaters?* Bloaters? Angus?

The first draft of *TUH* is more than half finished, and for some weeks its characters have been assuming a fitful and *cloudy* reality. Now a minor one named Glassglue has materialized at the head of the stairs as his creator is about to go down to dinner. Mr Earbrass was aware of the peculiarly unpleasant nubs on his greatcoat, but not the blue-tinted spectacles. Glassglue is about to mutter something in a tone too low to be caught and, stepping sideways, vanish.

Mr Earbrass has been rashly skimming through the early chapters, which he has not looked at for months, and now sees *TUH* for what it is. Dreadful, *dreadful*, DREADFUL. He must be mad to go on enduring the unexquisite agony of writing when it all turns out drivel. Mad. Why didn't he become a spy? How does one become one? He will burn the MS. Why is there no fire? Why aren't there the makings of one? How did he get in the unused room on the third floor?

Mr Earbrass returned from a walk to find a large carton blocking the hall. Masses of brow paper and then tissue have reluctantly given up an unnerving silver-gilt combination epergne and candelabrum. Mr Earbrass recollects a letter from a hitherto unknown admirer of his work, received the week before; it hinted at the early arrival of an offering that embodied, in a different but kindred form, the same high-souled aspiration that animated its recipient's books. Mr Earbrass can only conclude that the apathy of the lower figures is due to their having been deprived of novels.

Even more harrowing than the first chapters of a novel are the last, for Mr Earbrass anyway. The characters have one and all become thoroughly tiresome, as though he had been trapped at the same party with them since the day before; neglected sections of the plot loom on every hand, waiting to be disposed of; his verbs seem to have withered away and his adjectives to be proliferating past control. Furthermore, at this stage he inevitably gets insomnia. Even rereading *The Truffle Plantation* (his first novel) does not induce sleep. In the blue horror of dawn the vines in the carpet appear likely to begin twining up his ankles.

Though *TUH* is within less than a chapter of completion, Mr Earbrass has felt it his cultural and civic duty, and a source of possible edification, to attend a performance at Lying-in-the-Way of Prawne's *The Nephew's Tragedy*. It is being put on, for the first time since the early seventeenth century, by the West Mortshire Impassioned Amateurs of Melpomene. Unfortunately, Mr Earbrass is unable to take in even one of its five plots because he cannot get those few unwritten pages out of his mind.

In that brief moment between day and night when everything seems to have stopped for good and all, Mr Earbrass has written the last sentence of *TUH*. The room's appearance of tidiness and Mr Earbrass's of calm are alike deceptive. The MS is stuffed all anyhow in the lower right-hand drawer of the desk and Mr Earbrass himself is wildly distrait. His feet went to sleep some time ago, there is a dull throbbing behind his left ear, and his moustache feels as uncomfortable as if it were false, or belonged to someone else.

The next day Mr Earbrass is conscious but very little more. He wanders through the house, leaving doors open and empty tea-cups on the floor. From time to time the thought occurs to him that he really *ought* to go and dress, and he gets up several minutes later, only to sit down again in the first chair he comes to. The better part of a week will have elapsed before he has recovered enough to do anything more helpful.

Some weeks later, with pen, ink, scissors, paste, a decanter of sherry, and a vast reluctance, Mr Earbrass begins to revise *TUH*. This means, first, transposing passages, or reversing the order of their paragraphs, or crumpling them up furiously and throwing them in the waste-basket. After that there is rewriting. This is *worse* than merely writing, because not only does he have to think *up* new things just the same, but at the same time try not to remember the old ones. Before Mr Earbrass is through, at least one third of *TUH* will bear no resemblance to its original state.

Mr Earbrass sits on the opposite side of the study from his desk, gathering courage for the worst part of all in the undertaking of a novel, i.e., making a clean copy of the final version of the MS. Not only is it repulsive to the eye and hand, with its tattered edges, stains, rumpled patches, scratchings-out, and scribblings, but its contents are, by this time, boring to the point of madness. A freshly-filled inkwell, new pheasant-feather pens, and two reams of the most expensive cream laid paper are negligible inducements for embarking on such a loathsome proceeding.

Holding *TUH* not very neatly done up in pink butcher's paper, which was all he could find in a last-minute search before leaving to catch his train for London, Mr Earbrass arrives at the offices of his publishers to deliver it. The stairs look oddly menacing, as though he might break a leg on one of them. Suddenly the whole thing strikes him as very silly, and he thinks he will go and drop his parcel off the Embankment and thus save everyone concerned a good deal of fuss.

Mr Earbrass escaped from Messrs Scuffle and Dustcough, who were most anxious to go into all the ramifications of a scheme for having his novels translated into Urdu, and went to call on a distant cousin. The latter was planning to do the antique shops this afternoon, so Mr Earbrass agreed to join him. In the eighteenth shop they have visited, the cousin thinks he sees a rare sort of lustre jug, and Mr Earbrass irritatedly wonders why anyone should have had a fantod stuffed and put under a glass bell.

The night before returning home to Mortshire Mr Earbrass allows himself to be taken to a literary dinner in a private dining room of Le Trottoir Imbécile. Among his fellow-authors, few of whom he recognizes and none of whom he knows, are Lawk, Sangwidge, Ha'p'orth, Avuncular, and Lord Legbail. The unwell-looking gentleman wrapped in a greatcoat is an obscure essayist named Frowst. The talk deals with disappointing sales, inadequate publicity, worse than inadequate royalties, idiotic or criminal reviews, others' declining talent, and the unspeakable horror of the literary life.

TUH is over so to speak, but far from done with. The galleys have arrived, and Mr Earbrass goes over them with mingled excitement and disgust. It all looks so different set up in type that at first he thought they had sent him the wrong ones by mistake. He is quite giddy from trying to physically control the sheets and at the same time keep the amount of absolutely necessary changes within the allowed pecuniary limits.

Mr Earbrass has received the sketch for the dust-wrapper of *TUH*. Even after staring at it continuously for twenty minutes, he really cannot believe it. Whatever were they thinking of? That drawing. Those colours. *Ugh.* On any book it would be ugly, vulgar, and illegible. On his book it would be these, and also disastrously wrong. Mr Earbrass looks forward to an exhilarating hour of conveying these sentiments to Scuffle and Dustcough.

Things contined to come, this time Mr
Earbrass's six free copies of *TUH*. There are,
alas, at least three times that number of
people who expect to receive one of them.
Buying the requisite number of additional
copies does not happen to be the solution, as it
would come out almost at once, and everyone
would be very angry at his wanton distribution
of them to just anyone, and write him little
notes of thanks ending with the remark that
TUH seems rather down from your usual level
of polish but then you were probably in a
hurry for the money. If it didn't come out,
the list would be three times larger for
his next book.

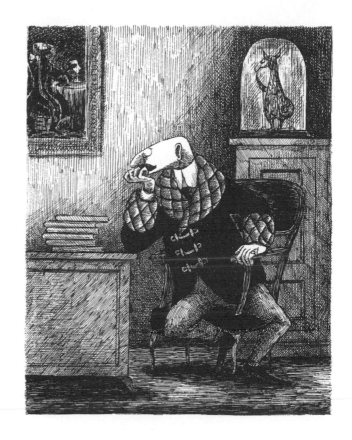

To-day *TUH* is published, and Mr Earbrass
has come into Nether Millstone to do some
errands which could not be put off any longer.
He has been uncharacteristically thorough
about doing them, and it is late afternoon
before he pauses in front of a bookseller's
window on the way back to his car. Having
made certain, out of the corner of his eye,
a copy of *TUH* was in it, he is carefully
reading the title of every other book there
in a state of extreme and pointless embarrassment.

Scuffle and Dustcough have thoughtfully, if gratuitously, sent all the papers with reviews in them. They make a gratifyingly large heap. Mr Earbrass refuses to be intimidated into rushing through them, but he is having a certain amount of difficulty in concentrating on, or, rather, making any sense whatever out of, *A Compendium of the Minor Heresies of the Twelfth Century in Asia Minor.* He has been meaning to finish it ever since he began it two years and seven months before, at which time he bogged down on page 33.

At an afternoon forgathering at the Vicarage vaguely in Mr Earbrass's honor, where he has been busy handing round cups of tea, he is brought up short by Col Knout, M.F.H. of the Blathering Hunt. He demands to know just what Mr Earbrass was 'getting at' in the last scene of Chapter XIV. Mr Earbrass is afraid he doesn't know what the Colonel is. Is what? Getting at himself. The Colonel snorts, Mr Earbrass sighs. This encounter, which will go on for some time and get nowhere, will leave Mr Earbrass feeling very weak indeed.

Mr Earbrass stands on the terrace at twilight. It is bleak; it is cold; and the virtue has gone out of everything. Words drift through his mind: *anguish turnips conjunctions illness defeat string parties no parties urns desuetude disaffection claws loss Trebizond napkins shame stones distance fever Antipodes mush glaciers incoherence labels miasma amputation tides deceit mourning elsewards ...*

Before he knew what he was doing, Mr Earbrass found he had every intention of spending a few weeks on the Continent. In a trance of efficiency, which could have surprised no-one more than himself, he made the complicated and maddening preparations for his departure in no time at all. Now, at dawn, he stands, quite numb with cold and trepidation, looking at the churning surface of the Channel. He assumes he will be horribly sick for hours and hours, but it doesn't matter. Though he is a person to whom things do not happen, perhaps they may when he is on the other side.

THE
LISTING ATTIC

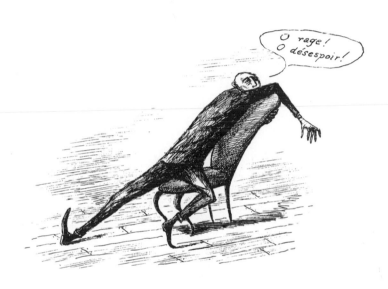

There was a young lady named Rose
Who fainted whenever she chose;
    She did so one day
    While playing croquet,
But was quickly revived with a hose.

A headstrong young woman in Ealing
Threw her two weeks' old child at the ceiling;
    When quizzed why she did,
    She replied, 'To be rid
Of a strange, overpowering feeling.'

They had come in the fugue to the stretto
When a dark, bearded man from a ghetto
    Slipped forward and grabbed
    Her tresses and stabbed
Her to death with a rusty stiletto.

A certain young man, it was noted,
Went about in the heat thickly-coated;
    He said, 'You may scoff,
    But I shan't take it off;
Underneath I am horribly bloated.'

A lady was seized with intent
To revise her existence misspent;
  So she climbed up the dome
  Of St Peter's in Rome,
Where she stayed through the following Lent.

There was a young woman whose stammer
Was atrocious, and so was her grammar;
  But they were not improved
  When her husband was moved
To knock out her teeth with a hammer.

A dreary young bank clerk named Fennis
Wished to foster an aura of menace;
  To make people afraid
  He wore gloves of grey suede
And white footgear intended for tennis.

While his duchess lay practically dead,
The Duke of Daguerrodargue said:
  'Can it be this is all?
  How puny! How small!
Have destroyed this disgrace to my bed.'

To a weepy young woman in Thrums
Her betrothed remarked, 'This is what comes
   Of allowing your tears
    To fall into my ears—
I think they have rotted the drums.'

A gift was delivered to Laura
From a cousin who lived in Gomorrah;
   Wrapped in tissue and crepe,
    It was peeled, like a grape,
And emitted a pale, greenish aura.

A clerical student named Pryne
Through pain sought to reach the divine:
   He wore a hair shirt,
    Quite often ate dirt,
And bathed every Friday in brine.

Il y a une jeune fille amoureuse
D'un homme qu'a une conduite honteuse;
   Il la mene chaque soir
    A son caveau noir
Et la bat avec plaintes crapuleuses.

'My trip? It was vile. Balaclava
I loathed. Etna was crawling with lava.
    The ship was all white
    But it creaked in the night,
And the band, they did not know la java'.

There was a young woman named Plunnery
Who rejoiced in the practice of gunnery,
    Till one day unobservant,
    She blew up a servant,
And was forced to retire to a nunnery.

A young man of acumen and daring,
Who'd amassed a great fortune in herring,
    Was left quite alone
    When it soon became known
That their use at his board was unsparing.

The partition of Vavasour Scowles
Was a sickener: they came on his bowels
    In a firkin; his brain
    Was found clogging a drain,
And his toes were inside of some towels.

As the breeches-buoy swung towards the rocks,
Its occupant cried, 'Save my socks!
    I could not bear the loss,
    For with scarlet silk floss
My mama has embroidered their clocks.'

An innocent maiden named Herridge
Was cruelly tricked into marriage;
    When she later found out
    What her spouse was about,
She threw herself under a carriage.

Les salons de la ville de Trieste
Sont vaseux, suraigus, et funestes;
    Parmi les grandes chaises
    On cause des malaises,
Des estropiéments, et des pestes.

Some Harvard men, stalwart and hairy,
Drank up several bottles of sherry;
    In the Yard around three
    They were shrieking with glee:
'Come on out, we are burning a fairy!'

An Edwardian father named Udgeon,
Whose offspring provoked him to dudgeon,
   Used on Saturday nights
    To turn down the lights,
And chase them around with a bludgeon.

The babe, with a cry brief and dismal,
Fell into the water baptismal;
   Ere they'd gathered its plight,
   It had sunk out of sight,
For the depth of the font was abysmal.

A lady both callous and brash
Met a man with a vast black moustache;
   She cried, 'Shave it, O do!
   And I'll put it with glue
On my hat as a sort of panache.'

A guest in a household quite charmless
Was informed its eccentric was harmless:
   'If you're caught unawares
   At the head of the stairs,
Just remember, he's eyeless and armless.'

A beetling young woman named Pridgets
Had a violent abhorrence of midgets;
   Off the end of a wharf
   She once pushed a dwarf
Whose truncation reduced her to fidgets.

A lady born under a curse
Used to drive forth each day in a hearse;
   From the back she would wail
   Through a thickness of veil:
'Things do not get better, but worse.'

Each night Father fills me with dread
When he sits on the foot of my bed;
   I'd not mind that he speaks
   In gibbers and squeaks,
But for seventeen years he's been dead.

There was a young curate whose brain
Was deranged from the use of cocaine;
   He lured a small child
   To a copse dark and wild,
Where he beat it to death with his cane.

A young man grew increasingly peaky
In a house where the hinges were squeaky,
   The ferns curled up brown,
   The ceilings flaked down,
And all of the faucets were leaky.

The first child of a Mrs Keats-Shelley
Came to light with its face in its belly;
   Her second was born
   With a hump and a horn,
And her third was as shapeless as jelly.

There was a young woman named Ells
Who was subject to curious spells
   When got up very oddly,
   She'd cry out things ungodly
By the palms in expensive hotels.

At whist drives and strawberry teas
Fan would giggle and show off her knees;
   But when she was alone
   She'd drink eau de cologne,
And weep from a sense of unease.

There was a young sportsman named Peel
Who went for a trip on his wheel;
  He pedalled for days
   Through crepuscular haze,
And returned feeling somewhat unreal.

A timid young woman named Jane
Found parties a terrible strain;
  With movements uncertain
   She'd hide in a curtain
And make sounds like a rabbit in pain.

Said a girl who upon her divan
Was attacked by a virile young man:
  'Such excess of passion
   Is quite out of fashion'
And she fractured his wrist with her fan.

Un moine au milieu de la messe
S'éleva et cria en détresse:
  'La vie religieuse,
   C'est sale et affreuse'
Et se poignarda dans les fesses.

Augustus, for splashing his soup,
Was put for the night on the stoop;
   In the morning he'd not
    Repented a jot,
And next day he was dead of the croup.

A young lady who lived by the Usk
Subsisted each day on a rusk;
   She ate the first bite
    Before it was light,
And the last crumb sometime after dusk.

At the Villa Nemetia the sleepers
Are disturbed by a phantom in weepers;
   It beats all night long
    A dirge on a gong
As it staggers about in the creepers.

There was a young lady named Fleager
Who was terribly, terribly eager
   To be all the rage
    On the tragedy stage,
Though her talents were pitifully meagre.

A lady who signs herself 'Vexed'
Writes to say she believes she's been hexed:
　'I don't mind my shins
　　Being stuck full of pins,
But I fear I am coming unsexed.'

A gentleman, otherwise meek,
Detested with passion the leek;
　When offered one out
　　He dealt such a clout
To the maid, she was down for a week.

While travelling in farthest Tibet,
Lord Irongate found cause to regret
　The buttered-up tea,
　　A pain in his knee,
And the frivolous tourists he met.

To his clubfooted child said Lord Stipple,
As he poured his post-prandial tipple,
　'Your mother's behaviour
　　Gave pain to Our Saviour,
And that's why He made you a cripple.'

From the bathing machine came a din
As of jollification within;
   It was heard far and wide,
   And the incoming tide
Had a definite flavour of gin.

As tourists inspected the apse
An ominous series of raps
   Came from under the altar,
   Which caused some to falter
And others to shriek and collapse.

Pour guérir un accès de fièvre
Un jeune homme poursuivit un lièvre;
   Il le prit à son trou,
   Et fit faire un ragoût
Des entrailles et des pattes au genièvre.

A nurse motivated by spite
Tied her infantine charge to a kite;
   She launched it with ease
   On the afternoon breeze,
And watched till it flew out of sight.

There's a rather odd couple in Herts
Who are cousins (or so each asserts);
   Their sex is in doubt
    For they're never without
Their moustaches and long, trailing skirts.

The Dowager Duchess of Spout
Collapsed at the height of a rout;
   She found strength to say
    As they bore her away:
'I should never have taken the trout.'

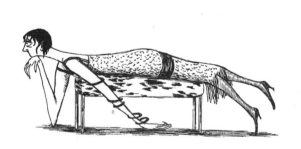

Said Francesca, 'My lack of volition
Is leading me straight to perdition;
   But I haven't the strength
    To go to the length
Of making an act of contrition.'

The sight of his guests filled Lord Cray
At breakfast with horrid dismay,
   So he launched off the spoons
    The pits from his prunes
At their heads as they neared the buffet.

An incautious young woman named Venn
Was seen with the wrong sort of men;
   She vanished one day,
   But the following May
Her legs were retrieved from a fen.

An indefatigable woman named Bavel
Had often occasion to travel;
   On the way she would sit
   And furiously knit,
And on the way back she'd unravel.

Having made a remark rather coarse,
A young lady was seized with remorse;
   She fled from the room,
   And later, a groom
Saw her rolling about in the gorse.

An old gentleman's crotchets and quibblings
Were a terrible trial to his siblings,
   But he was not removed
   Till one day it was proved
That the bell-ropes were damp with his dribblings.

There was a young man, name of Fred,
Who spent every Thursday in bed;
   He lay with his feet
   Outside of the sheet,
And the pillows on top of his head.

From Number Nine, Penwiper Mews,
There is really abominable news:
   They've discovered a head
   In the box for the bread,
But nobody seems to know whose.

There was a young man who appeared
To his friends with a full growth of beard;
   They at once said, 'Although
   We can't say why it's so,
The effect is uncommonly weird.'

Ce livre est dédié à Chagrin,
Qui fit un petit mannequin:
   Sans bras et tout noir,
   Il était affreux voir;
En effet, absolument la fin.

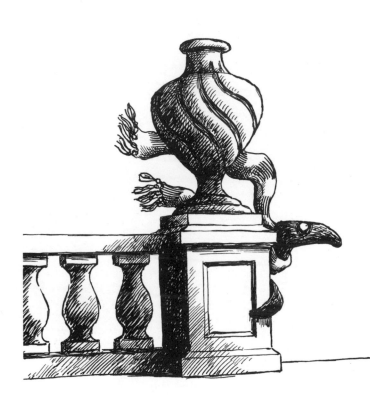

The Doubtful Guest

by Edward Gorey

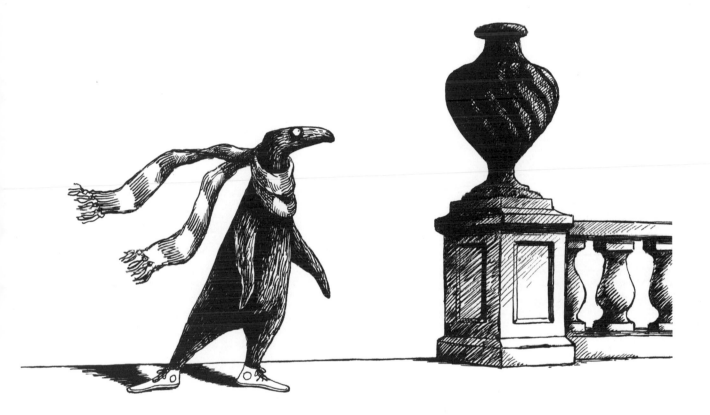

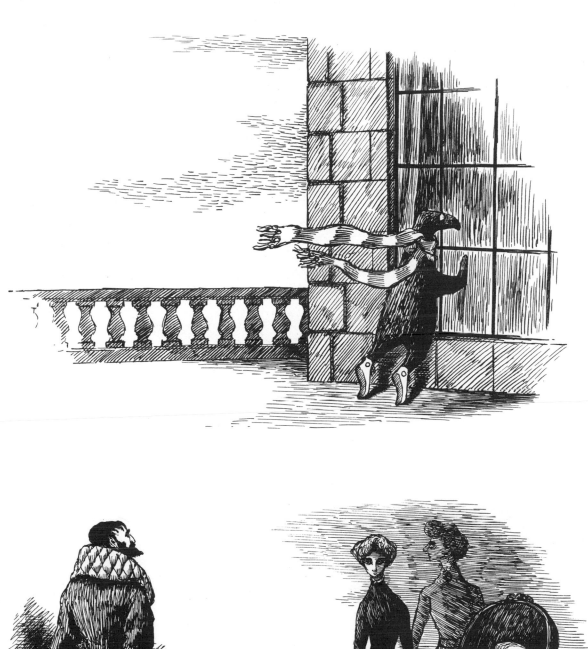

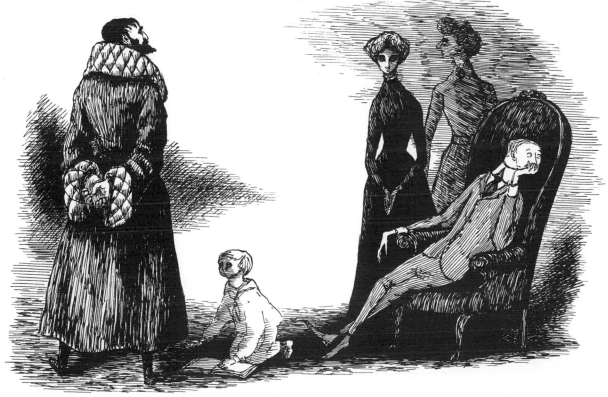

When they answered the bell on that wild winter night,
There was no one expected – and no one in sight.

Then they saw something standing on top of an urn,
Whose peculiar appearance gave them quite a turn.

All at once it leapt down and ran into the hall,
Where it chose to remain with its nose to the wall.

It was seemingly deaf to whatever they said,
So at last they stopped screaming, and went off to bed.

It joined them at breakfast and presently ate
All the syrup and toast, and a part of a plate.

It wrenched off the horn from the new gramophone,
And could not be persuaded to leave it alone.

It betrayed a great liking for peering up flues,
And for peeling the soles of its white canvas shoes.

At times it would tear out whole chapters from books,
Or put roomfuls of pictures askew on their hooks.

Every Sunday it brooded and lay on the floor,
Inconveniently close to the drawing-room door.

Now and then it would vanish for hours from the scene,
But alas, be discovered inside a tureen.

It was subject to fits of bewildering wrath,
During which it would hide all the towels from the bath.

In the night through the house it would aimlessly creep,
In spite of the fact of its being asleep.

It would carry off objects of which it grew fond,
And protect them by dropping them into the pond.

It came seventeen years ago – and to this day
It has shown no intention of going away.

THE
OBJECT-LESSON

It was already Thursday,

but his lordship's artificial limb could not be found;

therefore, having directed the servants to fill the baths,

he seized the tongs

and set out at once for the edge of the lake,

where the Throbblefoot Spectre still loitered in a distraught manner.

He presented it with a length of string

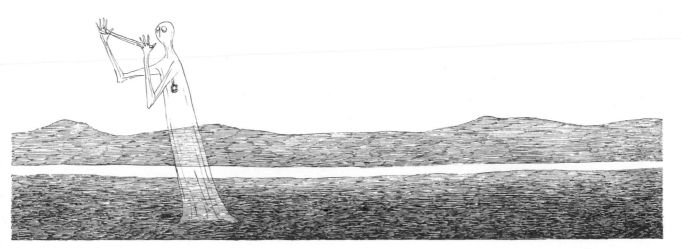

and passed on to the statue of Corrupted Endeavour

to await the arrival of autumn.

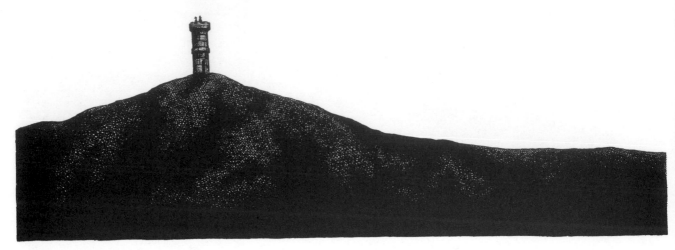

Meanwhile, on the tower,

Madame O——— in conversation with an erstwhile cousin

saw that his moustache was not his own,

on which she flung herself over the parapet

and surreptitiously vanished.

He descended, destroying the letter unread,

and stepped backwards into the water for a better view.

Heavens, how dashing! cried the people in the dinghy,

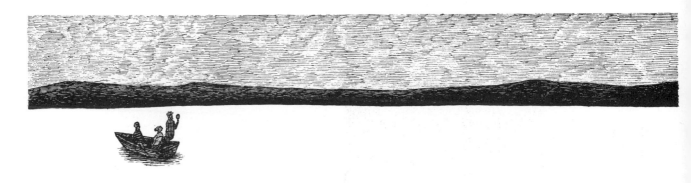

and Echo answered: Count the spoons!

On the shore a bat, or possibly an umbrella,

disengaged itself from the shrubbery,

causing those nearby to recollect the miseries of childhood.

It now became apparent (despite the lack of library paste)

that something had happened to the vicar;

guns began to go off in the distance.

At twilight, however, no message had come from the asylum,

so the others retired to the kiosk,

only to discover the cakes iced a peculiar shade of green

and the tea-urn empty

save for a card on which was written the single word:

Farewell.

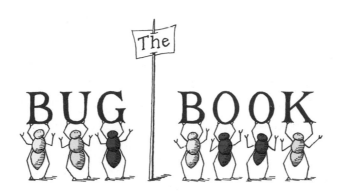

The BUG BOOK

by

EDWARD GOREY

There were once two blue bugs.

They lived in a teacup which had a piece missing from the rim.

They were frivolous, and often danced on the roof.

There were also three red bugs, who were cousins of the blue bugs.

They lived nearby, inside a
blue bottle, which made them
an interesting violet colour
when they were at home.

They were house-proud, and
frequently polished the glass
on both sides.

There were also two yellow
bugs, who were cousins of
both the blue and red bugs.

They lived a little further
off, on the topmost leaf but
one of a plant.

They were pensive, and sometimes sat on the topmost leaf and looked into the distance.

All the bugs were on the friendliest possible terms and constantly went to call on each other

And went on excursions together

And had delightful parties.

And then one day a black bug, who was related to nobody, appeared in the neighbourhood.

The other bugs were dubious, but nevertheless made an attempt to be friendly.

It was not a success.

After that, the black bug broke up their parties

And waylaid them whenever
they went visiting.

Social life came to a standstill.

A desperate secret meeting
was held.

At last they decided on
a plan.

The next morning they rushed
from their homes and dashed
to the top of a certain cliff.

The black bug followed them
to the foot of the cliff, where
he jumped up and down, and
shouted personal remarks.

Meanwhile, they were pushing
a large stone towards the edge.

It went over, and almost
at once a horrid noise came
from below.

Presently they descended and
rolled aside the stone.

The black bug had been
squashed quite flat.

To whom it may concern

They slipped the remains
into an envelope

And left it propped against
the fatal stone to be mailed.

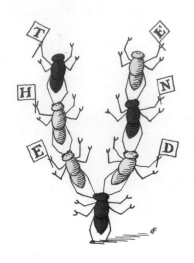

After which they had a party
complete with cake crumbs
and raspberry punch

And everyone enjoyed
himself immensely.

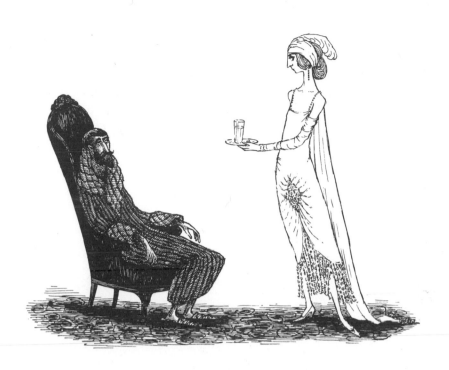

THE FATAL LOZENGE

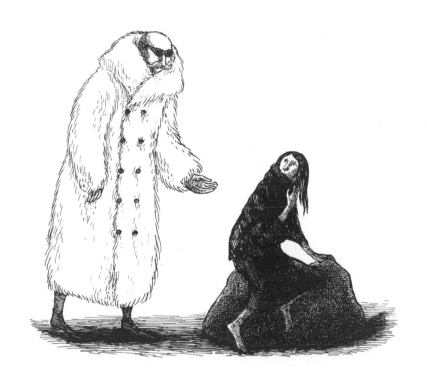

An Apparition of *her lover*
   She recognizes with dismay;
And later on she will discover
   That he himself had died today.

The Baby, *lying meek and quiet*
   Upon the customary rug,
Has dreams about rampage and riot,
   And will grow up to be a thug.

The Cad *decides he has grown weary*
   Of this affair, and that is that;
And so he tells her just how dreary
   He thinks she is, then leaves the flat.

The Drudge *expends her life in mopping,*
   In emptying and filling pails;
And she will do so, never stopping,
   Until her strength entirely fails.

The Effigy, *got up with clothing*
  Abstracted from the victim's room,
Is raised aloft to cheers of loathing
  Before it meets a flaming doom.

The Fetishist *gets out the hassock,*
  Turns down the lamp, and bolts the door;
Then in galoshes and a cassock,
  He worships It upon the floor.

The Governess *up in the attic*
  Attempts to make a cup of tea;
Her mind grows daily more erratic
  From cold and hunger and ennui.

The Hermit *lives among the boulders,*
  He wears no garment but a sack;
By slow degrees his reason moulders,
  The sun has long since burnt him black.

The Invalid *wakes up in terror*
   To feel his toes becoming numb;
The doctor's made another error —
   What unknown symptoms are to come?

The Journalist *surveys the slaughter,*
   The best in years without a doubt;
He pours himself a gin-and-water
   And wonders how it came about.

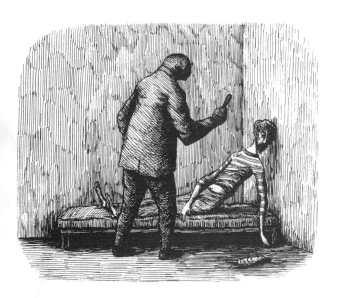

The Keeper, *when it's time for luncheon,*
   Flings down his charge upon the bed,
And taking out a home-made truncheon,
   Belabours him about the head.

The Lazar, *blessed with an appearance*
   Enough to give the strongest qualms,
Has little need of perseverance
   In prompting a display of alms.

The Magnate *waits upon the pavement*
    For his enormous limousine,
And ponders further child-enslavement
    And other projects still more mean.

The Nun *is fearfully bedevilled:*
    She runs about and moans and shrieks;
Her flesh is bruised, her clothes dishevelled:
    She's been like this for weeks and weeks.

The Orphan *whom there's none to cherish*
    Strays through the gloom on naked feet;
She presently will fall, and perish
    Unnoticed in some squalid street.

The Proctor *buys a pupil ices,*
    And hopes the boy will not resist
When he attempts to practise vices
    Few people even know exist.

The **Quarry**, *fleeing from the outing,*
   Sinks panting in the reeds and mud;
And hearkens to the distant shouting
   That tells him they are out for blood.

The **Resurrectionist** *goes plying*
   Without ado his simple trade;
Material is always dying
   And got with nothing but a spade.

The **Suicide**, *as she is falling,*
   Illuminated by the moon,
Regrets her act, and finds appalling
   The thought she will be dead so soon.

The **Tourist** *huddles in the station*
   While slowly night gives way to dawn;
He finds a certain fascination
   In knowing all the trains are gone.

The sight of Uncle gives no pleasure,
   But rather causes much alarm:
The children know that at his leisure
   He plans to have them come to harm.

The Visitor was somewhat pensive
   When she arrived to pay a call;
But now she's faint and apprehensive
   From hours of waiting in the hall.

The Wanton, though she knows its dangers,
   Must needs smear kohl about her eyes,
And wake the interest of strangers
   With long-drawn, hoarse, erotic sighs.

The Xenophobe grabs at the table,
   He feels his toes and fingers curl;
For he is only barely able
   To keep from striking down the girl.

The Yegg on rubber soles comes creeping
    Inside the house when it is late,
And while the occupants are sleeping,
    Removes the heirlooms and the plate.

The Zouave used to war and battle
    Would sooner take a life than not:
It scarcely has begun to prattle
    When he impales the hapless tot.

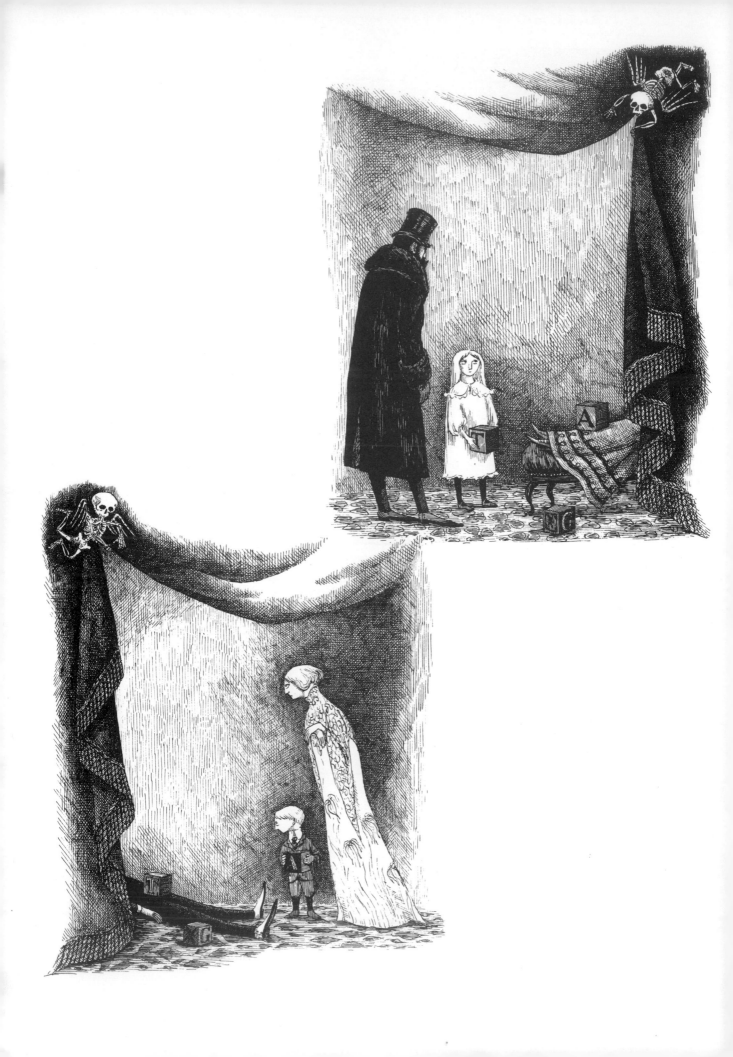

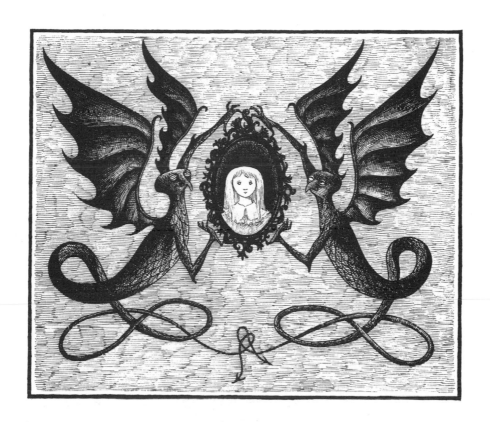

THE HAPLESS CHILD

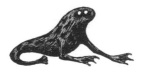 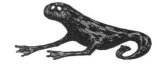

There was once a little girl named Charlotte Sophia.

Her parents were kind and well-to-do.

She had a doll whom she called Hortense.

One day her father, a colonel in the army, was ordered to Africa.

Several months later he was reported killed in a native uprising.

Her mother fell into a decline that proved fatal.

Her only other relative, an uncle, was brained by
a piece of masonry.

Charlotte Sophia was left in the hands of
the family lawyer.

He at once put her into a boarding-school.

There she was punished by the teachers for things
she hadn't done.

Hortense was torn limb from limb by the other pupils.

During the day Charlotte Sophia hid as much as possible.

At night she lay awake weeping and weeping.

When she could bear it no longer she fled from the
school at dawn.

She soon lost consciousness and sank to the pavement.

A man came and took the locket with her parents'
pictures inside.

*Another man came from the opposite direction and
carried her off.*

He brought her to a low place.

He sold her to a drunken brute.

Charlotte Sophia was put to work making artificial
flowers.

She lived on scraps and tap-water.

From time to time the brute got the horrors.

Charlotte Sophia's eyesight began to fail rapidly.

*Meanwhile, her father, who was not dead after all,
returned home.*

Every day he motored through the streets searching for her.

At last the brute went off his head.

Charlotte Sophia, now almost blind, ran into the street.

She was at once struck down by a car.

Her father got out to look at the dying child.

She was so changed, he did not recognize her.

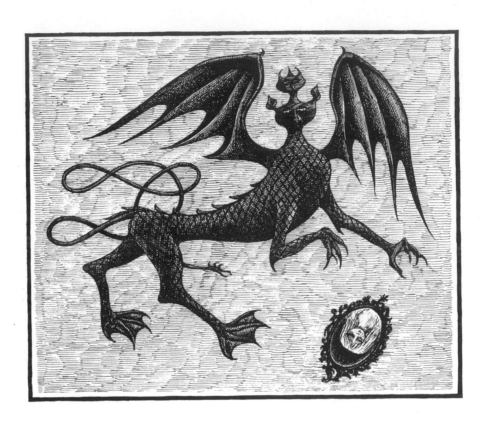

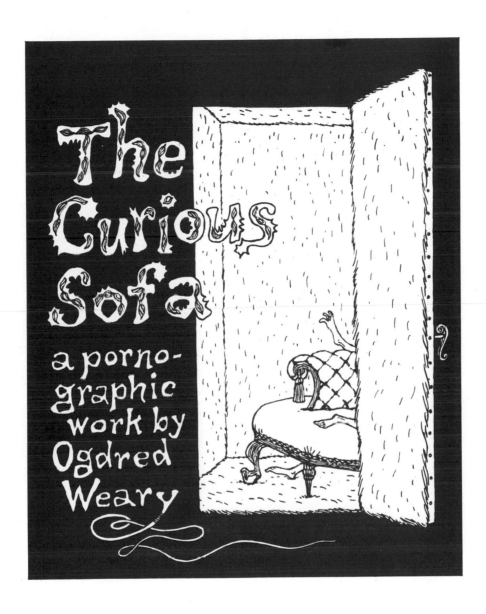

The Curious Sofa

a porno-
graphic
work by
Ogdred
Weary

Alice was eating grapes in the park when Herbert, an extremely well-endowed young man, introduced himself to her.

He invited her to go for a ride in a taxi-cab, on the floor of which they did something Alice had never done before.

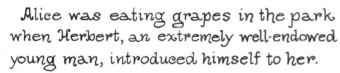

After they had done it several times in different ways, Herbert suggested that Alice tidy up at the home of his aunt, Lady Celia, who welcomed them with great cordiality.

Lady Celia led Alice to her boudoir, where she requested the girl to perform a rather surprising service.

Downstairs the three of them played a most amusing game of Herbert's own invention called "Thumbfumble." They then sat down to a sumptuous tea.

After he had finished the washing-up, Albert, the butler, an unusually well-formed man of middle age, joined them for another frolic. Herbert and Lady Celia had little difficulty in persuading Alice to spend a few days with them.

In the interval before dinner she perused an album of instructive chromolithographs entitled ‚Die Sieben und Dreißig Wollüste' which Lady Celia had thoughtfully set out.

Colonel Gilbert and his wife, Louise, came in after dinner; both of them had wooden legs, with which they could do all sorts of entertaining tricks.

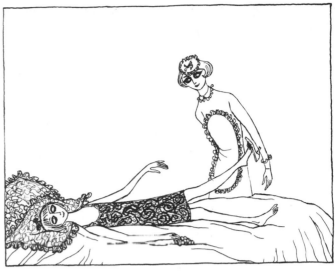

The evening was a huge success, in spite of someone fainting from time to time.

Alice, quite exhausted, was helped to bed by Lady Celia's French maid, Lise, whom she found delightfully sympathetic.

The next morning she was wakened in a novel fashion by Lady Celia in time for elevenses.

Looking out the window she saw Herbert, Albert, and Harold, the gardener, an exceptionally well-made youth, disporting themselves on the lawn.

They were soon joined by Donald, Herbert's singularly well-favoured sheepdog, and many were the giggles and barks that came from the shrubbery.

They called up to Alice, who, having put on an ingeniously constructed bathing slip, met them in the pool.

At luncheon, which was alfresco, Lady Celia announced they were invited to the Gilberts for the weekend.

To beguile the tedium of the journey Albert read aloud from Volume Eleven of the "Encyclopedia of Unimaginable Customs."

As they drove up to the house, Lucy, the Gilbert's daughter, and Gerald, her fiancé, an uncommonly well-shaped older man, emerged from an ornamental urn.

That evening in the library Scylla, one of the guests who had certain anatomical peculiarities, demonstrated the "Lithuanian Typewriter," assisted by Ronald and Robert, two remarkably well-set-up young men from the village.

Later Reginald, another remarkably well-set-up young man from the village, provided everyone with the most astonishing little device.

Still later Gerald did a terrible thing to Elsie with a saucepan.

The party split into twos and threes before retiring.

At breakfast it was learned that Elsie had expired during the night, and gloom descended on everybody.

When a change of scene was proposed, Lady Celia suggested a visit to the nearby seat of Sir Egbert, a dear friend of her youth.

When they got there, they found Sir Egbert, an extraordinarily well-proportioned old gentleman, and his friend, Louie, having a romp on the terrace.

They all went indoors and worked up some most intriguing charades.

During the light buffet supper Louie did a dance with a boa.

Sir Egbert offered to show them his famous sofa. Alice felt a shudder of nameless apprehension.

It stood in a windowless room lined with polar bear fur and otherwise empty; it was upholstered in scarlet velvet, and had nine legs and seven arms.

As soon as everybody had crowded into the room, Sir Egbert fastened shut the door, and started up the machinery inside the sofa.

When Alice saw what was about to happen, she began to scream uncontrollably....

THE WILLOWDALE HANDCAR

BY EDWARD GOREY

OR

THE RETURN OF THE BLACK DOLL

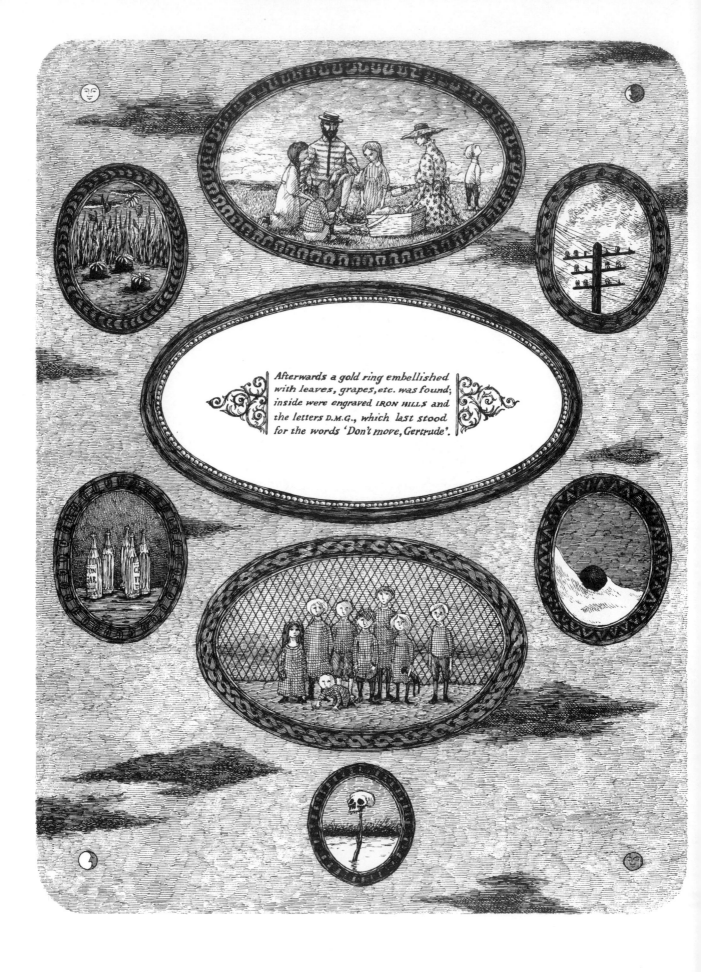

Afterwards a gold ring embellished with leaves, grapes, etc. was found; inside were engraved IRON HILLS and the letters D.M.G., which last stood for the words 'Don't move, Gertrude'.

One summer afternoon in Willowdale Edna,
Harry, and Sam wandered down to the railroad
station to see if anything was doing.

There was nothing on the platform but some empty
crates. 'Look!' said Harry, pointing to a handcar
on the siding. 'Let's take it and go for a ride.'

Soon they were flying along the tracks at a great rate. Little Grace Sprocket, playing in a home-made mud puddle, watched them go by with longing.

At Bogus Corners, the next town down the line, they stopped to buy soda pop and gingersnaps at Mr Queevil's store. 'How are things over in Willowdale?' he asked. 'Dull' they said.

A few minutes after they were on their way again,
they saw a house burning down in a field.
'Whooee!' said Sam. 'The engines will never
be in time to save it.'

The next morning they wrote postcards to everybody, telling them what they were doing and
didn't know exactly when they would be back.

At 10:17 the Turnip Valley Express rushed past.
A frantic face was pressed against a window
of the parlor car.

'Gracious!' said Edna. 'I believe that was Nellie
Flim. We were chums at Miss Underfoot's Seminary.
I wonder what can have been the matter.'

In Chutney Falls they hunted up the cemetery
and peered at the tombstones of Harry's mother's
family.

Later they ran into Nellie's beau, Dick Hammerclaw,
the local telegraph operator. He asked if they'd
seen her. He seemed upset.

Near Gristleburg they saw a palatial mansion on a
bluff. 'That's O Altitudo,' said Sam, 'the home of
Titus W. Blotter, the financier. I saw a picture in
a magazine.'

Several days later a touring car drew up alongside
them. The driver called out something unintelligible
concerning Dick before he shot away out of sight.

An undated fragment of the 'Willowdale Triangle'
they found caught in a tie informed them that
Wobbling Rock had finally fallen on a family
having a picnic.

In Dogear Junction they paid a call on Edna's
cousins, the Zeph Claggs. He showed them a few
of the prizes from his collection of over 7,000 glass
telephone-pole insulators.

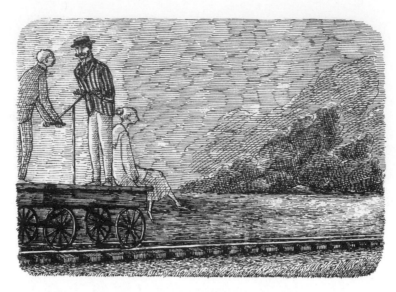

The following week Mount Smith came into
view in the distance; dark clouds were piling
up behind it.

During the thunderstorm that ensued, a flash
of lightning revealed a figure creeping up
the embankment.

*Some months went by, and still they had not
returned to Willowdale.*

*They visited the ruins of the Crampton vinegar
works, which had been destroyed by a mysterious
explosion the preceding fall.*

At Wunksieville they rescued an infant who was
hanging from a hook intended for mailbags.

'How much she resembles Nellie!' said Edna. They
turned her over to the matron of the orphanage
in Stovepipe City.

From the trestle over Peevish Gorge they spied the wreck of a touring car at the bottom. 'I don't see Dick's friend anywhere,' said Harry.

In Violet Springs they learned that Mrs Regera Dowdy was not receiving visitors, but through a window they were able to see the desk on which she wrote her poems.

As they were going along the edge of the Sogmush
River, they passed a man in a canoe. 'If I'm not
mistaken,' said Edna, 'he was lurking inside the
vinegar works'.

Between West Elbow and Penetralia they almost
ran over someone who was tied to the track.
It proved to be Nellie.

*Despite their entreaties, she insisted on being
left at the first grade crossing, where she got
on a bicycle and rode away.*

*That evening they attended a baked-bean supper
at the Halfbath Methodist Church. 'They're
all right,' said Sam, 'but they're not a patch
on Mrs Umlaut's back home'.*

A week later they noticed someone who might be Nellie walking in the grounds of the Weedhaven Laughing Academy.

On Sunday afternoon they saw Titus W. Blotter in his shirtsleeves plunge into the Great Trackless Swamp.

In Hiccupboro they counted the cannon balls in
the pyramids on the courthouse lawn.

At sunset they entered a tunnel in the Iron Hills
and did not come out the other end.

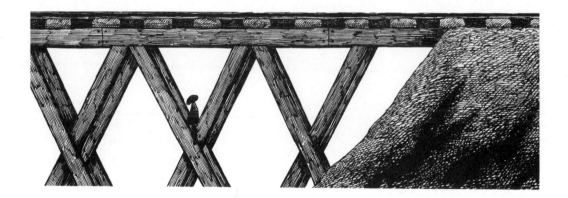

THE
VINEGAR
WORKS

THE VINEGAR WORKS

Three Volumes
of Moral Instruction

THE GASHLYCRUMB TINIES

THE INSECT GOD

THE WEST WING

by

EDWARD GOREY

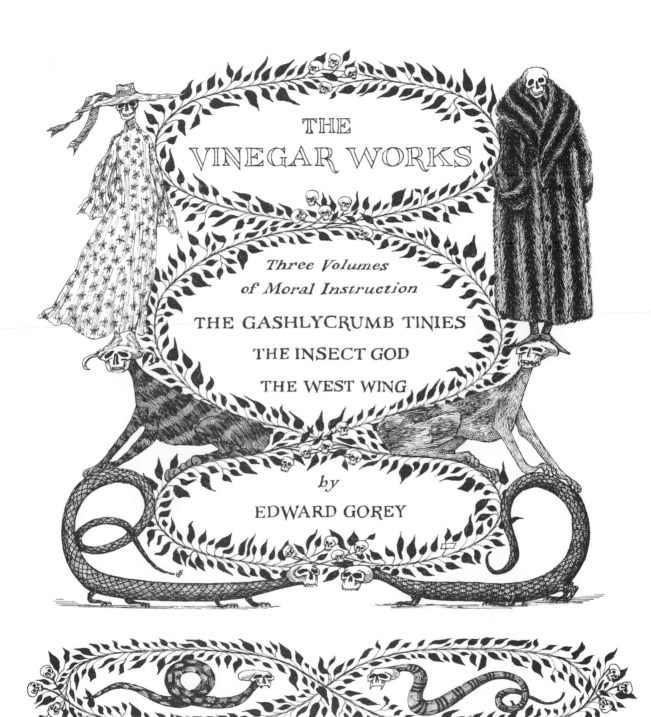

THE VINEGAR WORKS

Three Volumes
of Moral Instruction

THE GASHLYCRUMB TINIES

THE INSECT GOD

THE WEST WING

by

EDWARD GOREY

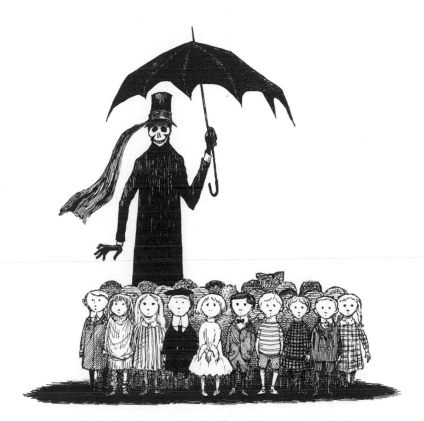

THE GASHLYCRUMB TINIES

A is for AMY who fell down the stairs

B is for BASIL assaulted by bears

C is for CLARA who wasted away

D is for DESMOND thrown out of a sleigh

E is for ERNEST who choked on a peach

F is for FANNY sucked dry by a leech

G is for GEORGE smothered under a rug

H is for HECTOR done in by a thug

I is for IDA who drowned in a lake

J is for JAMES who took lye by mistake

K is for KATE who was struck with an axe

L is for LEO who swallowed some tacks

M is for MAUD who was swept out to sea

N is for NEVILLE who died of ennui

O is for OLIVE run through with an awl

P is for PRUE trampled flat in a brawl

Q is for QUENTIN who sank in a mire

R is for RHODA consumed by a fire

S is for SUSAN who perished of fits

T is for TITUS who flew into bits

U is for UNA who slipped down a drain

V is for VICTOR squashed under a train

W is for WINNIE embedded in ice

X is for XERXES devoured by mice

Y is for YORICK whose head was knocked in

Z is for ZILLAH who drank too much gin

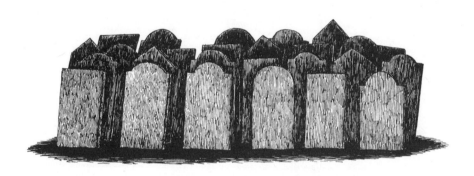

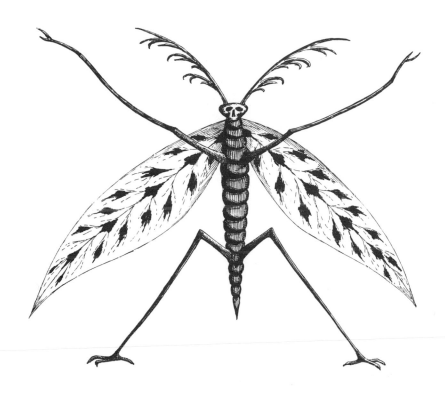

THE INSECT GOD

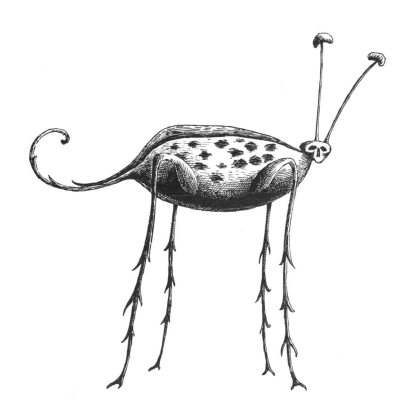

O what has become of Millicent Frastley?
Is there any hope that she's still alive?
Why haven't they found her? It's rather ghastly
To think that the child was not yet five.

The dear little thing was last seen playing
Alone by herself at the edge of the park;
There was no one with her to keep her from straying
Away in the shadows and oncoming dark.

Before she could do so, a silent and glittering
   Black motor drew up where she sat nibbling grass;
From within came a nearly inaudible twittering,
   A tiny green face peered out through the glass.

She was ready to flee, when the figure beckoned;
   An arm with two elbows held out a tin
Full of cinnamon balls; she paused; a second
   Reached out as she took one, and lifted her in.

The nurse was discovered collapsed in some shrubbery,
　　But her reappearance was not much use;
Her eyes were askew, her extremities rubbery,
　　Her clothing was stained with a brownish juice.

She was questioned in hopes of her answers revealing
　　What had happened; she merely repeatedly said
'I hear them walking about on the ceiling'.
　　She had gone irretrievably out of her head.

O feelings of horror, resentment, and pity
    For things, which so seldom turn out for the best:
The car, unobserved, sped away from the city
    As the last of the light died out in the west.

The Frastleys grew sick with apprehension,
    Which a heavy tea only served to increase;
Though they felt it was scarcely genteel to mention
    The loss of their child, they called in the police.

Through unvisited hamlets the car went creeping,
    With its head lamps unlit and its curtains drawn;
Those natives who happened not to be sleeping
    Heard it pass, and lay awake until dawn.

The police with their torches and notebooks descended
    On the haunts of the underworld, looking for clues;
In spite of their praiseworthy efforts, they ended
    With nothing at all in the way of news.

The car, after hours and hours of travel,
  Arrived at a gate in an endless wall;
It rolled up a drive and stopped on the gravel
  At the foot of a vast and crumbling hall.

As the night wore away hope started to languish
  And soon was replaced by all manner of fears;
The family twisted their fingers in anguish,
  Or got them all damp from the flow of their tears.

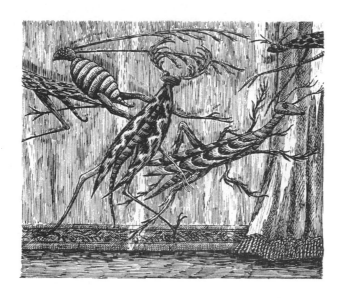

They removed the child to the ball-room, whose hangings
  And mirrors were streaked with a luminous slime;
They leapt through the air with buzzings and twangings
  To work themselves up to a ritual crime.

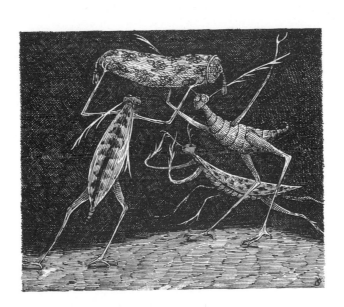

They stunned her, and stripped off her garments, and lastly
  They stuffed her inside a kind of pod;
And then it was that Millicent Frastley
  Was sacrificed to THE INSECT GOD.

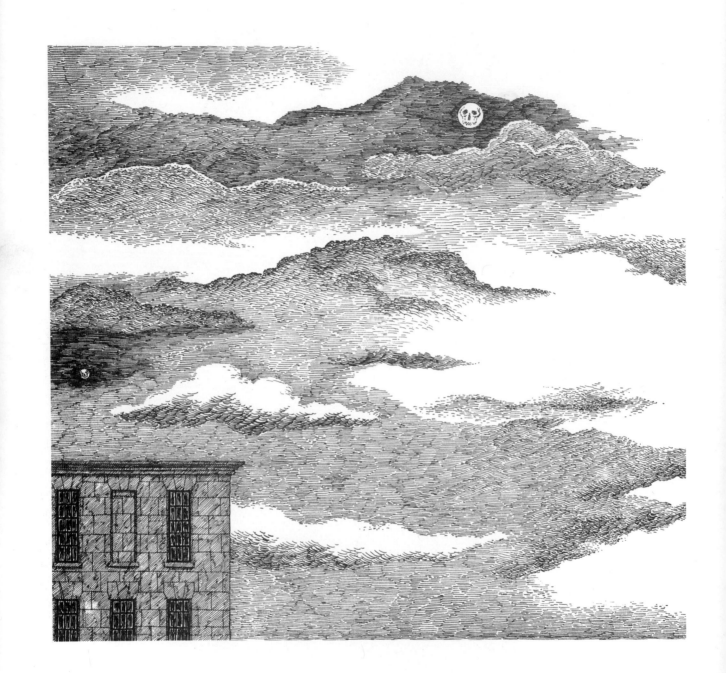

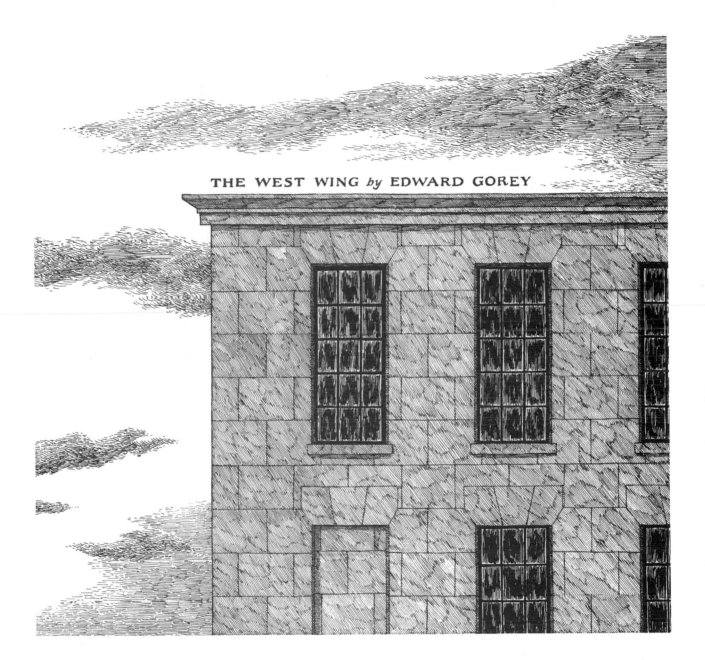

THE WEST WING *by* EDWARD GOREY

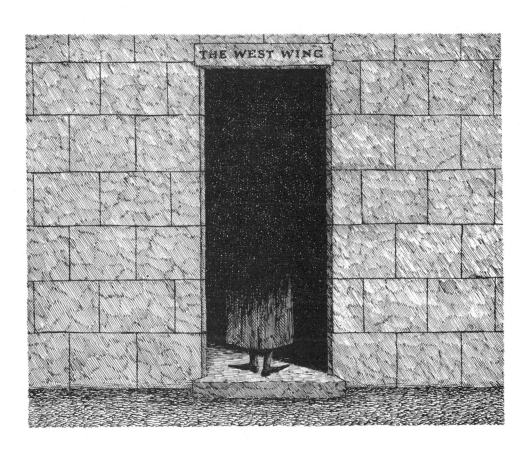

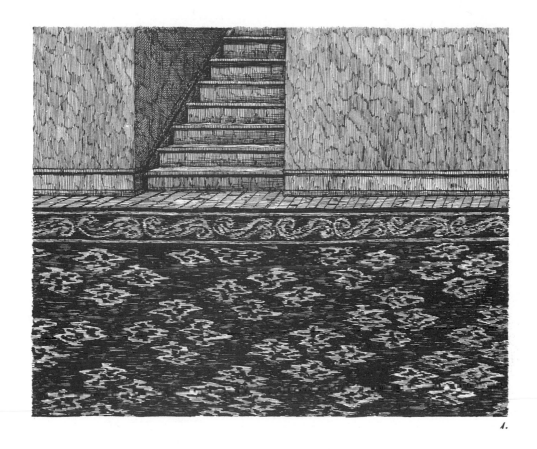

1.

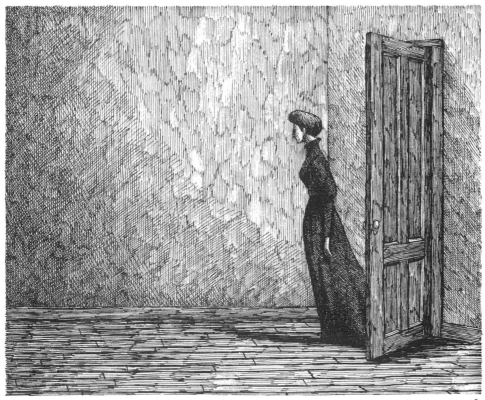

2.

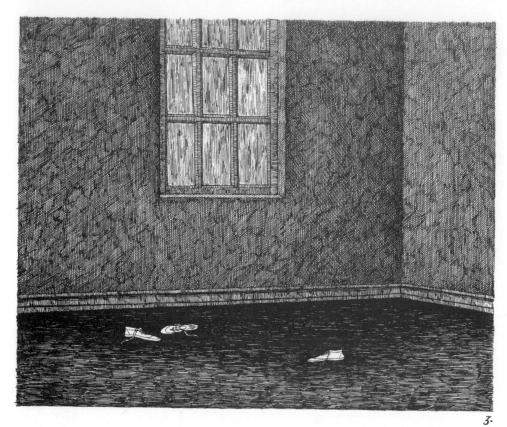

3.

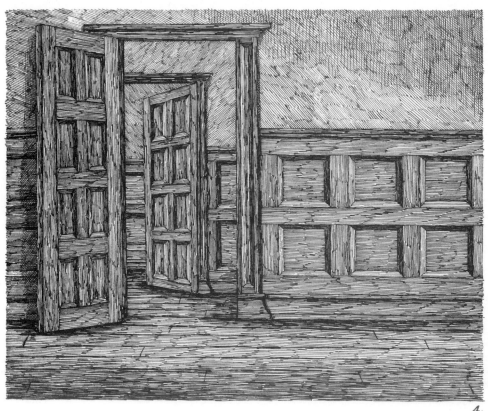

4.

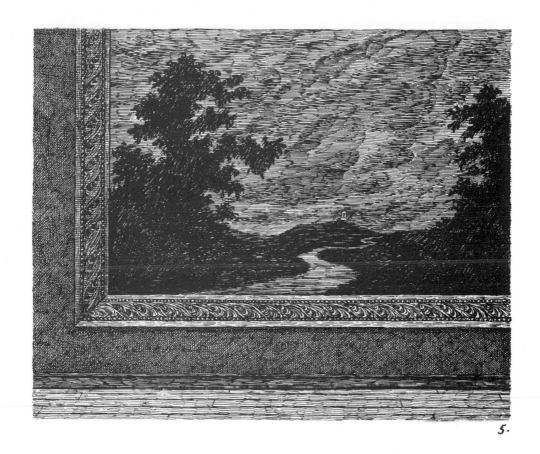

5.

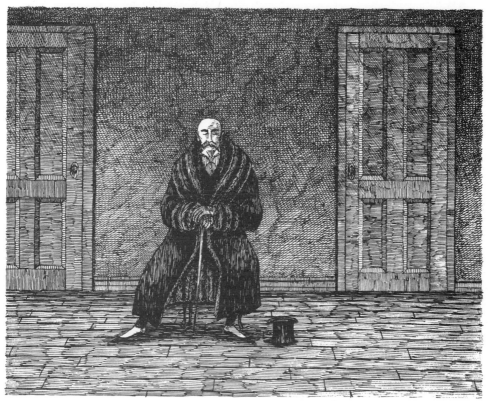

6.

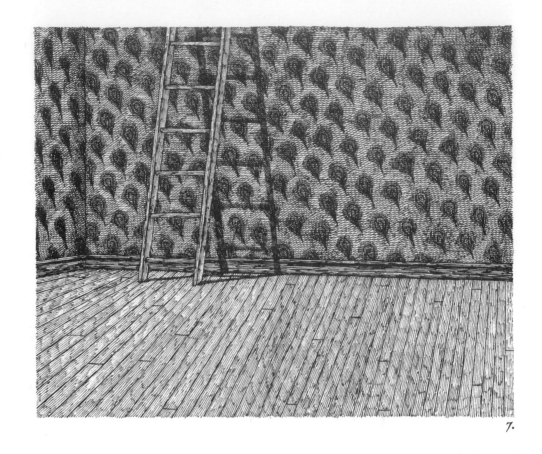

7.

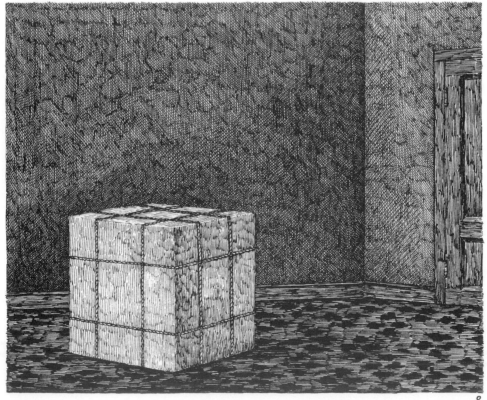

8.

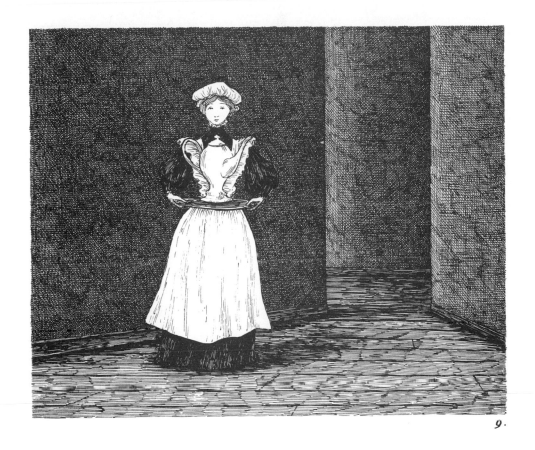

9.

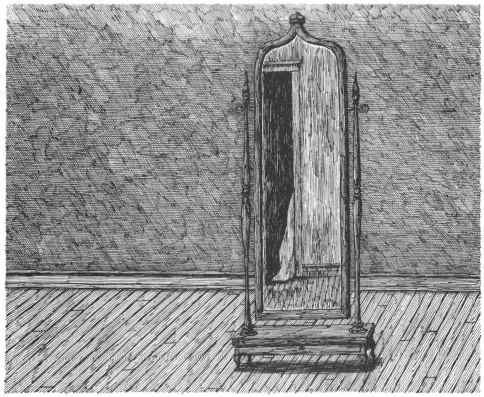

10.

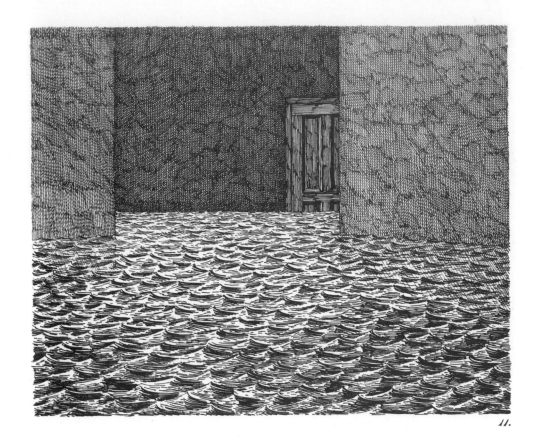

11.

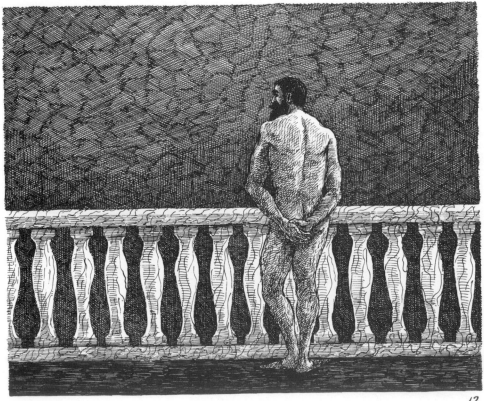

12.

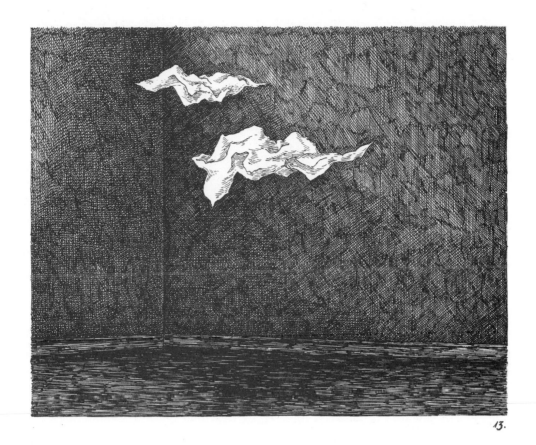

13.

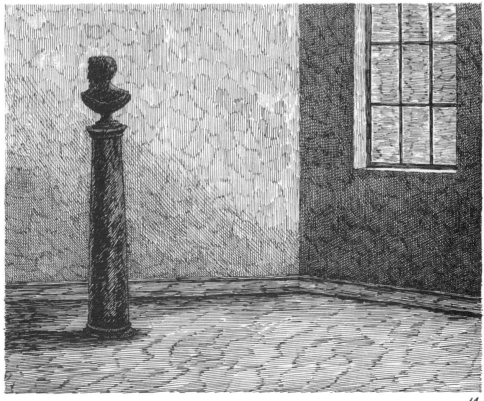

14.

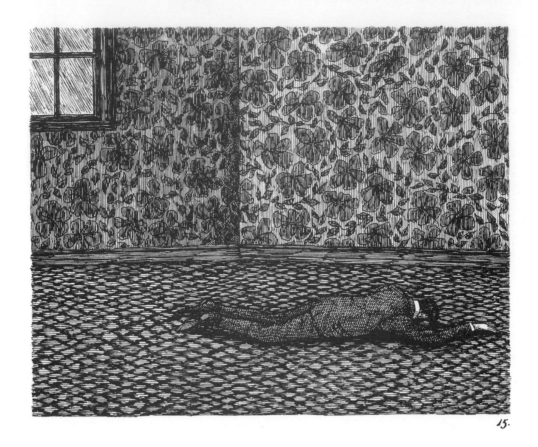

15.

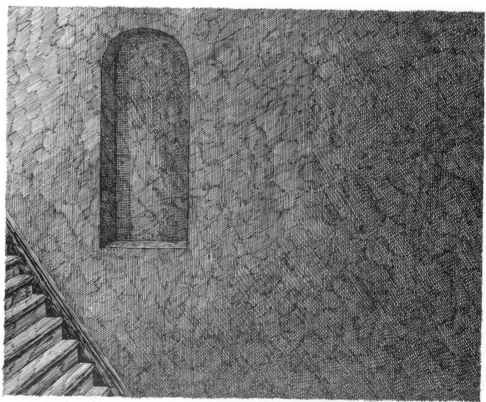

16.

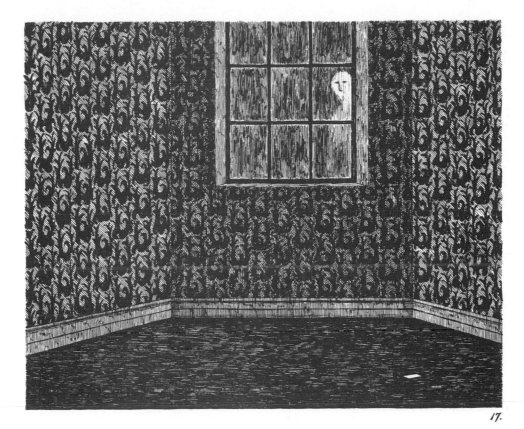

17.

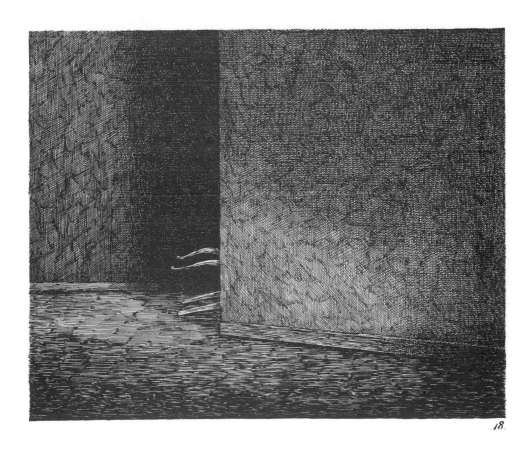

18.

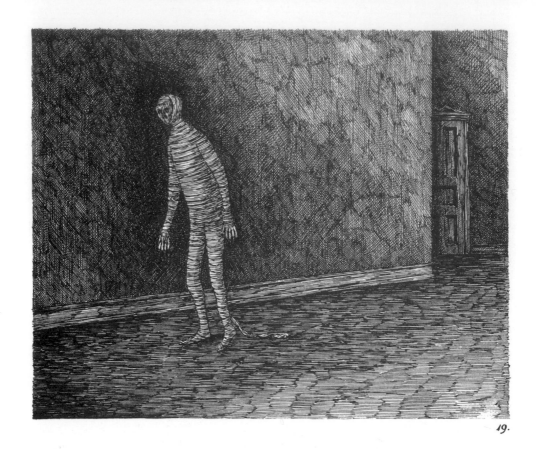

19.

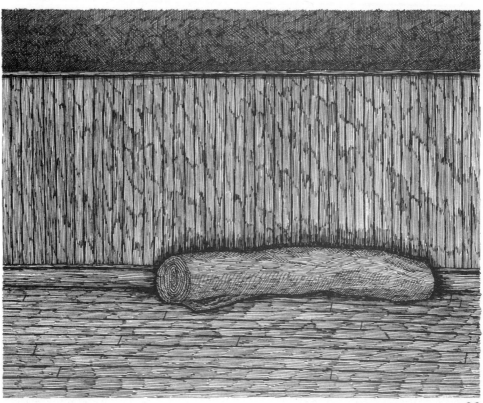

20.

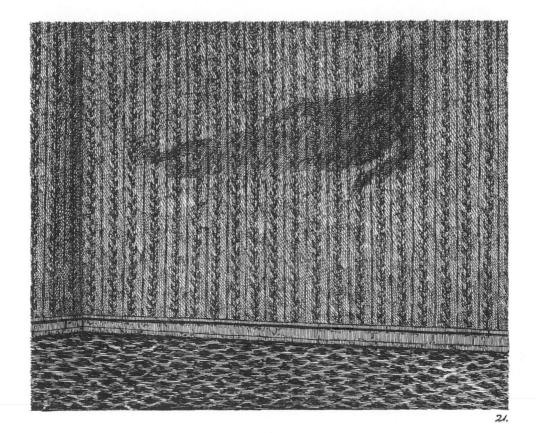

21.

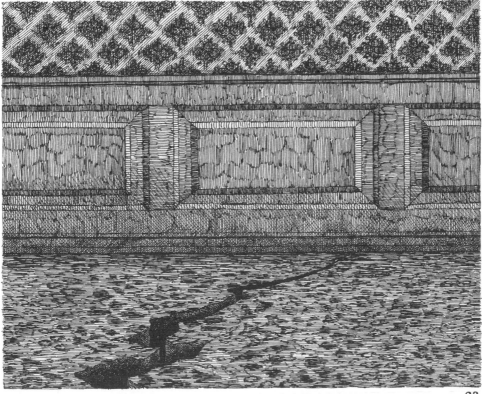

22.

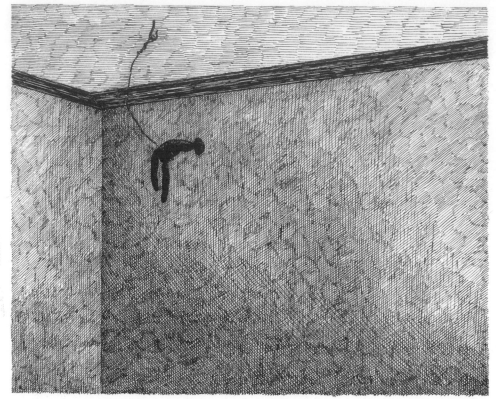

23.

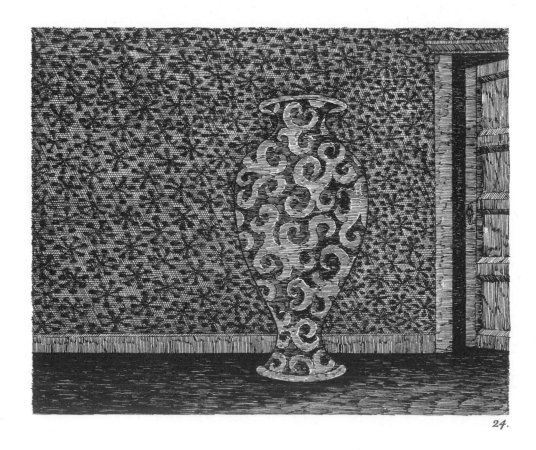

24.

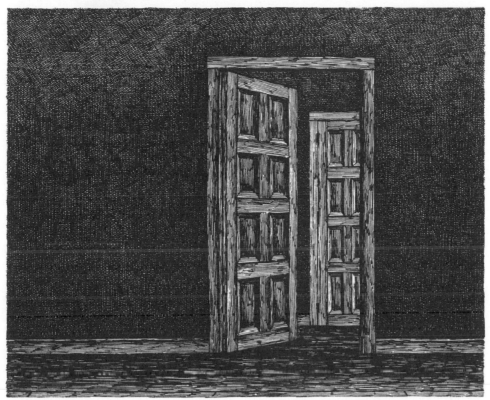

25.

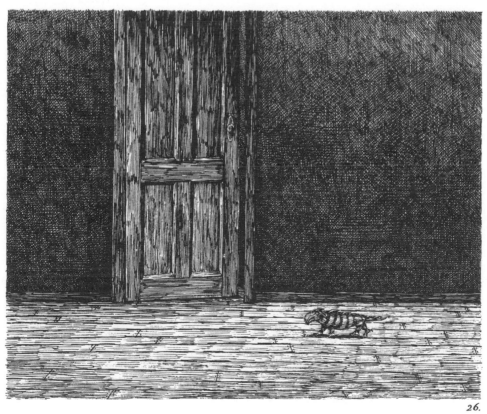

26.

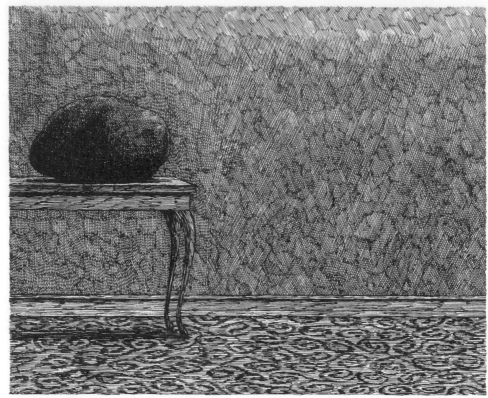

27.

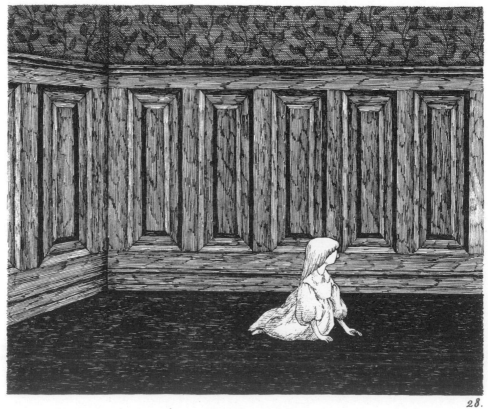

28.

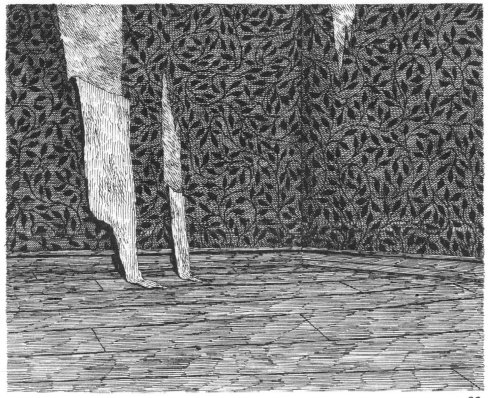

29.

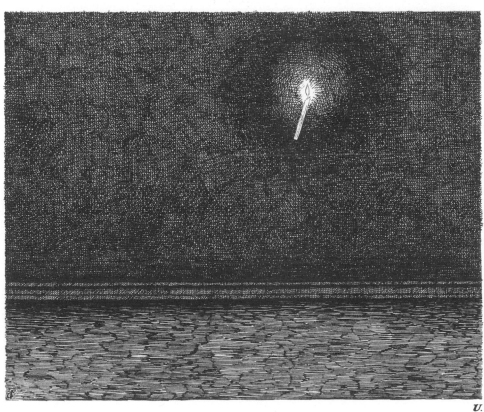

U.

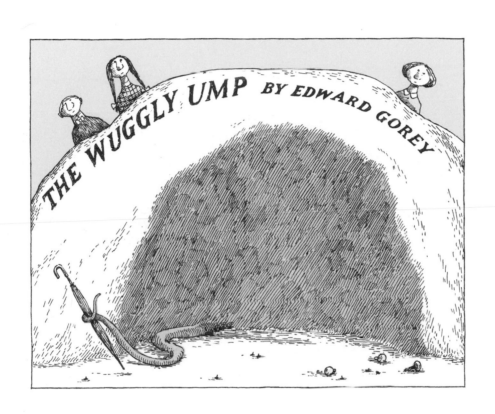

Sing tirraloo, sing tirralay,
The Wuggly Ump lives far away.

It eats umbrellas, gunny sacks,
Brass doorknobs, mud, and carpet tacks.

How most unpleasing, to be sure!
Its other habits are obscure.

Sing jigglepin, sing jogglepen,
The Wuggly Ump has left its den.

We pass our happy childhood hours
In weaving endless chains of flowers.

Across the hills the Wuggly Ump
Is hurtling on, kerbash, kerblump!

When play is over, we are fed
On wholesome bowls of milk and bread.

Sing hushaboo, sing hushaby,
The Wuggly Ump is drawing nigh.

The moon is full: its silver beams
Shine down and give us lovely dreams.

Sing twiddle-ear, sing twaddle-or,
The Wuggly Ump is at the door.

It's making an unholy fuss;
Why has it come to visit us?

What nasty little wilful eyes
For anything of such a size!

How uninviting are its claws!
How even more so are its jaws!

Sing glogalimp, sing glugalump,
From deep inside the Wuggly Ump.

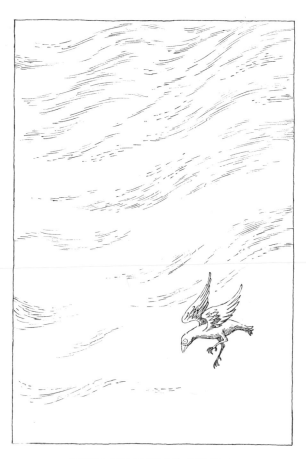

THE SINKING SPELL

O look, there's something way up high:
A creature floating in the sky.

It is not merely sitting there,
But falling slowly through the air.

The clouds grew pink and gold; its knees
Were level with the evening trees.

Morose, inflexible, aloof,
It hovered just above the roof.

It's gone right through, and come to rest
On great grand-uncle Ogdred's chest.

It settled further in the night,
And gave the maid an awful fright.

Head first, without a look or word,
It's left the fourth floor for the third.

The weeks went by; it made its way
A little lower every day.

Each time one thought it might have stopped
One found, however, it had dropped.

One wonders just what can be meant
By this implacable descent.

It did not linger, after all,
Forever in the upstairs hall.

It found the drawing room in turn,
And slipped inside the Chinese urn.

It now declines in fretful curves
Among the pickles and preserves.

It's gone beneath the cellar floor;
We shall not see it any more.

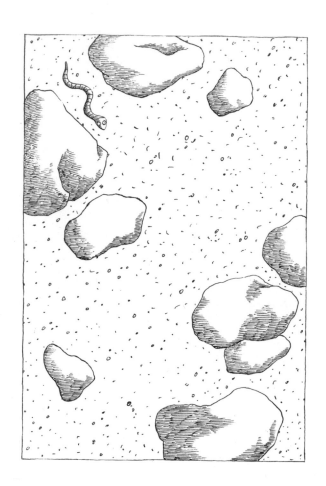

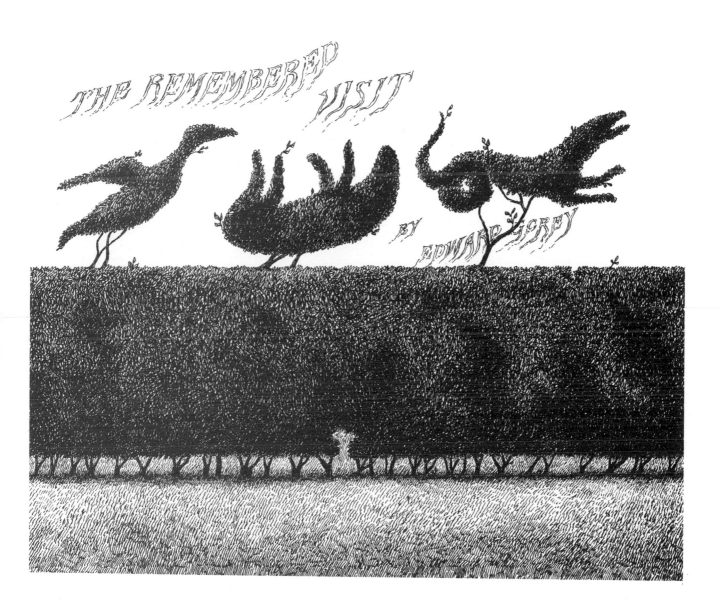

The summer she was eleven, Drusilla went abroad with her parents.

There she climbed endless flights of stairs.

She tried to make out the subjects of vast dark paintings.

Sometimes she was made ill by curious dishes.

She was called upon to admire views.

When the weather was bad, she leafed through incomprehensible magazines.

One morning her parents, for some reason or other, went on an excursion without her.

After luncheon an acquaintance of the family, Miss Skrim-Pshaw, took Drusilla with her to pay a call.

They walked to an inn called le Crapaud Bleu.

They were shown into a garden where the topiary was being neglected.

Drusilla was told she was going to meet a wonderful old man who had been or done something lofty and cultured in the dim past.

Eventually Mr Crague appeared.

He kissed Miss Skrim-Pshaw's hand, and she presented Drusilla
to him.

After they had sat down, Drusilla saw that Mr Crague wore
no socks.

He and Miss Skrim-Pshaw mentioned a great many people who had done things in their conversation.

Tea was brought: it was nearly colourless, and there was a plate of crystallized ginger.

Mr Crague asked Drusilla if she liked paper.

He said he would have liked to show her his albums filled with beautiful pieces of it, but they were upstairs in his room.

Drusilla promised when she got home to send him some insides of envelopes she had saved.

Miss Skrim-Pshaw said it was time they made their adieux.

On the way back a few drops of rain fell. Somehow Drusilla was hungrier than she had been before too.

Days went by.

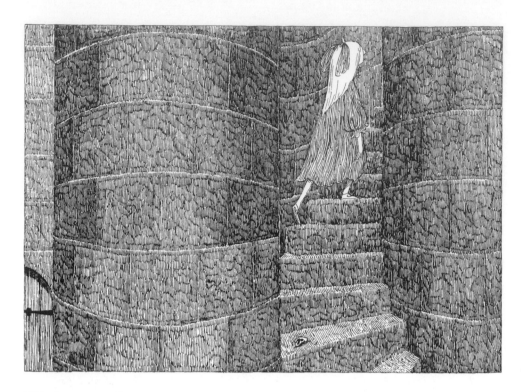

Weeks went by.

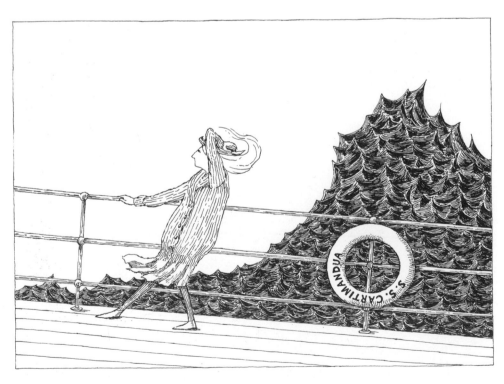

Months went by.

Years went by. Drusilla was still inclined to be forgetful.

One day something reminded her of her promise to Mr Crague.

She began to hunt for the envelope-linings in her room.

On a sheet of newspaper at the bottom of a drawer she read that
Mr Crague had died the autumn after she had been abroad.

When she found the pretty pieces of paper, she felt very sad and neglectful.

The wind came and took them through an open window; she watched them blow away.

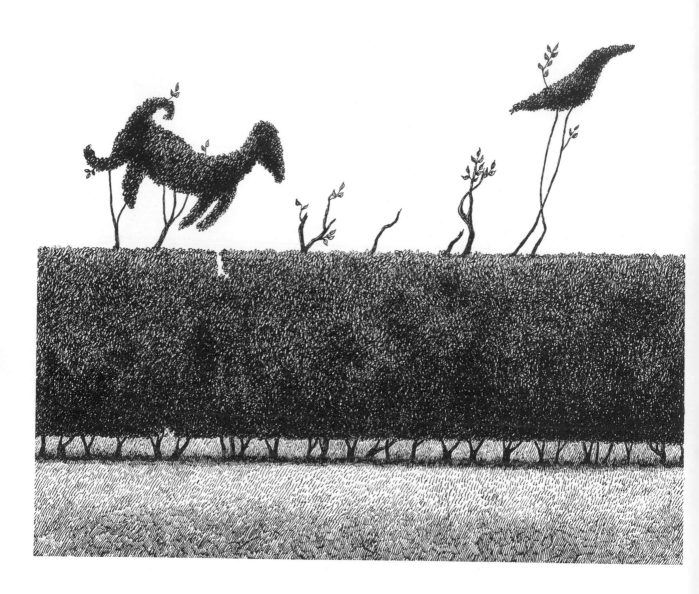

ALSO BY EDWARD GOREY

The Beastly Baby
The Nursery Frieze
The Pious Infant
The Evil Garden
The Inanimate Tragedy
The Gilded Bat
The Utter Zoo
The Blue Aspic
The Iron Tonic
The Osbick Bird
The Chinese Obelisks
The Epiplectic Bicycle
The Sopping Thursday
The Deranged Cousins
The Eleventh Episode
[The Untitled Book]
The Awdrey-Gore Legacy
The Interesting List*
The Admonitory Hippopotamus*

THE SECRETS

The Other Statue
The Night Bandage et al*

WITH PETER F. NEUMEYER

Donald and the ...
Donald Has a Difficulty
Why we have day and night

WITH VICTORIA CHESS

Fletcher and Zenobia
Fletcher and Zenobia Save the Circus

DRAWINGS FOR

The Jumblies, EDWARD LEAR
The Dong with a Luminous Nose, EDWARD LEAR
Story for Sara, ALPHONSE ALLAIS
The Salt Herring, CHARLES CROS
Irene Iddesleigh, MRS AMANDA M'KITTRICK ROS*

*In preparation

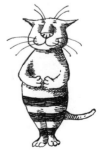